Entwining Lives

Channelled by
Irene Bays

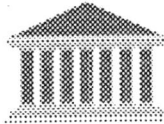

Stonecliffe Publishing
Welton - Lincolnshire - England

© Irene Bays 1994

ISBN 1 898086 01 X

British Library Cataloguing-in-Publication Data
A catalogue record for this book is available
from the British Library

Computer typeset by

Stonecliffe Publishing,
P.O. Box 11, Welton, Lincolnshire, LN2 3HY
England.

Printed and bound in Great Britain by
Antony Rowe Ltd, Chippenham, Wiltshire

This book is the first venture of The Eastbourne Christian Spiritualist Church, into the publication of works of importance to Spiritualists and any others who are seeking the Truth of Life and the Hereafter.

The Eastbourne Christian Spiritualist Church acknowledges its grateful thanks to the late Lilian Elwell, a past President of the Church, for her generous legacy enabling us to produce this book and also our extensive library of spiritual teaching tapes.

All the proceeds from the sale of this edition will be utilised for future publications of a similar nature.

The Eastbourne Christian Spiritualist Church
1a, Cavendish Avenue,
EASTBOURNE,
Sussex. BN22 8EW

Further copies of this book may be obtained from the above address at a cost of £8.50 plus postage and packing.
Quantity discounts are available.

Dedication

* * * * *

Dedicated to my dear husband Arthur, in
loving memory, and to Thomas our friend
in Light and Love.

Acknowledgements

My grateful thanks to Richard Slade for his support and for editing the original work with such dedication. And to John Parker, who has waited so patiently to set the wheels in motion.

My thanks also to Arthur, Diane, Bert, John, Rose and Maurice, the members of the Group, who sat with me for two years, during which time we learned so much.

My love and thanks to all the Teachers from spirit realms, who so generously shared their knowledge with us

CONTENTS

* * * * *

Part Two

Part Three

Introduction

At the age of ten I was told by a neighbour that I was a Healer, but of course at that time I had no idea what he meant.

Three decades later I found that by touching the forehead of a headache sufferer, the pain would be removed. I did not associate this with Healing.

When my husband and I moved to East Dean near Eastbourne, we were drawn to attend services in the Eastbourne Christian Spiritualist Church, where I became a probationer Healer; eventually becoming a Registered Healer.

One morning during my prayers, I had an experience which heightened my spiritual awareness, and from that day channelling commenced.

Later I was 'requested' to commence the Group, and the names of the proposed sitters advised. They were all well known to me and agreed to join me.

"Entwining Lives" is the result of the merging together in love and harmony, of the members of the Group with our teachers in spirit.

Peace be with you.

Irene Bays
Curry Rivel
Somerset
November 1993

PART ONE

We place ourselves in your
Loving care Father God,
May we walk side by side with
Those in Spirit Realms,
That we may all draw
Closer to Thee.

PREFACE

This is a message received by the Channel on 30th May 1980, and which was passed on to the Group on the occasion of their first meeting on 4th. July 1980.

It makes no difference at all whether you sit in a circle, oblong, square, or in a straight line, for you will still be a Group, and at this stage that is what you will be; a Group which is to have teachings.

The Group are all healers of different understandings, and each will receive the knowledge of their own type of healing ability. Of course it will take time to accomplish this, anything up to a year, but you will all be happy to give forth the power for each in turn. For as you already have the awareness my daughter, it is a case of one for all and all for one.

We would like you all to go into the Sanctuary at 8.15 p.m. that gives time for all to be together. Once seated and quiet, we request that you say the following to the Group.

"We are all equal, and we all have our own individual paths to tread, and it is up to each one of us to follow the teachings we will be given. We are met together at the request of Spirit, and our guidance and knowledge will be spiritual, for it is the commencement of the New Age, and this is the age of spiritual advancement for all peoples upon the Earth plane.

"There will be no phenomena, and there will be no antics. All teachings will be by the use of our channel at this stage. Will you please go now if you are not going to take heed of the teachings you will be given; for this is a Group who must dedicate themselves to service. Even Jesus the Nazarene dedicated Himself to service, and gave His life to prove that His Father God was real and could do all things.

"We are not requesting that you give up your lives, but we **are** requesting that you speak in truth at all times, and this is essential. Should there be things said or done that you wish to deny, then I say to you, if you deny in truth that is good, but if you deny something which is of truth — remember Peter? — Then it is best that you keep a still tongue for the sake of your own progression. I hope you all have the meaning? Truth must always be spoken between you. If you do not agree, if you do not understand then say so, and discuss it, for that is one of the important functions.

"I would remind you that not only were the majority of this Group, members of The Church of the Twelve Disciples, and have been visited by the Holy Spirit; but also these same members were brought together at a discussion group connected with the Church on the Rocks. So you can now perhaps see the beginnings of the part of the Master Plan with which you are involved. It is requested that at the end of each meeting together, you stay in the Sanctuary and discuss those things which you have been told or those things that have happened. And I say to you now, be honest, speak in truth, and if you do not agree, say so. Your comments will be noted, for we in spirit will stay with you until the ending prayer of Thanksgiving.

"You are requested to be of the understanding that you have self discipline, each one of you. If you undertake to be of this Group, then you must be of regularity. It is essential. I say again, be of love and truth, in order that the Light of God can be sent forth with understanding. Be of truth one to the other, and my children, you will have vibrations of a high level, and thus the teachings can surpass all that you have yet received. At a later time, this Group will become twelve, but not just yet.

14

Now I request that you say a prayer — send forth healing and send forth the twin circles of Light as requested many Earth days ago by Sister Agnes, for this is an instruction that has been given to all the other Groups. Then sit quietly with your eyes closed, sending forth your power to the centre of the Group — it will be used. First of all my channel will speak, for she will be used by me, for I intend to welcome you all. Then you must remain quiet."

Should there be a materialisation or manifestation then you will be told, but my daughter, never total darkness, for this is a Group of the New Age. My daughter, you will find that all members of the Group will have their progression, for even as the disciples went forth to spread the Light of God, so will you all go forth, when the time is right.

Chapter I

THE PLAN

G reetings my children — greetings. At last I have the pleasure of welcoming you. There has been much planning taking place to bring you all together. There have been errors of free will, and we in Spirit have had to work along different paths in order to bring you all together. It is essential that you are together and that you all have the teachings, for you are all to be channels for the healing Spirits to use you. You have differing gifts and between you, you will be given great knowledge and awareness.

Now I must introduce myself, I am Thomas. I was [1]Thomas à Becket in one life, and on the Earth plane I have also walked behind Jesus the Nazarene, and I have been on the Earth plane since the time I was Thomas à Becket, but I come to you as Thomas à Becket. Thomas — for it was whilst I was Thomas à Becket and Archbishop of Canterbury that I learned my lessons. I was Chancellor to Henry II. I was arrogant, I was greedy, I was domineering, I was ruthless. Oh yes, these things have been written of me, and they are true. I was made Archbishop

---

[1]Thomas à Becket - (1117-1170) Archbishop of Canterbury (1162) and Chancellor of England (1158) under Henry II; he successfully opposed Henry's policy in taxation and other matters, and was murdered by Henry's orders, in Canterbury Cathedral; he was canonised in 1173, and his shrine became the most famous in Christendom; it was destroyed in 1538.

of Canterbury by Henry II, for he wished to rid me from his Court. But my children, when I entered the portals of Canterbury Cathedral a great spiritual awareness came over me and I found my spiritual path, and I thank God that it was so. And that is why I come to you as Thomas, for that is the life in which I found my spiritual awareness, and it is to help you along your spiritual path that I come. And so you now know who Thomas is.

I want you all to be aware of the teachings you are given. You have already been told that you misinterpret, and you do, and so does our channel. So that you all really start on equal footing. And gradually we hope that you will find a greater awareness of those things that are told you from those who come to you from the World of Spirit. You cannot rely on anyone else within the Group to lead you along your spiritual path, for nobody but yourself can tread your spiritual path. I ask you to remember this, for it is important to each one of you.

I will tell you something about the plans that we have for this Group, but I must say to you, that of course, it does depend upon you. It is intended gradually as you become aware, that there will be manifestations within this Sanctuary. It is intended that Jesus the Nazarene will manifest. I will say to you that the Master stands within this Sanctuary at this moment, for it is His Master Plan that you are all part of.

There are many hundreds of Groups around the Earth plane that have been created in the same way as this Group has been created. They are of different denominations, they are of different creeds. They are of different beliefs in all manner of ways, but they meet together in groups of seven, at the guidance of the Nazarene. Though of course many would be very surprised, but nevertheless that is so, and these Groups have been brought together in order that the Brotherhood of Man can be spread across the Earth plane. For if it is not spread soon, there is going to be terrible devastation and much suffering, and I do not say this to frighten you, for it is a fact.

You sat together at varying times with another Group, and some of you here were sitting within that Group when Sister Agnes gave a message — a message in which she said, "Send forth a light, a light from your heart, and a light from your head. Send it forth, and we in the World of Spirit would use those lights to gradually build up the two circles around the Earth plane." Now of course, you are probably thinking, but the darkness is already within. And that is so, for as the light encircles the Earth plane and spreads it will drive out the powers of darkness. They will retreat before the light, for there is nothing else that they can do.

Now you probably think, what are the powers of darkness? The powers of darkness are the thoughts in the minds of men and women. Thought is all powerful, and it is by the thoughts that you send forth, that you can influence the thoughts of others. You are to plant seeds, which of course are thoughts. You will see some grow; you will realise that that person who you have been talking to has a greater awareness. They will ask questions, they may seek books to read, they might seek places to go to find out more, but some of those seeds, some of those thoughts, will take a long time to germinate. They will germinate, but with the teachings that you receive you will have a greater understanding of those things to say.

You will be given an understanding of those people to whom you speak, whether they will accept what you say or whether they will reject, and therefore you will concentrate more on the people who are accepting. But make sure that those that reject do have some knowledge to walk away with. For by their thoughts we perhaps can steer them very, very carefully upon their spiritual path, for all must have the awareness eventually. It will take a long time, but this is the beginning of the New Age. This is the beginning of the spiritual awareness, and by the time that the Age of Aquarius is ended, there will be no need for television sets or telephones, for all will be able to communicate by thought. This will happen, it will happen.

At the moment the Earth plane is very troubled, very troubled indeed. For there have been atrocities carried out upon Mother Earth, and she resents because the balance of her life is being changed. And unless something is done to stop these alterations of the balance, then Mother Earth is going to retaliate.

You will find my children, that there will be happenings, they are only murmurings really, but unfortunately lives will be lost and people will suffer. It is very doubtful whether much notice will be taken of the first grumblings unless the Groups that have been informed, the people that have been brought together, can link up in thought across the Earth plane, each sending forth their own thoughts of love.

My children, you know the conservationists are members of groups such as yours, for they meet together to discuss ways and means of bringing back life; of preserving those things which are being destroyed; of trying to bring balance back again upon the Earth plane. Have you ever thought of that? Or have you thought, perhaps they are cranks? They are not, for although they may not be aware, they are all guided by Spirit. The fishermen are striving to preserve their livelihood but also they are striving to keep a balance upon the Earth plane, for the fishes that swim in the sea and the creatures that live on the land, and the trees and the flowers are all part of the balance. The birds that fly, the rain that falls, the Sun that shines, the Moon encircling the Earth plane, are all part of the balance.

I will not come to speak with you every time, for there are others who will come to give you teachings. And there are others who will come to tell you, each one individually, of your own particular healing gift. There will be times when the whole period will be given to one individual, in turn of course; and when that happens I ask you all please to send forth your love and your strength to that individual, that those who come to help to guide and to teach may be given the power they will need. For you see, we are relying on the vibrations of the harmony that is between you all. Our channel lifts the vibrations with music before you come in order that the words that are spoken may be heard and understood.

There will be times when we will have discussions, when you will be able to ask questions and receive your answers; and there will be times when all the power and energy will be given to a manifestation — a High One, a Teacher, who will come to speak with you. There will come a time later on, when our channel will be taken over completely and will stand to one side, but she is not ready yet, although she is a very clear channel. I tell you these things in order that you may have an understanding of those things that will happen, and will also have an understanding of the reason that you are requested to have discipline. Discipline of attendance, the discipline of regularity. It is essential, you see. Otherwise the vibrations will be affected and it will mean that we in Spirit will have to devise a different plan for that particular meeting. But then we can do that, but it will not be the meeting or the teaching that you should have.

Now my children I will go, and I say to you all God's Blessings surround you, His Love and Light protect you all at all times. God bless you my children, God bless you.

Chapter II

THE POWER OF THOUGHT

reetings my children, this is Lauda. This teaching is one of great interest, for it involves those things which have happened through the ages on the Earth plane. Those things which have happened through the power of thought. The power of thought can do more good and more harm than is realised, for the power of good creates wonderful things, and the power of the thought of evil creates havoc.

The power of thought in the past was the power that was used to raise temples, to create many marvels. You know of course that [1]Stonehenge was, and is, a temple. A temple of very ancient things, but a temple also of love and truth. Even now those who are given the guidance by Spirit, although indeed they are unaware, are being taught the secrets of Stonehenge, for the secrets of Stonehenge of the past will become used in the future.

The knowledge that was placed within Stonehenge is today called 'common knowledge,' for it talks of the Moon and the Sun. It talks of the half year and the quarter year; it talks of the

---

[1]Stonehenge — Prehistoric stone monument on Salisbury Plain, Wiltshire, consisting of concentric circles of dressed stones erected mainly in the Bronze Age; some of the larger stones carry lintels and among the smaller are blue stones which apparently come from SW. Wales.

circles around the Earth plane from which energy comes. It talks of many things, but gradually these things are being unfolded by those who make a study of the matter. My children, Stonehenge is a place of great mystical power for there are many Spirits who tenant it, and at certain times they can be seen by those who have [2]The Gift. At certain times they mingle with the visitors and thoughts of spiritual matters are placed within the minds of certain of those visitors, which are taken away with them and talked about all over the Earth plane. And people ponder upon those things, and gradually inquiring minds start to think, and they gradually acquire the spiritual awareness which is necessary.

There are other places upon the Earth plane spread across the world. There are the wonders of Egypt, and indeed they are wonders, for the Egyptians had great psychic powers, and a great psychic awareness about things which had to be preserved and passed on, and there are certain things which are still preserved and which will be found when the time is right. There are secret chambers which have been built within the [3]pyramids, but when the time is right those who are to discover them will be guided to those secret places in order that the knowledge may come forth of those ancient times.

There is talk of a Sun God, and indeed there is a God of the Sun, for He is a Master too, and He is guiding the energy from the Sun to those places where it is most needed. At the moment it is within the area of the Middle East. The centre, the area where the rays of the Sun could reach if the Sun were placed flat upon the Earth plane, in the centre of that area now known as the Mediterranean, the area connecting the Red Sea — that is

---

[2]The Gift — A faculty looked upon as being given by Heaven — a natural endowment — a talent.

[3]Pyramid — Monumental structure of stone etc. with polygonal or square base and sloping sides meeting at apex, constructed by ancient Egyptians over a royal burial chamber and by Aztecs and Mayas as stepped platform for a temple.

the area where the powers of thought are the most destructive at the present time. The rays of the Sun stretch deep into the continent known as Africa. They stretch far across that continent, and there is a great deal of evil thought. The rays of the Sun, if laid flat upon the Earth plane, would reach up to the continent known as Russia. If they would reach up into the areas known as India, they would stretch across many countries. But if you look at your maps you will see that where the rays of the Sun would reach is where there is most unrest, most violence.

The rays of the Sun, the energy that is therein, must be used to cleanse out the evil thought — but of course it cannot be done without the help of the groups that are being set up across the Earth plane. For linking up with the Sun energy or the love energy, the thoughts of love that are sent out, the thoughts of compassion, it is these thoughts that will help to eradicate the thoughts of evil.

My children, the continent now called Australia was at one time peopled by those known as the Aborigines. The Aborigines were considered to be an ignorant band of savages by those who first alighted upon the shores of Australia. But the Aborigines are very wise people and stretch back in their ancestry for many many generations. They have been upon that continent for many ages of time. Oh yes, of course there have been refinements, but their knowledge, their spiritual knowledge of course I am speaking about, their spiritual awareness has at all times been very strong.

They lived as they had always lived by hunting the animals, by eating the herbs, the berries, the fruits of the trees. By spearing the fish within the water, by a very balanced diet. By a very balanced diet, that is as it would be known today, if all the various mineral elements were taken into consideration. Therefore, their body tissues were very strong, and thus they were very clear channels, and communicated with the Spirit world all the time. But now these people have been brought into so-called civilisation and their spiritual awareness has been dimmed. It has been, so to speak smothered, and this is a great pity.

I am telling you this, for I tell you things of the past ages. There have been many races, many tribes of people upon the Earth plane over the centuries, over the ages, and each one has discovered something new. But if each one could have seen into the past ages, they would have realised that nothing is new. For men's minds contain so much information, and past lives come forward of those things which were learned in past times, and are utilised again and again. So there really is nothing new, for old wonders that are so-called wonders, have all happened before, and wonderful cities and wonderful knowledge has always abounded in various parts of the Earth plane at various times.

Indeed at times there have been wonderful things upon the Earth plane and all are connected, for the [4]Incas worshipped the Sun, and the Egyptians worshipped the Sun, and the Maoris worshipped the Sun and their Spirit Gods, as they called them. For you see it was recognised that it was through the Sun that life survived. But of course the Sun would have dried everything up without the rain, and so there were rainbows. And so really and truly all peoples at all times have worshipped God the Father, for He is the Creator of all things.

May the blessings of the Beloved Father be upon you, and may the Light of His Love protect you at all times. God bless you.

* * * * *

Greetings my children — this is Lauda. I have listened with much interest to the discussion that has taken place upon the teaching that was taped. I have listened to those words that

---

[4]Incas — Inca — Member of American Indian Quichua-speaking people who at the time of the Spanish expedition which overthrew them in 1533 had a highly developed civilisation and ruled a large region of S.America with centre at Cuzco, Peru.

were spoken regarding the troubles upon the Earth plane. There are many troubles upon the Earth plane, and there is going to be much trouble. You were quite right to question the effect of the Sun's rays, and perhaps I have confused you, for to me it is quite clear, and I thought I had made allowances for the fact of the conscious mind.

When we speak of such matters we always bring the spiritual to the front, and the Sun laid flat in that area would not be able to send those rays to the distances that were commented upon, for the rays would be foreshortened by mountains. There are mountain ranges of course on the continent known as Africa, but there are points upon that continent where rays of the Sun would penetrate a very long way across that continent, for there are gaps right the way through in a direct line. This also applies should the rays of the Sun be sent towards the continent known as Russia. My children, there are places all around the Earth plane where, and I speak of course figuratively, where a string could be placed, and where it would pass completely round the Earth plane without any hindrance whatsoever.

There are several areas of this nature both longitude and latitude and it is these areas that are of the greatest value. I would very much like to list the names of these places that could be identified and linked, but it would take far too long. The thought that I may be romanticising is not correct, for it is possible that this would happen, and these are areas also of great danger. For my children, in the continent of Russia there are many secret places where great scientists with very destructive and evil minds have worked out many of these, 'passages' I will call them, where terrible weapons of destruction could be directed, and through these passages they could cause tremendous havoc at distances completely beyond conception.

I would say to you that this is possible, and this is why I also say that the energies and the love and the light must be used to stop these happenings. If I were to say to you that it is possible to send a missile, of the nature now being manufactured, constructed and hidden, and that it would be possible to send such a missile many many thousands of miles, you would not believe this to be true. But it is a complete truth that these passages, as I have called them, are used. It would be possible for you to research, but it would take you a very long time, but even in a small way you can research if you have an atlas of the world that is the full truth. It would have to be an atlas of perfection, and there are such atlases in the world.

My children, there are many things happening far beyond the knowledge of those on the Earth plane. There are things hidden away of great evil, and it is so necessary that a greater understanding be given to those people who are linked together in the Master Plan, and you have already been told that such groups have been formed around the Earth plane. By such knowledge peoples eyes can be opened to the dangers around them, and if through we in the World of Spirit these things can be pointed out, then it is hoped that a greater wisdom will spread and that people will become more enquiring and less lethargic. For all across the Earth plane the cry goes up, "We must not interfere, it is not our business." But, my children, it is your business. The safety and protection of the Earth plane is your business. You may say, "But what can I do, I am but one on my own?" You have already been told on the tape that the power of thought is all powerful, all embracing, and as you use thought, so you affect all that is around you, and you affect yourselves as well.

You are sitting together within this Group for progression, for a greater understanding and awareness of matters of the World of Spirit. And in order to progress you must have a greater awareness of those things that are going on around you. You must, in your way, endeavour to turn the thoughts of people towards a spiritual awareness, a giving out of love, a selflessness. By your example you can do this upon the Earth plane. There are those who have chosen to dwell amongst you from another Universe. They are living amongst you these Ones of high knowledge, for they are seeking to avert the dangers, they are seeking to bring about a unity. They are Ones of a greater intelligence, and in time they will be recognised, but at the moment they are lost in the crowd. Even now in the World of Spirit, there are those of a high level who have chosen to re-incarnate in time. But even now they are as children, but with a far wider knowledge than any child has ever had before. They will become known as Teachers of spiritual awareness, for they are the next stage in the Master Plan. And it is hoped that by their example those things which could so easily happen to Mother Earth, could be averted.

My children, I am afraid I sound like the voice of doom. It is not quite like that, but I am endeavouring to point out to you how easy it would be for Mother Earth to be completely destroyed. I hasten to say it will not happen. This will not happen my children, but I am saying to you, it could happen. There will be havoc upon the Earth plane for Mother Earth is going to cause considerable disruption, for as you have already been told the balance of life upon the Earth plane is being distorted, and she must protest in order to distract. I hope you have the meaning. But in so doing some of those free wide open passages will be blocked. for it was not intended that such evil and destructive weapons would be created. They have been created, I can assure you, they have been created, and they must therefore be rendered harmless, or perhaps I should say they must be rendered less destructive.

Now my children, when I spoke to you about the Aborigines this was merely an indication of the value of the correct food. For I did say that through their diet the Aborigines became clear channels, and that you my children, by your diet, you too could become clear channels. You must be clear channels and this is part of The Plan, you must all be clear channels. I would hasten to add my children, that you are not doing too badly now. The path will be made clear to you and you will find that those things that confuse you now will slip into place along with the other pieces of the jig-saw puzzle.

My friends, for I look upon you as friends as well as my children, I hope you do not find that confusing, but with all close relationships, friendship is very important. Perhaps there would not be quite so much dissension within the homes of many, if parents would be friends with their children, and their children would be friends with their parents.

Now my children, I feel that I have been speaking long enough. I hope that you have an understanding now about the rays of the Sun in the context that I used in my previous message. I hope now that you will discuss those things that I said. We are with you in this room and we will take those thoughts and those words that you speak and think upon them. And at a later meeting we will give you the opportunity to ask questions, and you will receive your answers, but now I go.

May the Love and the Light of The Beloved Father be with you, and surround you with protection, as indeed it does. God bless You.

* * * * *

Greetings my children, it is I Lauda. All around the Earth plane there are those who are busy predicting those things which will happen. There are those who speak in truth and there are those who enlarge upon the teachings of others. There are those who investigate the surface of the Earth plane. There are those who use scientific instruments and say that such and such a thing is going to happen on such and such a date. There are those who have been delving into the predictions of those of the past, who are now in Spirit. There are those who use astrology and there are those who just wet their finger and hold it to the wind, so to speak.

My children I say to you, many things will happen on the Earth plane. Many things will happen, for there is coming now a time of interplanetary action, a bringing together, so to speak, of a peak period, and it is during this peak period that many things will happen. But many more things could happen and many of those things that have been predicted could be stopped. The strength of the power of thought is not yet realised, for there are comparatively few schools of teaching upon the subject of thought.

There are those who do much good by simply sitting in prayer. But they do not all realise that it is the power of thought, the dedication, the concentration, the joining together in unity, which builds up the power. They do not realise the great force there is in thought, for each thinks of thought in an individual way, of MY thought. What can my thought do? I am but a small, a very small cog in the huge wheel of God's Plan, what can my thought do? But the thoughts of each individual play a very large part.

You can test this yourself. In your daily lives you come across those who snap back, who are aggressive. You could accidentally knock into somebody and if you turn round and say, "I am very sorry," and smile at them, you will find nine times out of ten they will say, "That's quite all right," and return your smile. You will of course come across those who will give you what is known as a dirty look and carry on, and it is those people that you must ask a prayer for. Ask a prayer that they may be relaxed, that they may become at peace.

You will also find that there are those who will be for everlasting complaining about this that and the other. I would say to you, do not agree with them but try to guide their thinking upon more positive lines, for nine times out of ten those people are told, "Oh yes — Oh isn't that dreadful," and so the thought goes down and down. It is not a trivial matter it is of great importance, for by going forth in this manner and by your thinking being positive, by your decisions being positive, you will do a great deal to help. You will do a great deal to take away the clouds of anxiety, of tension that surrounds some people.

I know there are times when you yourselves are feeling depressed or have an anxiety problem, but for you, you have the understanding; sit quietly in prayer and meditate for a while and you will be given your answers. If you have not tried this then I would suggest you do so. Send up your prayer to Father God. Tell Him your anxiety, tell Him your problems, and then sit quietly in meditation for just ten or fifteen minutes. Still your mind and let the words of guidance be received. You will find that if you have completely relaxed and cleared your mind you will feel very much better and there will be a solving of your problems.

There are those to whom you can say these words and there are those who would not understand, who would probably turn round and say, "I'm far too busy to sit down and meditate or whatever you call it." But there again it is an indication that that person needs help. You see my children, I am still talking of healing, of a different type of healing, of a day to day healing. One which does not require words, but prayers and thoughts of sympathy and compassion. But it does mean that you yourself must have positive thinking, for it would be very easy for you to turn round to the person who slammed the door in your face or bashed into you, so to speak. I must apologise for that is a slang word, but nevertheless it would be very easy for you to turn round and snap also, and this you must avoid doing. Try to smile more, try to send out cheery words more often and watch the results. It is quite surprising how people will react. Negative will react to positive and if you are positive then those with negative thoughts will react to you, will react to your thinking. Try it, it really does work.

Now I want to say a word or two about children, for those who are now coming upon the Earth plane have very many traumatic happenings ahead of them. Many of them have come down with this knowledge, which will in early childhood become a fact. They will know and they will understand their role. There will of course be those who will not become aware until a later stage, for you see the knowledge must come forth in steps. Thus it is increased and thus the power builds up, for there must be a tremendous power of positive thought to avert what could happen in the future. I would hasten to add that it will not be the future of any of you in this Group. You will by that time be in Spirit, for there will be much for you to do.

You are learning well, all of you, and the children who have returned who are now upon the Earth plane and those who are waiting to return to the Earth plane have much work ahead of them. There are many who will be lost in the wilderness of despair, and they must be led back upon the path of true love. There are those who are returning to the Earth plane who are termed, 'old souls.' Those with many experiences and great powers. There are new souls who have to learn, and unfortunately their teachings, their early teachings, are going to be of very great strength. I say unfortunately, for sometimes the approach slowly made is much more acceptable. But all things are as written and all things must happen that way.

Gradually you are going to see a chain of events happening upon the Earth plane, and you will be able to say, "Why, we were told this when we were sitting in the Group of healing," for there are many things that you have stored away in the spiritual mind. There have been teachings whilst in the sleep state, all knowledge of which is stored in the spiritual mind. And there are going to be times, not too far off, when you will bring forth knowledge which you do not even realise you have, and you will marvel, for you will not realise that you had such a depth of thinking. So we come back again to the power of thought. The power of thought, a power which if used for good, can create the safe keeping of Mother Earth.

I go now. God bless you. May the Love and the Light protect you at all times and indeed it does. God bless you, all of you.

Chapter III

THE CHAKRAS

G reetings my daughter, greetings my children — this is Lauda. It is a great pity that once again there are not the full members here, so we cannot give the same teachings, for again there are teachings that all must hear. I know the thought has gone forth from those who are missing, for the understanding has been given that they will not attend. Although I know that my words are on the machine it is but a one way system, for without the discussion and all being present we do not hear the words, we do not read the thoughts of you all. We know that they will discuss when they hear these words but there will be no record of their comments.

My children, you probably wonder why it is so important that the whole meeting is recorded upon the machine, particularly the discussion which takes place. You probably wonder why every word has to be recorded, and wonder why this is necessary when you each remember those words which you have spoken. But my children when once they have been said those words are gone, but captured upon a machine they are held. And there will come a time when those words will be of value, and all that which has taken place within this Group, within this little Sanctuary, will be of importance, for they will become teachings to others.

At this moment it may seem rather far fetched, but time will prove that this is correct, for the teachings that are given here will become teachings of tomorrow. There will be many enquiries upon the Earth plane in due course regarding those things of the World of Spirit, and I speak now of an open house. An open house embraces completely the Love and the Understanding of Father God, that the words that are spoken are sent forth from Groups such as this. And as I have already pointed out they are of many denominations and creeds of many understandings, of many diverse conditions upon the Earth plane.

I have already mentioned the conservationists — there are those people who are endeavouring to save the old buildings, that they may be kept intact as they were for future generations to study. And although they are made of bricks and mortar, or straw, or wattle, or hay, or beech branches, they will nevertheless be of great importance to spread an understanding across the Earth plane for those who are to come along seeking. There have always been those people upon the Earth plane, my children, who have been interested in history, and not only the history of kings and wars and invasions and such like. But the history of trees, of the birds, of the fossils, of the rock formations, of the ebb and the flow of the tide, of the invasion of the sea on certain areas, and the drainage of the sea in certain areas, of underground rivers, of unknown water supplies, and so it goes on. These people, my children, are seeking into history.

There has been an upsurge amongst certain groups of people to discover the burial places of the Ancients, to open up these burial places and to discover within the secrets that are hidden. There are such burial places within this country, but of course there are such burial places around the Earth plane. Whether it be India or Egypt, whether it be a remote island in the Pacific, whether it be vast continents, there are burial places of great interest and treasures of wisdom buried within, and all these interests will be recorded in various ways, and all the research will not be wasted.

So we come back again, my children, to this little Group. We are sitting together, seven people within a small room, but the words that we are speaking and the discussions that are held are recorded, and there will come a time when they will be heard outside of this Sanctuary. Not yet, but there will come a time, and so the words must be upon the machine. And so we come back to the point that if you do not attend with discipline and regularity, all the words and all the thoughts of this Group will not be upon the machine. I hope you have my meaning, my children. It may seem as if I have gone round, round the World if you like, to get back to the point, but it is important that you have the discipline and the regularity.

We know and we understand that there are occasions when your life upon the Earth plane must be regulated by other considerations, but my children, I would say to you, think before deciding to break your discipline. Now of course there can be another thought. There can be the thought that maybe those things are said at the Group meeting which you attend are not for you. It may be an evening where someone else is given the full concentration of power. But that is as it should be, for there will come a time when you are given the full concentration of power and so there will be a sharing, as indeed there must be.

Now my children, I would like to speak for a brief time upon healing. I would like to say a word or two about the [1]chakras, the spiritual centres of the physical body. The crown chakra is the opening to the secret places, within where lies hidden many treasure which you can bring forth if you sit in meditation and go deep within. All chakras must be in balance,

---

[1]The Chakras — are the vital force centres at the different levels of experience or consciousness in the human system. The word chakra means a wheel in Sanskrit and these centres of energy may be seen as wheels or vortices of force. The energies seated at these levels manifest through these vital force centres.

for if they are not then the physical body is out of balance, and this leads to various complaints and illnesses, to disabilities and pain. For if the chakras are in balance, then the physical body is in balance.

My children, the solar plexus, the [2]solar chakra, is very important also, for it is into that area that all things enter. It is into that area that the warnings will be given, of those things around you that are not as they should be. You will find that if you are in the company of people, I am talking of course on the spiritual level, if you are in the company of people who are not on the same vibration as yourself, it will always be registered in the solar chakra. There will be a feeling as of lead, a heaviness. Discuss this point amongst yourselves for it is of interest.

My children, I am not going to say any more at this time, for we would ask you to sit and discuss the knowledge that you have regarding the chakras within yourselves, the spiritual centres. We would like you to discuss and bring forward the knowledge that you have and then we will talk about those things.

And so, my children, I will say for now, farewell, but we will speak again after the discussion. God bless you. God bless you.

* * * * *

Greetings my children, this is Lauda. I have listened with interest to the rather frugal remarks passed regarding the chakras. It is, as has already been said, there are the main chakras and there are the secondary chakras, and the main chakra is the heart, for the heart is the atom. The atom is the part of God, for you are all part of Father God. My children, I know you have this understanding.

The chakras are very important in healing my children, very important, for as has already been stated the chakras must be in balance, and I am speaking now of the main chakras. It is true

---

[2]The Solar Chakra — sometimes called the Chakra of absorption, is located at the level of the solar plexus. This chakra is the seat of the element of fire in our nature.

all heal in different ways and there are many healers who are unaware of the importance of the chakras, but we wish this Group to be aware of those things that they can do, of those things that can happen if the chakras are misused through lack of knowledge. Yes my children, you are channels and there are those in the World of Spirit who use you, and they direct the God Power. And if the God Power is to be directed and used correctly, then my children you must have a knowledge of the chakras.

The atom is within. It has been said that it is possible for the human body to create more power than any bomb that has yet been devised, and comparatively this is so. My children, if the [3]pineal gland, the [4]crown chakra, is not functioning as it should be, then there is no real life within the physical body. Yes, there is the heart, but you see my children if the brain is not fed correctly it becomes damaged, and if it becomes damaged it does not trigger off the movable parts of the body and everything else that is controlled thus. So the physical body is just a shell, and people become what is known as 'a cabbage', which is very sad but it does happen. And this is brought about because the pineal gland is not functioning correctly, and the crown chakra — the spiritual centre is not able to come into alignment with the heart chakra.

Comment has been made about the thyroid chakra. The physical body does not affect the spiritual because my children, they are quite separate, and yet they are as one. The thyroid glands and the thyroid chakra are very important, but one does

---

[3]Pineal Gland — Pineal — shaped like a pine-cone; small conical body of unknown function behind third ventricle of brain.

[4]The Crown Chakra — the crown centre — is located at the top of the head corresponding to the position of the pineal gland. It is the seat of the highest frequency of energy vibration in ourselves. This vibration is often depicted by artists as a halo surrounding the head of highly evolved or holy people. Statues or pictures of the Buddha usually show the crown chakra at the top of the head. The tonsure practised by monks had its origin in the functioning of this centre.

not affect the other in this case, and so you see that if the physical is not as it should be the spiritual is not affected. I feel there may be some confusion from this, but I will make it clearer at a later time.

Above the eyes, to either side, are spiritual centres. Again these are important, as they are the centres of spiritual awakening. They are the centres that can affect your thinking; they are the centres that connect to the third eye, and they are the centres of great value. It is through these centres that psychics become aware of impressions. It is not clairvoyance as such, it is impressions of ones in the World of Spirit, impressions of those around, and yet you do not actually see. I hope you have the meaning.

The inner ear, the clairaudient faculty, is also connected with these centres, and altogether my children, the head is the most important part of the physical body. For within it also houses spiritual centres of great delicacy. The heart chakra has the most value for how could anything be of more value than that which is the creative part, the God within you, the part of Father God that makes all men and women brothers and sisters.

My children, I will now go to the basest part, and that is the [5]sacral. That my children, is where the sex organs are, and it is the lowest chakra of the main chakras, not only in position but in reaction, and it is that chakra that controls the lives of many people. It is that chakra which has to be brought under control. It is that chakra which is the cause of many evil happenings upon the Earth plane. For at the present time it is that chakra which virtually holds sway in the physical bodies and in the spiritual bodies of most people who seek revengeful ways.

I would say to you, my children, that the chakras are important. We will discuss them another time, but I would say, the chakras ARE important. They control so much of your

---

[5]The Sacral Centre — The sacral — is at the level of the sacrum on the spine. At this level we have the experience of fluidity in ourselves. This is called the element of water.

spiritual life. And if you have a greater understanding of the value that they are to your spiritual awareness and to the healing; if you could only have a greater understanding of the control that can be brought about by understanding the chakras, then my children you will know how the God Power flows through you when you are healing.

I would say to you, it is not always necessary to lay on hands, for absent healing is of great value. Absent healing can be given to those who have no knowledge that it is being given, and it is a wonderful thing to be able to send forth absent healing of great power. This can be done when you understand the God Power within you and the God Power that is sent through you.

My children, I was talking at the earlier message about discipline. You see discipline is necessary at all stages of spiritual progression, for you need discipline to sit regularly in meditation. We will have a meditation evening — we will sit in meditation and we will discuss. And I hope by that time you will all have achieved an understanding and an ability to go deep within. Deep within are where the treasures are stored and where you can bring forth great spiritual knowledge.

I would say to you, endeavour to use the knowledge that will be given to you and that which you already have. Seek and find out more of the power that is within. Read about the chakras. I do not mean great volumes, touch the surface, if you like. If you have knowledge of the chakras, then you do not need to study. But if you have no knowledge of the chakras I would say to you, read upon it. You will be surprised how valuable that knowledge will be as you progress in the healing.

Now I know that there are those who say, "I am a healer, I have done this, and I have done that." They forget that they are but channels. I do not decry the ability, for it is an ability that comes from Father God. There are different degrees of healing as there are different levels of spiritual knowledge. Ask yourselves, what degree, what level do you wish to obtain? Do you wish to just tickle the surface, so to speak, or do you wish to really understand that which happens? Do you wish to understand the spiritual centres, and do you wish to see a patient who has come to you in great pain? Do you not wish to see them get up and walk away with happiness upon their face? It can be done. It will be done, in time, if you have discipline.

Now, my children, I will go. Do think on these words. It is necessary that you have a greater understanding, it really is necessary. I will go now and leave you to discuss, if you wish to discuss.

May the Light and the Love of Father God surround you at all times, and it does. God bless you all. God bless you.

Chapter IV

HEALING
ABSENT HEALING

G reetings my children, this is Lauda. I come to speak with you about healing for this is your main concern. We spoke last time on the chakras. We did not cover the chakras to any depth, but I endeavoured to give you an understanding of the importance of the seven main chakras, the spiritual centres that must be brought into line if the physical body is to be kept in line — in attunement.

I wish to talk to you this time about the healings that are brought about by [1]absent healing. There have been many words said regarding absent healing and there are those channels who are used for the absent healing alone, for they feel that this is where they are of most use and of most service. This of course is very often the case, for there are those upon the earth plain who are not clear channels for clairaudience or clairvoyance, and there are those who are not clear channels for spirit doctors to use. Absent healing is brought about by the power of thought and concentration, and those who are used for absent healing,

---

[1]Absent Healing — Healing through the intercession of a healing medium (often but not always assisted by a dedicated group), by spirit doctors on behalf of patients who have no direct contact with the medium. Patients are often unaware that they are being treated, more especially if they are ignorant or known to be hostile to Spiritualism. The aim is to benefit the patient spiritually, mentally and physically, if possible, but no promises are given.

those people have considerable concentration. They are able to shut out completely the sounds and the every day thoughts around them, while they sit and concentrate their thoughts upon absent healing, upon those who are sick. Sometimes at considerable distances, even the other side of the Earth plane.

Absent healing is of course entirely the power of thought, the concentration of love, the concentration upon the person who is sick. Now my children in many cases the one who is sending forth absent healing has no knowledge of the life of the person they are seeking healing for. They have a name, sometimes they have an address, sometimes just a town or a village name and the illness, whether it be of mind, body, or soul. But they concentrate upon that name, upon that place, upon that sickness, and the thoughts are used, for the thoughts are carried towards that person.

The one who is receiving healing, the one it is intended should receive healing, may be completely unaware of these thoughts. They may be lying on a sick bed, they may be carrying on their daily lives, they may be in a gathering of people, but nevertheless those thoughts of healing are sent to them. On some occasions they are aware of a change within themselves. Sometimes they may feel happy. Sometimes suddenly they may feel as if a weight has been lifted from their shoulders, and sometimes they may feel nothing. But that does not mean to say the healing is not being given.

My children, there are those who send forth absent healing by sitting together in twos and threes or in large groups. There are those who send forth absent healing by linking together within their own homes, one in one place, two in another, three in another maybe. But they link together at a certain time and they link with a certain person. It is usually the medium of the Group, if there be one, or the strongest, the co-ordinator, so to speak, who will be projected to that one who is sick, and thus you hear of a sick person who says, 'There was a lady or there was a gentleman, or there was a child with me. I saw them quite clearly. They came and spoke with me. I do not know who they were but they were here and when they left I felt so much better." You will hear of these occasions. I expect you have already heard of such occasions, and that is the power of thought, projected by a group of people who have linked up at a certain time, and this of course can be very powerful and very strong.

There are occasions when absent healing can be used to steady the mind of a soul in torment. To concentrate upon the crown chakra, the pineal gland, is to concentrate upon matters of the mind, and a great soothing and a great relief can be given. And very often this type of healing is of the utmost value where there have been bereavements, particularly bereavements brought about by carelessness. For it is those who are left behind with the thought, "If only I had done this," or "If only I had said that." It is those bereavements that bring illnesses of the mind. And by absent healing, by concentrating upon that person, upon the pineal gland, much relief can be given, and a space in which to sort out that which is troubling and that which is causing the illness, and gradually it is dispersed.

Now there are those who concentrate on colours when giving absent healing, but absent healing through colours must only be given when there is a wide knowledge and understanding of the colours in relation to the parts of the body that need repair or healing. If a person of great strength concentrates the force of the wrong colour on to an organ or part of the body, then they can cause problems. Perhaps the thought will go forth, that surely we in the World of Spirit could do something about that. But we do not interfere, we cannot interfere, for it is your thought that is going forth. And so I would say to you, absent healing by the use of colour needs much study. Do not treat it lightly for it can be of considerable value.

Now my children, sometimes you can be working, carrying on your daily lives, and you will hear of somebody, maybe a neighbour who has an illness, and perhaps the thought will enter your head, 'I do wish I could do something to help.' The thought is used and very often does help, and you are bringing about a condition of healing within that person.

I know there is one amongst you who has considerable strength with absent healing, and we will listen with interest to the comments that are made in the discussion that is to follow. I will go now. God bless you. God bless you.

* * * * *

Greetings my children, this is Thomas. We have listened with great interest to those words which have been spoken regarding absent healing. And we have listened with great interest to those other words that have been spoken, for it shows that you have some knowledge of other subjects upon which we will speak, for from those other subjects, my children, there are healings also.

Much comment has been made upon the power of thought upon the absent healing in comparison to the laying on of hands. Absent healing, my children, is very powerful when used correctly. The power of thought is directed, as has been stated, to the [2]etheric body of the patient. It circulates the body, the physical body, it circulates in the etheric, it cleanses those parts which are damaged if it is the Will of Father God that those parts are cleansed. Now when I say the Will of Father God, I mean if it is as written, for in the [3]Akaishic records everything is written. At some future date we will have a discussion on the Akaishic records, although I am sure it is your understanding that nobody in the physical body can see the

---

[2]Etheric body — The Etheric body is a duplicate in appearance of the physical body, formed of a much finer substance which is invisible to the physical sight.

[3]Akaishic Records — An occult term said to be a cosmic picture gallery and record of every thought, feeling and action since the world began. Often advanced as an explanation of clairvoyant and psychometric perceptions. Yogis believe that this record can be contacted when in certain psychic states of consciousness.

43

Akaishic records when in the Astral body, for they are carefully guarded; but information is given when travel is made to the [4]Halls of Learning and Knowledge. But I digress.

Absent healing, when conducted through a group of people sitting together is of great value, but only if all people sincerely link. Where there is sincerity there is love, and where there is love there is power, and where there is power the healing is complete, if it is to be so. I trust you have my meaning.

A patient who receives a manifestation is usually completely unaware that that which they see is not of substance, although it appears to be. There have been occasions, my children, it has been known, that a patient when fully recovered, has sworn on the Holy Book that that which they saw really was there, when in fact it was a manifestation. Oh yes! It was there, but it was not there. I speak in riddles, but I know you have my meaning.

Absent healing is very worthwhile, for with absent healing there are no barriers, for you see my children, the patient is often unaware. With the laying on of hands there is often a barrier put up by the patient. Very often that patient has been persuaded, and by putting up a barrier they delay that which could happen, but that same person could receive absent healing entirely unaware. It does happen, it has happened, it will continue to happen, for when thought is sent forth with love then its power is many times increased. I would say to you my children, at no time send forth absent healing unless your heart is full of love, the love that is sent forth brother to brother. So called miracles have happened when love has been the key.

My children, you live in very busy times. You live in a period of time upon the Earth plane which you yourselves chose to return to. A period of time which lacks sadly in love, a period of time of absolute materialism. And so you see my children, how valuable, how very very valuable is the love that

---

[4]Halls of Learning — Places for instruction in the spirit spheres. Sometimes said to be visited by earth people during sleep–state.

you can send forth. In these busy times, you give that which is most precious, a part of your time upon the Earth plane to dedicate in service, to follow in the footsteps of The Nazarene. For to work in love, to be of service, to unselfishly give of your time is indeed of great value.

My children, Lauda spoke of absent healing using colour, and we are indeed gratified to hear the words that were spoken regarding colour healing, for it is treated too lightly. Colour healing must be studied. It is a healing which will be used much in the future. It is a healing which will be used by those who call themselves Doctors, but there will not be Doctors as are known now. There will be no need for vast expensive machinery, for those upon the Earth plane who are to follow you will have within themselves far greater ability than the machinery. I speak of course of times many years ahead, but colour healing will be used.

My children, I would say to you, the thoughts that you send forth on absent healing, the thoughts of love that you send forth, are used, will be used. But I would say to you — do not — do not be disappointed if the one to whom you have sent those thoughts does not become whole. At times it is necessary that suffering has to be endured. There is a reason, but believe me my children, Father God does not want any one of you to suffer. It is not His wish, it is not His desire, it is not His intention for any one of His children to suffer. There was perfection in the beginning, there will be perfection in the end. But there are lessons to be learned, there are mistakes to be rectified, and my children there must be a greater awareness of those things that can be accomplished through love, the pure spiritual Love.

My children, there will not be perfection for many many earth years, but there is an awareness spreading across the Earth plane. It is an awareness which is becoming of great value. It is an awareness greatly increasing within the early civilised countries, but also my children, there is much healing needed within those areas of great distress and turmoil. But if you think about it, in those areas there are those who are struggling to bring forth the right thinking for peace. Send forth thoughts of healing to those areas my children, indeed this evening in the prayer that was said, those thoughts were sent to those areas and that is good.

Now my children, I will go. I would like to make sure that you have the understanding that if you are a clear channel for a Spirit Doctor or those in the World of Spirit who wait to be used and who wait to use you as a channel, you save the energies of those in Spirit who do this work, for if you are a clear channel you do not cause your own thinking to disrupt the work that must be done. If you are a channel for absent healing, for you are still a channel, your concentration must be good, it must be complete, and you send forth your thoughts of love and healing to the patient. They go to the patient, to the etheric body, where they are picked up and utilised. I hope you have the understanding. It has been very nice for me to return once again to this little Sanctuary for it is a place that is very dear to me. I will go now my children, and I will say to you — God's Blessings upon you all. May the Light and the Love of Father God be with you as your protection, as you walk along your spiritual path. God bless you my children. God bless you.

* * * * *

Greetings my children, this is Lauda. I come to speak upon absent healing once again. I do not wish to be repetitive, but there were many questions, and many thoughts put forth at the discussion at the last meeting. There were one or two thoughts put forth which must have an answer, thoughts of complete misunderstanding.

The thought was put forward that free will can be used for bringing about a healing. No my children, free will cannot bring about a healing, for at all times the thought goes forth, and it is the thought of healing that is used and conveyed to the etheric body of that one concerned with the thought, no matter how trivial, my children, the thought of healing may be. It may be for a child who has fallen down and brought blood to the part that has been damaged. This is why mothers are considered to be healers of their children, for they say, "Oh never mind, we will soon make it better," or "Mummy will make it better." And the thought has gone forth, the request to make it better, and to have the pain removed. And those healers and helpers who stand by, come forward to do their work, and it is through the love that the mother gives to that child by clasping it in her arms and comforting it, it is the compassion that soothes. It is this in all things, my children, whether children or adults, whether those who have lived a few earth days or those who have lived many earth days, the same thing applies to all. Compassion and love; the thoughts of healing that are sent out all combine to bring about comfort, healing, a sense of peace.

Now my children, there was also a comment put forth regarding that which is known as black magic — those who conjure up the evil spirits. My children, it is the thought that conjures up the evil spirits, for evil spirits are banished below a certain dimension, but thought will bring them forth. And so it is with that which is known as black magic. Here we can combine a previous teaching on the chakras, a teaching in which I told you something of the sacral chakra, the base chakra. I told you at that time that it is those who have revengeful thoughts and thoughts of hate who are on the level of the evil ones, for the more evil the thought the lower the dimension. I am sure you have my meaning.

Those who practice the art of so-called black magic, delight in desecrating the name of Father God and Jesus the Nazarene. They delight to humiliate and degrade, they delight to make sick, to bring about suffering, to cause derangement of the mind. All these things my children, are evil thought which is practised by those who are within that dimension. It is possible, by concentrated thoughts of evil intent, that a power can be built up which will cause evil, but again I must emphasise — it is the power of thought. You will say, "Surely the powers of darkness can be overcome by the light." My children, the light does not penetrate that dimension, for it is within that dimension that a great desire has to arise, to lift those souls into the light. I know that our daughter has the understanding, for in an earlier initiation she had the task of lifting into the light those who so desired, and I am sure she still remembers the reluctance that she felt to touch those dark forms. So I hope that I have made it quite clear, that it is the power of thought, whether it be for good or evil, that is the dominating factor.

I will now speak about the healing power of flowers. Flowers have a wonderful healing power, for the colour of flowers embraces the whole spectrum, and of course it is the power of the [5]Devic people. My children, I am sure you have all heard of fairies, and pixies, and elves, and these are a fact. Although I expect it is beyond the understanding of two or three of you, but it is of course your privilege to accept or reject according to your understanding. I would say that there are Devic people who tend the flowers, who take upon themselves this work, for it is a work of love, and it is this love which is sent forth in healing from the flowers.

There is one amongst you who has recently lost a dear one, and when I say lost, I mean from the physical touch, for that one is not far away. She has passed through the veil and she is now in the World of Spirit. And I may add, she has a wonderful understanding and therefore there is no need to worry or wonder about her for she is near. I would say to that one, fill your rooms with flowers. Oh, I do not mean great masses, but a few in one corner and a few in another, and so on, so that wherever you go about your home you will see the bright colours of the flowers and you will know that as you pass them, you are also receiving healing, for the Devic people will do that work. There is no need at any time to have masses and masses

---

[5]Devic — The Devas — Eastern word for angelic beings, or of that order.

of flowers about, but there are occasions when it is best to have a large display, and this is at a time of remembrance. At a time of remembrance the brightness of the flowers filling the room with their colour and perfume gives energy which will enable those in Spirit who do not have great power, to draw close to you. For my children, it does take considerable energy to stand by your side.

There are plants, also the greenery of shrubs and trees, that of course are healing and strength giving. You all have the understanding that to place your arms around the trunk of a strong tree is to revitalise yourselves. For from the power within that tree, the vitality and the energy is coursing up towards the heavens, towards the Sun, towards the cosmic rays. So you too will draw up the vitality, and receive strengthening and healing.

My children, there are some schools of thought, Health Farms I think some are called, where those who seek, walk upon the dew laden grass in the early hours of the morning with bare feet. This is a very good practice, for from the early dew and the early risings of the vitality into the grass, you too will be revitalised. But my children, I would say to you, make sure it is dew laden grass that you walk upon in your bare feet and not snow. For although this too would assist greatly, you would receive just as much benefit by scooping up a bowl of snow and taking it inside and rubbing your feet in it. For within would be warmth and protection and without you could well catch a very serious cold.

My children, endeavour to have within your homes a plant of green, for green is tranquillity, and you will find that to have one or two plants of green where you can see or touch them will bring you a calming effect. Now my children I will go, for it is time for you to discuss those things that have been said. We will listen. God bless you.

Healing

* * *

ACUPUNCTURE

Greetings my children, my name is Tooskio. I come to say Hello, and I come to give you a lesson on [1]acupuncture. You have heard of acupuncture I don't doubt, and you know that it is an old Chinese healing. It is a healing which works upon the pressure points. It is a healing which links up with many parts of the body from areas which seem to have no connection whatsoever. It is a healing of great delicacy, and it is a healing of much ancient wisdom.

My children, all over your body you have special points, special areas linking up with the nervous system. You have minute nerves all over the body all linking up to a central point. These points are of great healing value. There is a point in the sole of the foot which links up with the heart. Also in the sole of the foot there is nerve linkage with the ears and with the eyes and with the kidneys. The soles of the feet are of great delicacy, and greatly misused. You have already been told of the value of walking on the grass, and perhaps if I tell you that the soles of the feet have these acupuncture points of linkage with the whole body, perhaps you can understand how necessary it is to obtain vitality from Mother Earth.

---

[1]Acupuncture - Chinese practice of pricking areas of skin with needles for therapeutic purposes.

There are points behind the ears of great delicacy which can be used to cleanse away tumours on the brain. There are points in the neck which can be used to help the kidneys and the liver. There are points in the thighs which can be used to bring into attunement problems in the area of the bowels. In the top part of the elbow there is a very delicate point which can be used to cleanse cataracts of the eyes.

My children, I wish that I could give you a demonstration of acupuncture. I wish I could give you a greater knowledge through that demonstration. For acupuncture is of great value for healing, and acupuncture is a healing which will be, and even now, is much used in the Western world. My children, hair that is falling out can be brought into luxurious growth by the use of acupuncture. Limbs which are encased in crystal can be cleansed, for by activating the nerve centres the crystals can be dispersed. Spinal problems can be corrected by acupuncture. Of course I am not talking of acupuncture by just one usage, of course one has to have a series of treatments, but it does not take long.

I would say to you, you might find it of great value to study something of acupuncture. But I would say to you that just a casual glancing at a book is not enough. You must have instruction, for the needle or the pin or whatever you like to call it, must be placed at the right angle, otherwise you could cause great discomfort. To have a knowledge of the acupuncture points could assist very much the difficult patient.

My children, I would like you to think upon what I have said. I would like to have elaborated more, but I must go. And so I say God bless you. God bless you.

Healing

* * *

HEALING OF ANIMALS

Greetings my daughter, this is Lauda, and greetings to you all. Our teaching tonight is about the healing of animals. The healing that is given to animals is a healing of complete understanding, for no word can be spoken from the animal; but the animal healer, the one that is used for the healing of animals, the instrument, is given a greater understanding of the thoughts that are sent forth from the creature. There is a link-up, there is a bondage between the two, and one is brought up to the level of the other in order that they may commune.

When healing is being given to an animal there must first of all be a complete oneness one with the other. The animal must trust completely the one who is healing, and to do this it is best to sit quietly caressing and whispering gently into the ear of the animal. I must interject here, for I keep referring to the animal, but of course the healer is used for the healing of birds of flight, and other creatures, for a snake can be healed through the Love of God, and so I must say — All God's creatures.

My children, there have been many wonderful healings of animals, many wonderful healings of the creatures of the Earth plane. It has been known for a healing to be given through a channel to a tiger of very ferocious nature, and it has astounded those who have been privileged to watch how docile the animal has become from the touch and the gentle words of the healer, for you see, he speaks the words from God. It is absolutely essential that when a creature is brought to you for healing that you spend time speaking to it, caressing it, and making sure that you are linked. You will know when you are linked, for as a healer you know these things. I would say to you that it is always a good thing to link in understanding with any creature.

It is always a good thing to whisper gently in its ear, and I am sure you have the understanding that it is possible by blowing gently up the nostrils of a creature, to bring about the unity. But I would say to you my children, do not try and blow up the nostrils of a ferocious creature for you may find that your head has become its lunch.

It is best when healing to start at the head, for that too is the crown chakra, and the spiritual centres can be reached from the spine in the same way as ordinary healing. For the spine whether in the physical body, whether in the body of a creature, which of course is also a physical body, the spine is the centre from which the psychic centres can be reached, and you start at the head and follow the pattern of healing as for humans. I use this word in order to make it easier for you to understand which is which, and as in the healing for humans, so for the little creatures.

By gently moving your hands down the spine and bringing into line, you will bring about a soothing, but nothing must be hasty. To gently caress and to gently envelop in your hands that area which is damaged, can be of great value. For those who are instruments of Veterinary Surgeons, I would say that there are many who wait in the World of Spirit to come forward to help the little creatures on the Earth plane.

There is a creature who is much loved who has lost the sight of the eyes. I would like to say to you that if you place your hands around his head covering the eyes, and hold them there for a time, he will receive benefit, but I would also say that he will never see more than shadows, for the control nerve is very badly diseased, you have the understanding?

My children, there is one amongst you who is greatly interested in the healing of creatures upon the Earth plane. And I would say to that one to concentrate on that line of thought, for as you have already been told, thought is all powerful. Concentrate upon that line of thought to bring into play those things which have been said, and in time you will find that you will become used as a pure channel and in time you will be sought by many. Bear in mind that at all times you are a channel and that the love and the understanding that you give to the little creatures will be returned a thousand times, for the little creatures do not forget.

I would like to say to you, that there will come a time when you will look back upon these words, all of you, the words that are spoken within this Sanctuary. You will look back and you will say, "It was quite right, it has happened," and it will happen that each one of you will use the gifts of healing to bring about a greater understanding between peoples. It is the understanding that you are given, and the understanding that you will send forth, which will help to bring about that which must be brought about.

There will come a time when the peoples upon the Earth plane will link with this understanding. But there will be areas which will shut their ears to that which must be, and then there will come about a great concentration of thought upon those peoples, and they will be made whole.

And now my children I will go. It is possible that you will say, "I have heard all that before." It is possible, but I would say to those, that there are others amongst you who have not heard it all before. And so perhaps this has been a teaching especially for them. But as you have already been told, each one will receive a teaching especially for them, and so it is written, and so it will be. Now my children, I will go in order that you may discuss those things which you know. God bless you. God bless you.

Healing

* * *

ACUPRESSURE

This is Lauda. I will not stay with you for long. I come to introduce one who has not communicated in this manner. He has not returned to the Earth plane before and he has come particularly to speak to the one known as M....

Hi there. My name is Philip Chitou. I've come to speak to you mate about healing. You've had a few lessons at it. A good understanding I believe you have. I've come to talk with you to suggest that you have a look into [1]Acupressure, 'cos I thought you'd right enjoy doing that. By the way I suppose you've guessed I'm an Aussie. I used to work in Melbourne. I went there with my parents when I was a nipper and I got interested in Acupuncture and Acupressure. But I think for you mate that Acupressure would be a good idea. I think you'd find it interesting. In fact I know you'd find it interesting. Of course there's the other one which you could do which is to do with the muscle reaction, reflexes. You'd probably enjoy that too. You could combine the two.

I suggest that you have a bit of research on it. You can't pick it up mate by just reading about it. You gotta have some

---

[1]Acupressure — A practice of applying pressure to various parts of the body with the tips of the fingers, for periods of half a minute to four minutes. Acupressure will cure or relieve a variety of ailments from anxiety and apoplexy through cystitis and earache to toothache and tetanus.

instruction on it. You gotta know what you're doing 'cos you can do a lot of harm, but I guess that you'd enjoy it.

There's a lot to learn, you have to go ahead slowly, make sure you know what you're doing, but you can get some pretty good results. What I used to find was such a joy was the expression of peoples faces. They used to come in and they didn't know what they were going to go through, but gosh they went out looking mighty pleased with themselves.

You see you're going to need something to do and you're going to need to earn a bit of cash one way and another, and that way mate you can do it. Mind you I' m not saying that you should charge the prices they charge in some of these posh places. But you could earn a living at it and enjoy doing it, and at the same time you could help those who needed help, and you'd like doing that too.

You see your type of healing isn't the sort of healing that's the laying on of hands. That's a different type of person altogether does that. But your sort of healing is an under-standing of the muscles and the pressure points, and the results that you can get! I'm not going to tell you anything about it because its up to you to research, but you know you can ask me some questions later on if you want to. But you know its a pretty wonderful thing.

The way I started was some old chap, he was out in China. Oh I don't know what he was doing out there, trading I think, but he learnt about this Acupressure and Acupuncture. Mind you he was a good 'un at Acupressure and he was a good 'un at Acupuncture, but I could never get on with those pin things. No way! But he taught me a lot — he really did. Got me interested. Helped a lot too, gave me a great deal of instruction and stood by me while I was practising. Cor! you should have seen some of them when I hit the wrong spot, they used to leap up. But never mind, it happened and they didn't mind. They said they realised that I was learning, so all round it was a pretty good do.

So I say to you mate, have a go. See how you like it. I reckon you'll like it real good. Have a go sport, I reckon you'll enjoy it. I'd like to say to you, "Any time you're over in Melbourne come and see me," but that wouldn't do any good. But still I reckon this is a real good way of communicating. I hope sometime I'm allowed to come back again to find out how you're getting on. So I'll go now. Good luck mate. You'll enjoy it. Cheerio.

Healing

* * *

HEALING OF THE MIND

Greetings — it is with much pleasure that I speak with you. It is with much pleasure that I join you in this Sanctuary. I am a visitor who has been round to many such Sanctuaries upon the Earth plane. I come to bring you a teaching, an understanding of yet another healing. For you are a group of healers and there are many such as you upon the Earth plane.

I come to speak to you about a healing of the mind, for there are many upon the Earth plane at this time who suffer problems of the mind. Many of these problems arise through the agitation's that are caused by the actions of others, for upon the Earth plane at this time there are many who wish to be the leader. There are many who wish to make all subservient to them. I am not talking about countries; I am talking about small areas; I am talking about businesses. There are many problems caused through the actions of others during the business life. There are anxieties and tensions that are set up, and these in turn cause mental disorders. Mental disorders which indeed should not occur. Mental disorders of cruelty, of mental cruelty.

The mind is a very delicate instrument. I am speaking of course of the conscious mind, though I hasten to add that the spiritual mind is also a delicate instrument. But that of course has special protection, particularly with those who are of service and those who have understanding of the protection that they can and do receive. The conscious mind is an instrument that is very delicately balanced. It is an instrument which needs very careful handling. I am sure you know, you have heard instances where people have been driven completely insane by the words that have been spoken by others.

I would like to give you an example. The occasions when it is said, "Where have you put my book?" "I put it on the table." "But it is not there now," and subsequently it is found hidden away in some ridiculous place. These sort of things do happen and there are those in institutes of mental disorder all across the Earth plane where this sort of treatment has been given. It takes away the balance of the mind; it takes away the balance of the physical body; it destroys completely the consciousness.

You, I am sure, all have an understanding of the trouble, of the mental trouble, the mental disorder that is caused by the loss of a child or a loved one through an accident that has been inflicted by the one who grieves. I hope I have made myself clear. This is such a pity, for there is no need for this type of mental disorder. If only an understanding could be given that the loved one is by their side grieving for them because there is nothing they can do to help, for one is in Spirit and one is in the physical body.

If you should come upon one who suffers thus I would say to you, endeavour to help them to the understanding that accidents happen and when you love somebody you do not in any way intend them harm. You could help by giving a loving understanding of the sorrow that they bear and you could lead them along to the doorway that they could open to walk along their Spiritual path.

There is the mental disorder caused by fatigue through nursing somebody who is very demanding, for fatigue causes mental disorders. Fatigue is a draining of the energy from the physical body, and there are occasions of fatigue where if you just relax and rest, the energies pour back into the physical body. There are instances of fatigue where the energy has been drained by somebody else who has survived upon the energy they have drawn from you. And this can cause mental disorders, for there is no reserve to build up resistance.

The best remedy for such people is complete rest in a completely different environment with people of interest. Who can take them out of themselves, so to speak, away from the environment that has caused the disorder. And as the energies return, and they will return with the right attention and the right understanding, then the mental disorder will disappear. So you see, if you should meet somebody in a similar situation, there might be an opportunity to take them away, to take them out of themselves, to give them pleasure and you would also have pleasure, for you would see the energy returning. I am talking of people with fatigue from nursing, from looking after someone for a considerable time.

Now there is another mental disorder and this is the disorder which is brought about by the taking of evil drugs. By the mishandling of herbs placed upon the Earth plane by Father God for a reason, a reason of healing. Herbs which are misused can cause a great deal of mental disorder. It is such a pity that man has found a use such as this for God's gifts. There are many upon the Earth plane who suffer greatly because somebody has given them a drug to take which has brought about a false world. It is dreadful to see how many young people upon the Earth plane have closed down their spiritual path because they have taken drugs. I cannot say to you too strongly what a dreadful mistake it is, because the physical body becomes as nothing and the spiritual consciousness is completely locked away.

When there are hallucinations brought about by taking these drugs, sometimes there are glimpses of the spiritual path, for there are many in Spirit who endeavour to help by showing fragments of what could be, but it is very very difficult. Those who take drugs, and there are many young people, they desperately need a friend, someone who will understand. I would say to you, this takes much knowledge, it takes a great deal of love and it does indeed take dedication, for it is a very demanding situation.

Mental disorder brought about by taking drugs is something that has gone on through many hundreds of years, thousands of years. It is not new, but where it was confined to a comparatively small area, now the knowledge has spread across the Earth plane because of the transport. Because the Earth is shrinking, not in actual size, I know you have the understanding, and unfortunately the good and the bad things are spread as well.

There are many good things which are taken from one place to another. There is wonderful knowledge, wonderful teachings. There are teachings that have come from the Chinese, there are teachings that have come from the Indians, the Tibetans. So many teachings from so many areas upon the Earth plane. Some of the areas really quite small, but the knowledge has spread around the Earth plane. But unfortunately also those happenings which it would have been best to have been confined to small areas have also spread.

The taking of drugs was spread around the Earth plane by those who came in ships. They adopted the idea for they spent many hours upon the water and there was great boredom. And so those who went out to the Eastern countries in their ships acquired the use of opium, and it was used while they were travelling, and inevitably it spread. It was not as now of course, for there were not the facilities to spread these drugs. There have of course been refinements one way and the other, but now there are so many young people who suffer because of these drugs.

It might be at some future time that one of you may become involved with a clinic. A clinic which will deal with young people, and you will come across this problem, and there will be given spiritual healing. As yet spiritual healing has not been used, for the problem has been contained, so to speak. But there will come a time when there will be spiritual healing given, and there are those in Spirit who wait to work through those who are chosen.

There will come about an awakening to the knowledge that spiritual healing will and can be used, and will be successful. There will be something in a newspaper which will tell you something of the success of one of the healers upon another continent. And when you read this notice you will remember my words, and you will have the understanding that help will be given to these young people from a source that is beyond their understanding at the present time.

Now of course there is the mental disorder which is brought about by an accident at the time of birth. An accident brought about by human error. An accident that should not be, for it is an accident caused by free will, for human error is part of free will. It is extremely unfortunate when this happens but we in Spirit endeavour to give an understanding to the one who has received this damage. We endeavour to give them an understanding in the spiritual mind, of the reasons for their return to the Earth plane.

It has been said on many occasions from many platforms that the task before one is chosen before returning to the Earth plane, and this is so. Some have been told they have returned for they must undergo pain because in their previous life they inflicted pain. But this is not always so. In fact it is very rarely so, for it is not a [1]karmic condition as a rule. Very often one undergoes pain through the free will of others or the free will of ones-self. It is not intended that a young man should drive a motor car at great speed in order that he can crush the physical

---

[1]Karmic Condition — Karma — The Hindu Law of Action. It is bound up with the traditional religious views of the Hindus regarding the inexorability of reincarnation either higher or lower in the animal human scale. The only release according to them, is by a process of ascetic withdrawal from the world of passion, the techniques of Yoga. Sum of person's actions in one of his successive states of existence viewed as deciding his fate in the next. i.e. DESTINY.

body. Oh no — that is free will, and there is a lesson to be learned there, but it is not intended. So the accident that happens to one at birth through the free will of another is not intended. But from the behaviour, from the lesson that they learn, they can gain much value. Oh no — such things are not intended. It is not intended that you return to the Earth plane in order that you may have an immediate accident. Oh no — it is not so.

I would say to you all, for you are all healers in your different ways, that you are indeed learning from the teachings that you are receiving. We know that there are not to be startling results. We know that you are not to go forth suddenly with great skills, for you have your own thinking to do and your own sorting out. However I would say to you, when you meet somebody who has a problem of the mind, spare them a little extra time. Send out love to them, help them.

There are so few people in the ordinary walk of life who have the understanding. They just ignore them or laugh at those who are slightly mental. I say to you, you are healers, spare a little of your time to help them. You will have no idea of the extent of the help that you will give by just a kind word, a smile, a little understanding. There will be those with them who will say, "They do not understand, they will have forgotten by tomorrow." It is not so, for the knowledge is sent through to the spiritual mind and is held there to come forth from time to time.

It is now time for me to go. I would ask you to think upon my words. It is good I know that they are held upon the machine and that you will be able to hear again the words that I have spoken. I ask you to read them carefully and to discuss. Discuss with others, hear their views. Far too few people think of those who have problems of the mind. The Love and the Light of Father God protect you all at all times. God bless you all.

Healing

* * *

ANCIENT HEALING

Greetings, greetings, I come to you from many aeons of time ago. I must say to you in advance that this is the first time that I have spoken through a channel of this nature, and therefore I ask you to be patient, for I have those things I wish to say to you but I am afraid that I cannot say them to you in a rush.

I come to you from far off China from many aeons ago as I have already said. I come before you because it is important that you have an understanding of the healing of those times. For you are all healers and it is necessary that you have understanding of all types of healing, both of the present day upon the Earth plane and of the types of many many aeons ago. For as then so it is becoming now, for healing has passed through many stages. Healing has passed from knowledge to ignorance, for what other than ignorance was the use of leeches on those who were already desperately ill? Can you say to me, "That was knowledge?" Indeed it was not. It was laziness, for it was easy to obtain leeches, and it was easy to apply them to the person who lay sick in their bed. And if they died it was too late to help them, and if they lived of course the one who applied the leeches was considered wonderful. And that was nonsense.

Healing has to be done all through the body. The human body is a wonderful piece of machinery and of that you have the understanding. How many times have the workings of the human body been used for great machines? And the systems are exactly the same whether they be made of flesh and bone or whether they be made of steel, metal or other substances. There is a feeding and there is a waste. There are areas that have to be oiled and there are areas that have to be cleansed. There are areas that have to be renewed. And it is the same with the human body, and so it has been all the time.

There have been fevers and there have been diseases that have needed investigation. There has been research and there have been those who have risked their lives, so to speak, to take upon themselves the illnesses of others that they may use themselves to test and try. In China at the time that I am speaking of there were many wonderful men of medicine. Men of medicine who knew about the human body. Who studied the workings of the human body, who knew about diseases of the bones. For even in those times there were diseases of the bones, even as there are now. Things have not changed, it is just that as time progresses things are eliminated and what was of great concern in my China does not happen now. And there are diseases which happened within your living memories which do not happen now, and that is because of the research and the care that has been taken to decipher and test and try.

There are within the human body, parts which are constantly wearing out, and these parts must have the correct nutriment to assist them to be ever changing. There are those foods which must be eaten, for in all foods there are those minerals and vitamins and salts that are used by the human body. And if you will take the time and the trouble to read those books which have been written, particularly those books which have been written in ancient times regarding the use of herbs, of nature food, you will find that God has supplied food of all kinds to feed all parts of the body.

There is now on the Earth plane at the present time, a great searching for a change in the foods that are eaten. A greater understanding of the workings of the human body, and a greater desire to study the whole body. Holistic Living it is called. It is a way back and yet it is a way forward. To really commence healing one needs to know about the human body, for there are parts where great control can be given.

There are many who are healers — who call themselves healers — who know very little of the human body and know even less of the spiritual body. And yet they call themselves healers and excuse themselves by saying, "I am a channel through whom the Spirit works and therefore I need to know nothing about the human body." But if they do not learn about those things that can go wrong, and those things that can be put right, and those things which cause the problem, they cannot talk to the one who comes to seek healing.

The China in which I lived was poor. There were great wastes and there were, even at that time, centres of culture and understanding. The living for some was very artistic, a very slow gentle life. And yet because of this, the human body rebelled, for a machine likes to be used and if it is not used it seizes up. Thus in the China of my time one would see those who were of the age of thirty who could not walk far, for they had not lubricated those parts which needed lubricating, and they had remained in sitting positions for too long at a time. Because of this there developed great problems with the knees and with the feet, and in some cases there was a withering disease which had to be researched into, for one would find that the legs would not function.

So it came about that a young man decided that he would investigate the reason for this and he went off to a Monastery high in the mountains, for there have always been those of prayer, always. I call it a Monastery, but you would probably say that a Temple had been constructed. The young man went to the Monastery and spoke to those men of prayer and asked them if he could be given some knowledge from the Gods. They sat together in that place in a circle, and in the centre was a small fire which had been carefully constructed to a certain shape. For the flame had to be a single flame and it had to be a flame of blue, and this was achieved by the wood, the roots that were burned. They sat in vigil for two days and two nights. They had exercise of course and returned to their vigil, but all did not leave at the same time, every other one in the circle was maintained.

At the end of that time the Elder of the Monastery said that he had received a message from the Gods, and he told the young man to go forth. And on the way down the mountain side he would see a bright yellow flower growing, and he was to pick the heads of the flowers and put them in a safe place and take them with him. The flower heads were discovered and they were large and he put them carefully in a cloth made of woven grasses and he carried them back with him. He removed the centres of these large flowers and he boiled in water from the running stream, the remainder of the flower. It was mixed with a meal — a local food — and then the centre seeds of the flowers were placed into the mixture. Not all of them of course for this was to be a treatment, this was to be a gift from the Gods.

There were six people chosen, six who had the withering disease in their legs. They were chosen for the treatment and they were told to eat the meal, and they were afraid for they thought they were to be poisoned. Indeed there was only one who would take the meal without protest. The rest were tied so that the meal could be forced into their mouths, for there was a determination that they should have this which had been directed by the Gods. After a time the withering disease ceased and the legs started to recover and the muscles too became firm. And because of this the young man decided that he must go forth to find cures for other illnesses, and so he did. He was one of the very first of those ancient times to seek herbal remedies and holistic medicine, for he realised the cause and effect. The cause of the wasting disease — inactivity, and the effect of course was — inactivity. I have spent more time upon that story than I intended but I want to make you understand that there are reasons for the body to seize up. And very often through carefully studying the diet and the foods that you eat, those who come to you for healing can be shown the means of returning to activity those parts of the human body that have become inactive.

In China at the times that I speak of, the young men very rarely grew old. And when there was one who grew old, he was revered, for it was considered that he was one of great strength, and one who was blessed by the Gods with wisdom. I say to you, I would like to bless you, I would like to ask that you be given wisdom. I would like to ask that you be given an understanding and I would like to say to you, look upon the human body as a machine of great value. Do not neglect the parts that seize up, for the human body should run smoothly and sweetly, performing all those things that a good machine performs.

Have wisdom, have understanding, have compassion, but above all have knowledge and have faith, for all work together. There will come times when you will have a patient who you would dearly love to make whole, but remember there are times when the parts are too worn out. And it is then that the compassion and the understanding that you have gathered along your spiritual paths can be given to that one, and you may not realise just how valuable will be that understanding to that one. It cannot be that all are made whole again, it cannot be, for there are many reasons why this is not to be. But in your healing you will help, and by your healing those who come in contact with you will receive a greater understanding. A greater understanding that there is more within you and therefore there must be something within them also. For from your eyes will shine the Love of God and they will see.

I would like to stay longer but I have said all that I have to say at this time. I will go and it is with pleasure that I say thank you for letting me be with you, and I say, God's Blessings be upon you and I ask that wisdom be given to you all.

Chapter V

FREE WILL

I bring you greetings, this is Lauda. You are still two short of those who should be sitting in this Group. We have given those who withdrew time to consider and it is obvious that they have decided to follow free will, and this is quite in order, for all have free will and all can use it. It is a great pity that they have withdrawn for with patience they would have learned that which they are seeking, for all things do not happen as quickly as we desire. This applies not only to the Spirit upon the Earth plane, but the Spirit of the Spirit World.

We walk side by side and we cannot hasten anything. Indeed it is better to have a gradual awareness than to plunge and completely submerge oneself, for that way there can be a drowning. To gather information gently is of much greater value, for if one thing follows upon another in quick succession, then very often that which happened first becomes lost. And it is important with spiritual awakening that all things are remembered, for as you learn so you can teach. You can only teach those things that you truly know, for in teachings free will must not be used. The teachings that you give forth must be of true spiritual value and not something which has been concocted by yourself.

Those who have withdrawn would have learned a greater understanding, a greater understanding of their path, but undoubtedly in time they will have a greater understanding. It is entirely their own choice. For the present you will remain but five and you are in harmony one with the other, and we are able to come to give you teachings, but of course it is impossible for manifestations. I am sure you have the understanding, for manifestations require great energy, and at this present time there is not sufficient energy. However you will have a manifestation as promised. It will happen my children for it is written, and indeed as yet it is early days and there are many teachings to go, during which time you will gradually be led along your spiritual paths.

It is up to you to take note of the teachings you receive, to take unto yourself that which you understand. For each teaching that you have been given has been a teaching if you read the words carefully, for you have to seek on the spiritual level. We do not waste our time by just coming to give you a chat. That would be of no value to you or to us, but each time the teaching is a teaching. I will not explain further, for I am sure it is not necessary.

There will be those who will come to you to tell you of happenings past, and those happenings which are yet to come. You will each have the opportunity of asking questions and you will each be given replies. You will be given an understanding of the healing paths that you can follow if you so desire. I do not say you must follow, for I am ever mindful of free will. It is always a great pity when there is a disruption, withdrawal, from the Group, for it does cause a disruption of greater intensity than you think. For it takes time to knit a group of people together, that the energies can be used to the greatest advantage.

There is work which goes on behind the scenes, so to speak. The spiritual work which is not visible to those on the Earth plane. There are some mediums of great strength and great vision who have seen these energies at work and have commented upon the strength. But generally it is not realised, and so at the moment the energies are reduced. But when a certain matter has been decided, then the two who are to join the Group will come and there will be harmony as there was before, and the energies will be built up.

At the moment however, I must ask you to be patient and to accept the teachings which are given to you. To spend a little time reading between the lines, so to speak, so that you can each, in your own particular way, take your own meaning from those teachings. It would be a good idea if at sometime you put your ideas together to see if you were all following along the same lines. For there are many diverse opinions of the one subject and there are many interpretations of comments made, and I know that you have already discovered this. It is really very interesting at the different interpretations that can arise from one simple comment.

There are games that are played upon the Earth plane for amusement, for entertainment, to pass the time, and there could be a very interesting game devised, a discussing game if you like where there could be a comment made and everybody gave their interpretation. You will be surprised at the different number of comments that are made. There will be those who will say, "I never even thought of that," and so it is with the teachings that are given from those in Spirit. For those upon the Earth plane put different interpretations upon the same comments and very often this is the cause of arguments between mediums and between different groups. But really and truly it all means the same.

If everybody was to come together to discuss that particular point, it would be found that by elimination there would be but one truth. And so my children it is possible that by elimination gradually there will come but one truth and an understanding of that one truth. And there will be but one centre point, and that of course will truly be the brotherhood of man. There is nothing wrong with people having different ideas. There is nothing wrong with people following different cults, different beliefs, so long as all speak in truth, for if all speak in truth then it can only lead to the truth. One God, one Creator. To reach that understanding there must be many discussions and many eliminations, and of course this will take many earth years.

There are those who do not believe at all, who follow their own selfish path. For unless they are of service it is a selfish path, for they are entirely wrapped up with themselves. There are not really very many upon the Earth plane who are not of service one way or another, for a Mother is always of service to her children. Perhaps I should correct that and say, should be of service to her children. For to prepare a meal for them, to make a bed for them is being of service. There is the person behind the counter who hands out stamps. These are paid for, but that is the beginning of a service. The stamp is put upon a letter, the letter is posted, somebody collects it. That is a service. They take it where it can be stamped and where it can be directed to the person for whom it is intended, and that is a service. That service involves several people and several changing hands of monies. But to be of service with love, is as a Mother for her child or a Father for his child, for there is no payment required. All are done with love, with a sense of responsibility. And so you see that all that happens in the name of God. All that is done for the love of God, for the Father. All that the Father does is of love. There is no exchange of monies, but that does not mean to say that the service is of no value, for the service of love is of the highest value.

It has been said on many occasions by many people, it has been quoted many times, that to obtain wealth one must give everything one owns away, and of course we are speaking here of the material and the spiritual. But if you give all the material away, you would be left with nothing, and if you are left with nothing then it could be that you would be unable to give of the spiritual. It could be, for it could be that you would be worried about those things of the material that are necessary. It sounds like a vicious circle but it isn't really. One does not have to give away all one's earthly possessions to be of service. For one must have food and clothing and one must have a roof above one's head, but one can give all of oneself in service. One can devote much time in service, and many things can be achieved.

I say to you, be of service to your brother and sister and to Father God. It is really the only way to true love. The understanding that is deep within. The understanding, the awareness if you like, for which you are searching, you will find that gradually. You will progress and if the going is slow do not lose heart, but remember it is better that you learn slowly in order that you may teach properly those words which will help those with whom you come in contact. You will find that people will come and speak to you, and you will recognise those who are searching and give them a gentle understanding which will flourish and grow.

I go now. The Love and Protection of Father God surround you at all times. God bless you, God bless you.

Chapter VI

ANCIENT TIMES
TIBET

reetings my children, greetings. I come to you to speak of ancient times. My name is of no consequence. I come to tell you something about Tibet. I come to tell you of that ancient land wherein are housed many many secrets. I am sure you have read in your present day world about happenings in my land, but unless you have read from the actual writings that were made at those times you have not been told all the truth.

In the ancient land of Tibet, surrounded by high mountains where people have lived for many centuries in what is today known as rarefied air, there have been those who have lived for over 200 years. They have lived simply on the minimum of food, for you will have the understanding that there was not much to sustain them. They lived upon the pure spring waters that came from the snowy peaks, and they lived upon the herbs and the berries and the nuts that were to be found even in those bleak conditions.

You will have the understanding that even at such heights there are always pockets of soil, pockets that are sheltered, and although the soil is not of very much depth, nevertheless Father God made sure that all His children were fed. Of course in those ancient times we did not say Father God for we worshipped various Gods. I am speaking of ancient times, but we knew that there was someone, a God who provided. Who sent the Sun; who controlled the rain; who made sure there was enough food, for you see we were very spiritual. Even in those days we communed with the World of Spirit. You may say, "In those ancient times, who were the Spirits with whom you communed?" There are ancient times, beyond ancient times. I do not intend to confuse but think upon it and you will have the understanding. For there had been [1]Atlantis and there had been other lands, other peoples, all of whom had fallen from grace and were endeavouring to seek that perfection which they had lost.

Our ancient wisdom's, our teachings, for we had teachings, our teachings were to look deep within. Our teachings were to sit in meditation for many hours at a time. And we were not allowed in our teachings to move at all, for we had to learn of complete and utter control of the physical body. If you could sit in solitude for several hours without moving, I was going to say without moving a muscle, you would find that you would forget the physical body. You would feel no discomfort whatsoever, and you would lose yourselves deep within. For there are many many secrets and many many wonders that are hidden along that spiritual path.

To look deep within is not easy. It takes time, it takes supreme concentration. And yet one must not be aware that one is concentrating, for one must clear the conscious mind completely. One of these meetings within this Sanctuary I will come to you and we will sit in meditation, and I will endeavour to teach you the way to go deep within. It will of course be entirely up to each one of you whether you follow the teachings I will give, but of course it is up to you, but during that teaching

---

[1]Atlantis — (Greek legend) Fabled island in the ocean West of the Pillars of Hercules; it was beautiful and prosperous, the seat of an empire which dominated part of Europe and Africa, but was overwhelmed by the sea because of the impiety of its inhabitants.

it is hoped that you will remember the words that will be said. It is hoped that you will take those words away with you, and that you will endeavour to sit in meditation in the manner that will be taught, within your own Sanctuaries. But I would say to you never sit in darkness, for there is no need to sit in darkness. In ancient times we did not sit in darkness, we had a tallow light.

There were plants in the mountains. I beg your pardon I should say there were plants found in the small plateaus, high in the mountains. They were plants from which we were able to beat a grease of kinds. It was an oil of delicate perfume, unlike the oil or grease that is produced from animals. It was of a delicate perfume and it helped in the meditation. We would have small pots made from the little branches of trees. I suppose one would say really, the trunks of trees, for the trees were never very high. We would scoop out a small hole into which we could put the oil, and we would light them by the rays of the Sun. Now I expect you are rather confused, but we would have a large bowl of the oil into which were placed these small twiglets in order that they could soak up the oil, and there was a fire which was always kept burning into which we would place a twig, and we would very carefully use that to light our lights, and we would be very economical for we could not afford to be otherwise.

We used to write those things which had been revealed to us, and each one was given a different revelation. We have hidden, within the mountains, our writings. There was a time when they were all taken to a special place where they were guarded, a place which penetrated deep into the mountain. It was in the first place a cave of great depth, and we built outside the entrance a Temple, and we placed within that Temple the one who was chosen, and thus it was for many many years.

We found within the mountains, minerals. Minerals which today are given the name of gold and silver and platinum. We made vessels from these minerals for our use. We adorned ourselves with a piece of the metal known as gold, for we used it as means of communication. Each one wore around their neck a thong of leather from the skin of the goat. For you see we had goats in those ancient times, and there are still descendants of those creatures that served us with their milk and their meat. We had around our necks a thong of this leather and hanging from this we had our large disc of gold, cleansed and beaten to reflect the Sun. And this was our means of communication, and we could reflect the words, the symbols, the signs for many miles, and thus we knew when danger approached.

There are many sacred scrolls within Tibet, and they are still there, there are many hiding places. Many have been discovered and removed. Many have been destroyed by those who desecrated our country, many have been destroyed. I would say to you that there is one who has written about the opening of the [2]third eye. I think you all have my meaning of the one of whom I speak, for it is this one particular person to whom I refer. He was one of experience, but he is one also of a very vivid imagination. Many of those things of which he has written were of truth but many were of fiction. And so I would say to you that the Tibet of which he speaks is not the Tibet of which I speak. I hope that you have the understanding, for it is rather important. It is rather important because there can be misunderstandings.

Within the Temple that was built, there was a crystal of extreme beauty. It was a crystal that had been discovered deep within the mountain. It was a crystal that was comprised of many centuries of dripping water. No one knew how it was formed. No one knew how such exquisite beauty could come about in a place of complete darkness, for it was deep within the

---

[2]Third eye — An occult organ of psychic vision situated in the forehead. Attempts have been made to identify this fabulous organ with the pineal gland, at one time considered to be the seat of teaching. This idea is inconsistent with Spiritualist teaching, as the etheric or spirit body is a duplicate of the physical body, and contains only the usual compliment of eyes.

mountain, and was discovered purely by accident by one who had had an accident and fallen down a shaft within the mountain. It was a shaft that must have come about by water dripping, dripping, dripping through. The crystal was taken to the Temple and it was placed upon a plinth. It was large and of exquisite beauty. It remained within that Temple for many centuries, and then one day there was a war of bloody intensity and the crystal was destroyed, and with the crystal went the heart of Tibet. And that heart will never be restored.

So I come to you with my story, for I wish it to be a teaching, as indeed it is. The teaching that within each one of your there is a crystal of great beauty, a crystal of many facets, a crystal of divine right. A crystal which you must cherish and in no way desecrate. And so, when I come to you at a later time to give you a teaching on meditation, remember the crystal within and see if you can see its beauty.

I will go now, thank you for the energy that has permitted me to come to you. God bless you. God bless you.

Ancient Times

* * *

FRANCE

Greetings to you. My name is of no consequence, but my country when I was upon the Earth plane was France. A France very different to that of this present day. A France of vast bog–land, of forest, of mountains and waters. A France wherein abounded many creatures of the wild. Creatures that would spring upon the unwary traveller and tear them to pieces, creatures of very evil intent. But they were there for a purpose, for as with all things there is a reason, and as with all things there must be a balance.

When I lived in France it was a case of being very wealthy or very poor. A case of walking on clouds of silk so to speak, or a case of grovelling on the floor on your belly. There was plenty for some, very little for others. But those who had little found ways of sustaining themselves, for they would hunt, they would plant seeds, grow a bit of corn, search for berries, make a rough bread. But they knew how to sing, and their voices would ring out as they enjoyed one of their festivals. For there were very few means of pleasure apart from wenching, but they liked to sing and they liked to drink. They drank what you would call a bitter concoction, but to them it was a nectar for there was no tea or coffee. There was very little milk, in fact some would go most of their lives without knowing what milk was, for there was only goats milk and not all could afford to keep a goat.

In the Chateau life was very different, but of course there were not the comforts of the present day world. There were not the soft beds, for most slept upon the ground upon piles of hay. Although those who owned the Chateau had their hay beds sewn up in a rough sacking which was covered with the skins of animals. Their lives were really wasted to a certain extent, but even then there was knowledge of a spiritual path for there had to be progression, and one would find the mistress of the Chateau would tend to her servants, those who were close to her.

She would visit the sick and take remedies, herbal remedies, ointments which she had made, balms, perhaps a special delicacy, a pheasant or some other tasty morsel to help them along their way. And by her compassion and thoughtfulness she was progressing along her spiritual path. Her lord would go out hunting. He would be away with his retinue for two or three weeks at a time, for there were always hunting lodges. Not the fine constructions that are put up these days. They were roughly made from the trees of the forest, and they were thatched, so to speak, with the branches and the leaves. They were adequate to keep out the wild animals and the weather, and they would hunt. They would eat quite a lot of that which they caught, but then the remaining animals would be strung on to poles and carried back to the Chateau where there would be much merriment. Not all the animals would be used for that feast, for many of them would be hung and they would be smoked and they would be stored. For during the Winter period no one ventured out beyond the walls of the chateau.

Of course the poor people had to venture out whatever the weather, and many perished in the bitter winds and the snows, and many were rescued by those in the village or hamlet, for they would send out search parties and they were indeed a sight to see. There would be huge torches lit and there would be kindling wood taken along, for that would be dry, to set off the fires that would be needed to protect them from the wild creatures at night, and there would be great searches going on for those who were missing. Sometimes they would be found alive and well, nine times out of ten perched up at the top of a tree, for that was the only place of safety at night. But of course in the bitter weather that would have been of no avail and they would be crouched perhaps in a cave if they were lucky. But very often all that was found would be a pile of bones. Oh no! my children, times were not easy for the poor in France in those days. Oh no! they were not easy.

There used to be a weed which grew in the hedgerows. It grew very tall and had very thick fleshy leaves. It produced a bloom, but it also produced seed heads which were as of silk, and these used to be collected and dried. And when it was dried it was very coarse, although as a seed head it had been like silk, but it was very strong. When the harvest was collected and all was prepared then the spinning wheels would come out and the ladies would sit and spin and they would make yarn. The type of yarn, the cloth, the fabric was what you would call flax, and they used to use this as a backing for the embroidery, the tapestry work.

They used to sit and work at their tapestries for many hours, sometimes for several years. And they would adorn the walls, (I am speaking of course of the Chateaux and larger dwellings,) they would adorn the walls with these tapestries, and they would help to keep out the draught. They would be hung across the windows, if you could call them windows, for they were but mere slits. The ladies would do their embroidery, maybe a scene they could see when sitting in the garden, maybe a scene of their own imagination. There are still one or two fragments of these tapestries in France in museums, and they are of great interest, for the colours are still quite bright and yet they were produced by weeds and nettles and berries.

I would like to take you back to the France of those days. I would like to take you on a journey. You would have to walk of course, unless you were well off enough to own a horse, and very few ordinary folk had horses in fact, unless they found a wild horse somewhere. But that was not very often, for if they were seen upon a horse the local lord would say they had stolen it from him and they would be hanged. So you would have to make the journey on foot and the journey would be very slow for there would be no shoes upon your feet and you would find, to start off with, that your feet would be very sore and very cut. But to bathe your feet in the streams was to strengthen them, for there were many minerals in the waters. And you would find that gradually your feet would become quite hard, and there would be little discomfort. But you would not be able to stop to have a cup of coffee or a cup of tea, for you would walk many many miles across uninhabited country.

Oh no! the France of those days was very different and if it had not been for the monks and the friars who welcomed you to the Monasteries and the Abbeys, many a wandering traveller would have starved. But always you see there was a light and always there was love handed out to you by those who had the understanding that there was a God. That there was someone who really cared, and there was someone who heard your prayers. My France was very different but the Love of God was just the same. God bless you my children, God bless you.

Ancient Times

* * *

ROME

Greetings to you. I come to you this earth evening to speak with you. I come from the old Rome, I come from [1]Pompeii. I was a Senator for many years, but I had, like many, an estate and villa in Pompeii.

The Pompeii of those times was indeed a gay place to live, for it was a place of pleasure. It was a place to go when moving out of Rome during the hot Summer for the air was cool in that place. We had our baths, as indeed all Romans had their baths, for they were places where we would go to sit in the water and talk and discuss business. It was surprising the amount of business that was talked while sitting in the water up to one's neck. But it was refreshing and it cooled the brain.

I was in Pompeii when [2]Vesuvius erupted. I was in Pompeii at that ill-fated time. I had just commenced a very important meeting, a very important meeting which of course took place in my villa. A meeting of important personages who were discussing those things that had to be done in Rome. For at that time there was much difficulty with the Emperor. We had met and we had a feast before us when news was brought that

---

[1]Pompeii — Ancient town of Campania, Italy, buried by eruption of Mt. Vesuvius in AD. 79 and since 1755 gradually laid bare by excavation.

[2]Vesuvius — Mt. Vesuvius — Active volcano near Naples, Italy.

Vesuvius was rumbling. We took no notice for we thought it was just a rumbling and we carried on with our discussion, and the wine flowed and we talked.

There was a lot of noise outside for the chariots were racing up and down the piazzas. We thought it was the younger ones enjoying themselves, we felt no fear. Then my wife came in. She was quite distraught for our young daughter was out. She was afraid because of all the people that were out on the piazzas. We decided that it would be as well if we went outside to see what was happening, and from my garden we could see Vesuvius. It was not close you understand, it was not on top of us, but we could see it in the distance with a great red light coming from it, reflecting up into the sky.

Of course it had been rumbling for several days but there had been no other sign, no fire. We stood and watched for some time and thought it was quite safe. We went back to our meeting, we thought that was more important. My wife came out quite concerned, she was organising search parties for our daughter for she had been to one of the Temples to a display of art, a display of artistic dancing. These dances were very beautiful and the young ones were learning to walk gracefully. But we were not to see our daughter again. We decided that she must have gone to stay with friends, and I endeavoured to comfort my wife and encouraged her to go to bed saying that there was no danger from the volcano for it was too far away. So my wife went to bed, and we continued with our meeting.

It had been arranged that my guests would stay, for there was too much activity outside for them to go to their own villas. And so rooms were prepared for them. We would have liked to have gone along to the baths but there was no possibility of getting there, and so we stayed in the garden for it was cool. We sat there and supped upon wine and made our way to our beds. I awoke in the night to a feeling of suffocation, but I could find no reason. Then I heard my wife calling me and I went out into the garden where she was waiting. She was very distraught for she said that she could not breathe. I said I felt like that too and we partook of wine. It was a dreadful experience for we gradually suffocated. I now know that all my household and all my guests also suffocated, and I now know why. Pompeii was no more.

There were some of those who had gone for their holiday, as you say, and they had gone down to the sea and they stood in the water and they were saved. But Pompeii was covered in time, and yet Vesuvius was not close. You see something had to be done, for Pompeii was very gay and beneath all the ashes that came from the volcano there were many beautiful treasures buried, there were many beautiful works or art. But they were of no value to us for we had left the physical body and that was of no value to us either.

I would like you all to think upon these words, to see if you can get the understanding of value. God bless you.

Chapter VII

THE ETHERIC BODY

I come to you from many moons ago. I come to you in greeting. I come to you from the Land of Gold, and I bring to you treasures, for I was a member of a proud race.

When last I was upon the Earth plane many moons ago we carved our way through the tropical jungles. Many of my people were swallowed up in the swamps but we had those amongst us who knew the paths, even though they had never been there before within their recognition. Slowly inch by inch we carved our way through those forests till we found our haven. Our place of peace where we could live, where we could set up our temples and where we could follow our rules of life which had been laid down for us by the Sun, for the Sun was our means of worship.

We built mighty temples. We built those temples lovingly with much hard work stretching over many years. We grew our own food for we had discovered those things which had been supplied to us through the care of the Sun. That was our belief then. I know differently now of course, but I am speaking of the time many moons ago when I was on the Earth plane.

We had found a haven, a place of beauty, for we made it so. We had found a place where from the very ground there welled up pure water which we could drink without fear of fever or plague. We treasured that water. We directed it to huge chasms beneath the ground. We did not build them they were there. They had been discovered by those amongst us who understood such things. We directed the water to them that it may be stored and kept cold, for the Sun was very hot. We created a lake from the overflow. We created a lake and we discovered that where the lake was created, as the water flowed towards it to fill it, we discovered a curious mineral. I know it to be gold now.

We found that it could be fashioned and so the young men went forth and investigated. They went into the hills and found there the mineral known as gold, and we fashioned all things from it, for it was beautiful and it was like the Sun. It reflected the rays of the sun and it was beautiful. We lined the walls of our temples with vessels of different types which were beaten from the gold, for there was gold in abundance. We were indeed happy that we were able to adorn our Temple to the Sun.

The Sun's rays could be reflected all around by carefully placed openings high up within the Temple, and by this cunning we could create a Sun within our Temple. There were many wonderful happenings within that Temple, for there were miracles. There were those who were laid there in death, who when they received the rays of the Sun directed through one of the openings, they would rise and walk away, and yet they were still there. There were two and it was a miracle for they were of strength once again.

We trained our young men in the art of strength. They would run for many miles around the perimeter of our haven of peace. We had cleared a vast area and we had our stores wherein we kept the food which would be needed for the months of rain. For remember I have already told you we cut our way through a rain forest. So you will have the understanding of the rains that would fall for days and nights. We were of course upon raised ground for that was where the

Sun had led us when we were seeking and so we did not come to any harm. It was a life of vast experience to me, for of course I now have the understanding as indeed you have the understanding, that those who were laid within the Temple and those who were, but who were not, were in fact two, for that which rose was of the Spirit, the etheric body.

I know also that the Sun is powerful, but there is One who is even more powerful. I know now of course of God, the Creator of all things. I come to you to tell you these things. I say to you that when I passed from my earthly life I passed as a very old man. I was indeed blessed that I was allowed to stay in that beautiful place until I was an old man. I passed from that place at the age of 97, which was a very long time. I was held in great esteem, and when I passed I too was laid in the Temple and the Sun's rays were reflected upon me and I felt a freedom such as I had never felt before.

I arose from that which had covered me for all those years and I stood within that beautiful Temple and looked at that which was lying there. I was amazed and I was puzzled, but I felt a wonderfulness. I was taken to a place of great beauty. I was welcomed and I was given the understanding that the Spirit had been freed from the body and that I was now one with God. I say to you all, it was wonderful. I say to you that it has given me wonderment to be able to speak to you in this way. It is not the first time that I have spoken through a channel upon the Earth plane, for I have spoken before in the South Americas from whence I came.

I hope that at some future time I may be permitted to return, for I would like to tell you more of the experiences of those who cut their way through that jungle, and I would like to tell you more of the great reunion we had when we all finally met again in the World of Spirit. I would say to you that some of those who were with me in that beautiful place have returned to the Earth plane on two or three occasions to bring about an understanding, and I hope that perhaps by my visit you may have an understanding. But I tell you that although we worshipped the Sun as our God we were of course worshipping Father God.

And so I give you a Blessing — May the Sun's rays pour down upon you. May the Sun's strength be your strength and may the Blessings of Father God be with you always.

Chapter VIII

THOUGHTS OF LOVE

reetings my daughter, this is Lauda, and greetings my
children. Tonight we will have a teaching on the
harmonies brought about by sending out thoughts of
love. We will have a teaching regarding the helping of
people who need so much to feel loved, to feel that they are
drawn into the community, to feel that they are necessary in the
pattern of things.

There is one amongst you who has the gift of listening, and
believe me my children it is a gift, for to most people it is a case
of, "Oh! I must just tell you this." But the listener who gives
healing is the one who really does listen. For that one carries
within their mind those words that have been spoken. And they
retain this information until such times as they can bring about
a union or a meeting or a drawing forth or a bringing together,
not only of the physical body but of the spiritual consciousness.
There is one amongst you who has already developed well into
this field of healing.

It is possible, indeed it has happened, it happens many
times and indeed it has happened to all of you at some time or
the other, that you are sitting upon a bus or a vehicle of public
transport and somebody gets talking to you. And you will find
that all they wish to do is to pour out that which is within their

mind. They do not really mind if you listen or not — I beg your pardon — I should say if you are interested or not. They do not really mind, their main concern is that they tell someone. It may be that you are on a journey of several hours and the voice goes on and on and you wish they would be silent. But my children during that time you have been used for healing.

Very often you can be amongst a group of people and one person will jar considerably upon your senses. For they will appear to be shouting and laughing and generally being the life and soul of the party, I think it is known as. But if you could look deep within that person you would find that there is a sense of insecurity, a sense which has been formed during childhood, of being out on a limb, a desire to be noticed. For in childhood they have never been noticed. I am not saying that in every case this is so, but in the majority of cases it is so. There is always the person who in their own way are completing a healing by jollying up, drawing out those who are reticent. But of course you will recognise the difference, for it is the actions that follow which will make it quite clear to you.

There is the person who is an introvert who holds everything close within them, the person who never says a word, the person who suffers considerably. It is proposed that there should be a teaching on how to bring forth that which is bottled within. For once the cork is off the bottle then gases, so to speak, can escape. And once the bottle is empty, so that person receives full healing. It is a person of that nature that I can give you a picture to carry within your mind, for likening to a bottle is as it should be, but when the cork is removed gases are released. The bottle, a vast empty space, fills with golden light and a greater love and understanding pours within it. And this is really what does happen to the soul of the person who is an introvert.

Again there is the person with a vitriolic tongue, the person who carries past injuries within them, but not deep within them, for they are always repeating those injuries that have been done or are assumed to have been done. You see my children over the years these become larger and larger until in the end they can completely change the spirituality within, for it is completely tied up as a parcel and just cannot escape. This type of person is very difficult to heal, for they really do not heed the words that are spoken to them, because they are so busy with their own bitter thoughts. Their comments and their accusations can go on and on spilling out one after the other from the conscious mind.

I would say to you that you must check this flow of resentment, and I do not mean squash, I do mean you must check. You must put a barrier across the stream and direct the flow in another direction. And to achieve this is not easy, for time and time again you will feel you are wasting your time. But if gradually you can cleanse the resentments within, can cleanse away that which has been held tight over the years, then the string round the parcel will become untied, and the spiritual path will become clear.

It is a great pity my children, that over the years, and I am talking of many many years, there have been those who have reincarnated for the very reason that they have borne within resentments gathered over the years on the Earth plane. They have returned time and time again, and have commenced upon the Earth plane with a spiritual knowledge, for the knowledge always remains. But again they have built within them the resentments, gradually gathering each little detail, each little comment, each little spoken word that is forgotten by the other person, and so it builds up, and so the task of cleansing is not completed and they go back again. It is a great pity. And so you can see my children, how important it is to deal kindly with a person who has such a tongue, for you can help them greatly by stopping the flow and directing it in another path. I would say to you however, that you will receive no thanks, but you will know that within yourself you have accomplished part if not all of the healing.

And now my children there is another healing, another type of healing within the same field. It is the word that you speak yourself. For the words that you speak, the thoughts of love, can penetrate even the most prejudiced consciousness. It is so easy to say the harsh words and not so easy to virtually turn the other cheek. You are all here to follow in the footsteps of Jesus the Nazarene, and His words were, "Turn the other cheek, walk away." I say to you that it is not easy to bite back the remark, the retaliation which springs quickly to the tongue. But by so doing you can complete a healing, for you see it makes the other one think.

Perhaps you will say, "Yes, they will think I am stupid or they will think I am a coward," but does that matter? You know yourself the reasons behind your action, and you know yourself that by turning the other cheek wars can be stopped before they start. Think upon these words for there is much common sense. And that is what is needed upon the Earth plane, besides the love and the light and the brotherhood of man, for all can be brought about by common sense.

And now my children I will go. As always we are here within this little sanctuary and will listen to your words, and I would say to you please discuss this matter and do not go off on other paths, for we are here to learn and receive teachings. We are here to give teaching, but we too learn from your comments, and we know that from your comments you are all joining together in love and thought. And so you see it is important to discuss the matters that have just been spoken about. The Love and the Light of Father God is with you always. God bless you — God bless you all.

Chapter IX

PRAYER

G reetings my brothers and sisters, my name is Cecilia. I have spoken with you before, those who sat together in the small group of meditation. I come to you today to speak with you about the necessity to sit in prayer. I come too that you may have the understanding of how important prayer is.

I was a member of a very silent Order in France, and we sat for hours in prayer in our own individual cells. We had set times for prayer which were very important times. Although as a young girl when I first entered the Convent I did not understand the necessity for prayer at certain times. But it is most important and now I have the understanding, I wish to pass it onto you.

There are times when those in the World of Spirit come to you, there are times when those who take up the thoughts of prayer come to you. Although it has been said, and it is the truth, that prayers may be said at any time, anywhere. It is not necessary to close the eyes for one can pray just as devoutly when bathing the baby or gardening or doing other menial jobs about the house. One can pray when sitting quietly at the desk in an office; at the counter in a shop; having a cup of tea; taking a quiet walk. Prayer can be said at any time and it is always heard. For you have your guides with you at all times, those who keep with you at all times, for they are guides. They take your prayers to those who will use them, those who will convey them, and so you will receive answers. But I am talking more about the prayer of love that is sent forth perhaps for the Earth plane, for guidance or thanksgiving.

It is better for those times of Universal Thought to be always at the same Earth time. And so it is far better to say to yourself, "At eight o'clock in the morning promptly I will say a prayer for the safety of Mother Earth," or "I will say a prayer for all those who are sick," or "I will say a prayer for the ones who are bereaved all around the Earth plane." Do not forget the prayer to ask for guidance in your daily life. Then to give a regular time at night for thanksgiving, perhaps at ten thirty. You will find that at those times you will gradually feel a peace around you, and you will find also that within yourselves there will come a relaxation. If you truly give your thoughts to the prayers which you are saying, if you truly give your thoughts to those who wait to receive them, you will find a great inner peace. But I must add, it is not of any use saying the words with your lips and having your mind focused on something else such as you have this, that, or the other to do.

In the past there have been many great Teachers who have come to the Earth plane to teach the art of meditation and prayer, for meditation commences with prayer. Meditation is of prayer, but it has become something that must be, for there are those who sit in meditation who forget the prayer. There are those who sit in meditation who say in their thoughts, who send forth the thought — I want to look in — I want to see within — I want to bring forth those treasures from within. That is mainly a matter of ego, for if sitting together with several other people, and if not of the experience of prayer, they misconstrue; for all are linked together in prayer and meditation, and the spiritual awareness of those gifts within which can come forth, does come forth when there is the understanding.

Prayer is of great value, prayers sincerely sent forth unselfishly with compassion and love. Prayers that are sent forth because of a fear, because of a confusion are answered. They are always answered, and sometimes the answer is not recognised, and the thought then goes forth that God has forsaken me. But no, He does not forsake any of His children. There is a reason for all things and the answers that are expected are not always received, and very often the answers that are given are not understood, as I have already said.

I would say to you sit quietly in prayer at a time that is convenient to your own daily life. Send forth a prayer of compassion perhaps, or a prayer for guidance on a spiritual matter, or even a prayer for guidance upon a material matter if it is of unselfish origin. Then see if you have the understanding when that prayer is answered, for it will be answered. I am not suggesting my brothers and sisters, that you play games with prayer, oh no! It is not a game. One does not play with the power of thought, for one will not receive and one will only impede the spiritual progress. Sincerity and love, they are the key words, they are the key words of Spirit. They are the key words, and your prayers will be answered.

To recognise the answer of a prayer is the beginning of an awareness of a very wonderful nature. When I was in the Convent as a very young person, I loved Father God, and yet I rebelled at the time spent in prayer. For I could hear the birds singing outside the building and I could see the Sun shining in the blue sky on many occasions, and I longed to be out there. I am afraid that my prayers were not of the subject and not of the thought that they should have been, for my thoughts were outside that window with the birds. But I learned in time that my prayer, my thoughts about the Sun and the birds and the longing to be outside, were to a certain extent answered, and I spent several years working in the gardens of the Convent.

But I still said the prayers at regular times, for that was part of the Order. But I spent so many happy hours out in the gardens working. It was hard work but it was very pleasant, and I worked through all the seasons and came to realise that every season has its own beauty. Though the wind may be blowing and the air cold, to work in love and with a will and a knowledge that as one worked on the land so ones life was so created. I wonder if you have ever thought of that. You work in your gardens, you work hard to turn the soil over to get the air and the light into the soil, particularly those soils that are heavy and blocked and no light penetrates. And you place upon that soil something which will lighten it, something which will open it up, something which will allow the light and the air to penetrate.

Then there comes the time for the seeds to be planted, and in order to do this the soil has to be broken down very fine, and you plant your seeds. But it is of little use planting seeds and going away and leaving them, for you have to make sure that they receive water and nourishment. They have to have sustenance in order to survive. They have to have protection from the sharp eyes of the birds who after all, like tasty morsels. Then gradually the little growth comes forth, and it has to be protected from the scorching rays of the Sun until it has its roots firmly into the soil and has gained strength. And then it blossoms forth and it grows, with your tender care and the tender care of God, the elements, the rain, the Sun. So they grow and grow and produce their fruits, and you partake of those fruits, for they are fruits of love, the loving, tending and concern. Thus you reap your harvest and proceed on your way sustained, and then the cycle starts again. Liken that to your lives upon the Earth plane, for your lives may be of longer duration than the seed that you planted, but never the less they are the same.

I do ask you to spend a little time in prayer and silence. You do not have to spend many hours as we did in the Convent, for that was our work, to send forth our thoughts and prayers. Your work, all of you is that of healing. Your work is not to stay indoors behind high walls. Your work is to go forth and plant those seeds. Your work is to bring about healing. And as you have already been given the understanding there are many types of healing, but to give ten minutes in the morning and ten minutes at night at regular times in prayer is not to give up very much of your life span, and the prayers that you send forth will be answered.

It would be of much interest to each of you if you discussed the knowledge that you have acquired through prayer. Have you sent forth a prayer in true sincerity, compassion and love, and have you recognised the answer? Discuss it amongst yourselves. We will listen with interest, for we know that there have been such answerings, but you will help each other if you voice these truths.

Now I will go. I hope you have found my words of interest. I hope you will act upon them. I hope that now you have an understanding. Indeed I expect you already have the understanding, but to put into action that understanding is what is needed upon the Earth plane and amongst you. Thank you for listening to the words that I have said.

God's Blessings are with you at all times. God bless you, God bless you.

Chapter X

PREDICTIONS
VISITORS FROM ANOTHER SPHERE

G reetings my children, my name is Onifer. I come from a small island that used to be off the Seychelles. I have spoken through my channel before, she knows me well. I come to tell you of the times in which I lived many moons ago. I come to tell you of those things that happened and I come to warn you that such things are indeed happening now. I come to tell you that there must be a great caution upon the Earth plane, for if care is not taken a tinder box will be lit. But I tell you the end before the beginning, and that will not do.

I lived on my island which was of great beauty. It was an island populated by a people who lived on [1]nectar. We had our rules, we had our ceremonies, and we loved our God. We lived by the rules laid down many moons before I returned to the Earth plane. We lived a simple life, we lived in harmony and love, we respected each other. We fished in the waters, we ate the vegetation, the berries, the fruits, the herbs, and the other fruits that come from Mother Earth. There was a mountain upon our island, for our island had risen from the sea in a

---

[1]Nectar — (Greek Mythology) Drink of the gods; any delicious drink. Sweet fluid or honey produced by plants.

mighty storm and it was of great fertility, and it was clothed in vegetation in a comparatively short time. The mountain was the symbol, and on the side of the mountain there was a large cave which became our hall of ceremony. We worshipped there our God, we adorned ourselves with shells. We were indeed simple folk.

But one day it was shattered, for across the sea there came large ships of curious design. We thought that they had been sent by our God, we thought that they were Gods. We welcomed them, but they ransacked our island. They took our maidens for slaves, they took our young men to work upon their ships, they killed our old folk and they left nothing but desolation and grief behind them. There were but a few of us left, and I was one for I was left for dead. Of course when we realised that our maidens were being taken by these strange looking people, then of course we tried to stop it, but we were helpless.

And so those who were left tried to build up once again, the love and the beauty of the life we had known. It was not easy. We buried those who had been slain, and we cried out to our God, "Why did you let that happen? What did we do wrong?" But of course we had not committed a crime, it was progress, a progress from another country, for their civilisation was far advanced of ours. They knew how to build these large ships and we in our simplicity, living upon our simple island, eating the fruits of Mother Earth, knew nothing of the civilisation which could dig into the ground and find minerals which could be made into weapons. We knew nothing of this, and so these days, your time upon the Earth plane, we would probably have been considered rather like the ostrich, but no, for we knew no different.

I would say to you, as has already been said in a previous teaching: there are things upon the Earth plane, there are happenings of which you know nothing. But also I would say to you there are happenings upon other Spheres of which you know nothing. And I would say to you that the work that is being done within this Sanctuary, the knowledge that is being given to you, will at some time be of great value. For you will have an understanding of that which will appear from another sphere. And as we upon our island gazed upon those ships that sailed across our waters, so too will you gaze upon these ships, I will say, that will come across your skies. But I would say to you that the ships that come from other Spheres are not all of evil intent. For some come to investigate, to assess what will be done, to assess what must be done, and also to assess those upon the Earth plane who send forth light and thoughts of love. For you see radar will not be necessary, for telepathy will guide. The thought has gone forth, "That will not be in my time," and I would say to you do not be too sure, for progress is being made in many directions, and upon other spheres there is a great advancement.

You will be given proof of these words, for in the vicinity of the Seychelles there will be a happening of great magnitude. A happening which will cause much comment, and I come to say to you that as it began it will not end. It is not a riddle, think upon it. It has been a great delight for me to be with you this earth evening. God bless you all. Aloha.

Predictions

* * *

CLIMATIC CONDITIONS

Greetings my children it is I, Thomas. There are many things about to happen on the Earth plane, for there must be warnings. The warnings are intended to show Man that God is the stronger. This will be shown through Mother Earth, for Mother Earth is to undergo several changes.

There has been a tragic happening brought about by [1]earth tremors. There have been lives lost and much suffering. This is of course very much regretted, but there is much more suffering than need be. Those people who are in that area should put their trust in those who are trying to help them, but they are clinging — I cannot say to bricks and mortar, for it is but rubble — but they are clinging to things of the past and they will not let go, and this is unfortunate for it is best to let those things of the past go when the happenings arise to give you an indication that this must be.

I am not saying that those people who have lived simple lives high in the mountains could adapt themselves to the life in the towns below, for they would be very unhappy and completely out of place and harmony. But it is best to leave the area, move further away, for there is much space upon the mountains and it would be best if they moved away for it will

---

[1]Earth tremors — These earth tremors refer to the earthquake in Italy in 1980.

not be long before Vesuvius will start to rumble. It will only be warning rumblings, but if those people who are near take heed of those warnings, there will be no lives lost. There will be devastation of course, for that is unavoidable, but there will be no lives lost if they will only heed the warnings that will be given to them by Mother Earth.

The time is now coming when the area known as Los Angeles and the surrounding country will be devastated also in a mighty quake. There will be throwbacks from the sea and mighty waves will roll in and crash down on those houses that line the shore. There have been many warnings given to people in this area. Mother Earth has given many warnings, but they do not heed, and so there will be lives lost of great magnitude, it is inevitable. One can only warn and guide, and if those warnings are not heeded then it is free will which will cause the loss of the lives. It is very unfortunate but it will happen for it has to be.

There have to be changes upon Mother Earth for the time has now come for those changes, and a fresh cycle in the life of Mother Earth will be commencing. In the past there have been great changes on the Earth plane, for there were at one time colossal mammals roaming the Earth plane. But gradually these have died, they have become extinct as the word is used now. But there are still places upon the Earth plane where mammals can be found, lost in the mountain regions of the Himalayas. Lost in the mountain regions in the areas known as China and Russia. For there are areas in Russia which are as yet un-navigated, in fact one could say un-navigable.

Of course there are aeroplanes now, but aeroplanes are limited in what they can see. They cannot see under great crags and they cannot see down into the ravines. Even with the wonderful equipment for extending the vision they still cannot penetrate rocks and caves. So I say to you, there are still mammals and from time to time there will be discoveries, and people will marvel. There was the change of the Ice Age. The movement of the planet Earth caused this. This was a melting and a freezing in various parts of the world, of changing areas. Once again this will happen, but not just yet, but it will happen and there will be a changing of the climatic conditions.

A few Earth years ago there was great excitement and great experimenting with atom bombs and similar destructive weapons. There was a great race to see who could produce the first one, who could produce the second and so on. There was a race to demonstrate how clever they were in letting off these bombs. They were let off in areas that were safe, the scientists said. They were let off in areas of vast waste, so the scientists said. But my children there is life everywhere, and those areas that were subjected to demonstrations of the atom bomb were areas of considerable mineral life, minerals which have been activated and minerals which are quietly expanding.

There will be a strange happening in the area of the Pacific Ocean where atom bombs were dropped to the sea bed. For in those experiments there has been considerable damage done to the crust of the Earth. Scientists seem to have forgotten that although the oceans may be deep there is still the Earth crust at the bottom, and to interfere with that crust has caused a lot of damage. Damage which as yet has not been realised, for there is a mighty chasm opening up across the Pacific Ocean. It is gradually widening and there will be considerable surprise at what will happen in the Pacific Ocean.

The time is coming when Man must look into the future rather than planning for today. That sounds a contradiction of previous teachings, but you already have the awareness that people are now saying that if one removes the oil from the sea bed and does not fill it with something else, the cavities will gradually crumble and cave in, and indeed they will. And they are saying that we must not take all the oil out, that we must leave some for future generations. There is so much oil taken out and so many cavities left beneath the crust of the Earth plane. In some areas they have looked ahead and have filled those cavities with water and this is good. But there are other areas which are just sucking the oil out, the minerals, the life that has taken millions of years to protect the Earth crust.

Oh! there are to be so many changes upon Mother Earth, so many changes, and they are beginning to commence now. Vesuvius is already beginning to awaken. It will not happen tomorrow, but you will hear in the not too distant future that there are wisps of smoke rising from Vesuvius. And you will also hear in the not too distant future that quite serious earth tremors have been felt in the vicinity of Los Angeles and that area. Of course earth tremors are not confined to just a mile or two, for from Los Angeles it will run into the ocean and there will be a breach in the sea bed. The crust of the Earth is already damaged.

It is wise to let you know these things, for it gives you an understanding that those things which are told you from the World of Spirit are told you in truth. They are told you not to frighten you, for there is no need for you to be afraid, because you have the awareness that in any case the physical body will be discarded when the time is right. So you have the understanding that there is nothing to fear. But it is wise to remember these things and it is wise to note when the succession of events really commences. I speak in truth when I say that the quake which has just occurred is but the beginning. The volcanic eruption near the coast of Canada and America was also a beginning. The quake which will occur in the area of Los Angeles is also part of the beginning. Note these things down, put down dates and you will see a pattern emerge. A pattern of time, for these things will happen in succession.

You have the understanding, the spiritual understanding. You have the awareness of the Spirit within and the unity with Father God. You have the awareness that that which is written will happen, and indeed it will, for it is determined that the Earth plane will be cleansed in order that perfection may be reached. There is much darkness on the Earth plane at the present time and there is a tinder box waiting to be lit, as you have already been given the understanding. But it is hoped that by the action that Mother Earth is taking, that tinder box will never be lit. For it is hoped that Man will realise that survival is more important than power, and that a love and understanding of one's fellow beings and creatures is more important than the hoarding of gold.

You are all at this time upon the Earth plane with a particular mission, and there are those who are as yet unaware, and there are those who do not heed. But I would say to you there are thousands who sit in prayer to send out the love and the light to protect Mother Earth, and to try to carry out a cleansing and a healing. Join them in your quiet moments, join them and choose a time — you have already been told this — choose a time to sit quietly in your own homes. Sit at the same time once a day, once a week, once in two weeks. Always the same time, and unite with those who sit in prayer, for you have already been told that the power of thought is very powerful and can achieve much. Remember the power of thought in your daily lives.

I will go now. May the Blessings of Father God surround you and His Light and Love, and may you be truly protected, as indeed you are. God bless you, God bless you.

Chapter XI

THE SEARCH FOR SPIRITUALITY
SPIRITUAL AWARENESS

reetings my daughter, greetings my children, this is Thomas. I come to speak with you for this Group meeting. I come to speak with you for there is much to be said and much to be done. There will come about soon a great upheaval upon one of the continents upon the Earth plane. There will come about a great upheaval in which many lives will be lost. Their lives will be lost, for that is the way it must be, otherwise there will be a greater suffering if they were to remain upon the Earth plane, a physical suffering. Of course I know you have this understanding.

My children all of those in the Spirit World who have been allotted the task of teachings and of guidance, to bring about a greater understanding with all the groups around and across the Earth plane now have to say, "The time has come when you must sit in thought, you must send forth thoughts of love." These thoughts must be sent out in order that they may be used to bring about a calming of an area of great upheaval. For you see the area of upheaval is an area of change of thought, and where lives were orderly and therefore thoughts were orderly.

There have been great changes and people are very confused, and in this state of confusion there can come about a breaking of the pattern. And thus within that area there can come about great upheavals. I am sure you have the understanding. You are asked to sit quietly, to unite in thought with all the Groups around the Earth plane who are at this time being asked to unite in their turn.

You see you already have the awareness that times differ around the Earth plane. That when some are asleep others are wide awake, and when some are going to bed others are just rising. So you can see how the Groups that have been formed around the Earth plane are continually watchful and continually sending forth their thoughts, their prayers, and the light and the love. And so it means that the thoughts of love are going out all Earth day and all Earth night, wherever it is night and wherever it is day.

So my children I will ask you to please sit in silence and concentrate on Mother Earth. I ask you to visualise the Globe, the World, the Earth plane, revolving on the axis. I ask you to visualise the Moon on one side and the Sun on the other. I ask you to visualise the dark side of the Globe and the bright side of the Globe, and I ask you to visualise the dark side gradually revolving towards the bright side. This of course is symbolic. I ask you to send out thoughts of love for all mankind and for Mother Earth. I will speak when the time is enough. (The Group sit in silence.) Thank you my children, I would say to you that you have indeed sent forth help. Your thoughts will be used.

My children you will find that gradually within yourselves you will have a greater understanding of your spiritual path, for you are all beginning to awaken to an inner self, the spirit self. You are bringing forth from within some of those things which have been locked away. If you sit in quiet meditation you will be able to bring forth some of those treasures that are locked deep within, for you are beginning to have the understanding. You are beginning to have an awareness. An awareness which is gradually developing; an awareness which will gradually come forth, until your conscious mind will register those things that have been hidden deep within. Those treasures will come forth slowly, for each one must be understood and you must, each one of you, know deep within what must be done.

We are now approaching a time of much difficulty upon the Earth plane, a time of turmoil, a time of unrest. It is really a levelling off. And when once the levelling off has been completed then all will go forward into the New Age. For when once this barrier of turmoil is passed then there will be smooth waters. Of course it will take many Earth years, but now is the time when the thoughts are spread. Now is the time when an understanding must be given. Now is the time when there are those who have returned upon the Earth plane to bring about changes of thought; to bring about a concept of love one with the other. A concept of give and take, a concept of sharing, a concept of understanding, a concept of compassion.

Lessons will be hard and there will be some who will return to the Earth plane several times before they even become aware. For they have built a hard shell around the spiritual, and although they discard the physical body they take back to the World of Spirit a spirit which is encased. And of course you have the understanding that as you are now, so you are reflected when you discard the physical body. When in the World of Spirit unless you return with your spiritual mission completed, then back you come again, for you see each incarnation is a cleansing. Perhaps I should say, ought to be a cleansing. But I digress.

Within this Group there is an understanding of the power of thought. Within this Group there is a harmony, a harmony which has been built up over a period for longer than you are aware. It is possible that there will be changes within this Group, it is possible, but nevertheless the harmony will remain. And when finally the last words are spoken and you follow your own spiritual paths with the understandings and the teachings which you have received within this Sanctuary firmly established within your conscious mind, you will still all be linked in harmony, for you will all have been given the same teachings and understandings. You will find from time to time you will communicate with each other, because from each one of you teachings will be given to others. So from seven people there will be many who are given the understanding and the knowledge of the power of thought, of the love and the light that can be sent out to each and every on of God's creations.

I thank you for the love that you have sent forth. I am afraid that you may be disappointed with my words, but there must be deviations sometimes from the set pattern, and this is one of them.

May the Love and the Light of Father God surround you at all times, and it does. God bless you, God bless you all.

The Search for Spirituality

* * *

SPIRITUAL GUIDANCE

Greetings my friends, greetings to you all. It is my turn to speak with you, it is my turn to give you a teaching. I come my friends from Canada as it is now called. My name was Red Star, I was a [1]Cherokee of that great tribe. I come to tell you of the spiritual knowledge that we had in those times long before the white man came to our country, long long before.

We lived and we roamed the vast plains of that country. We set up our camps where there was water and where there was lush greenery for our beasts. We stayed for many long months before moving to other hunting grounds. We revered our ancient ones, our forbears, we revered their spirits. We would speak with them, for they never left us. Although they had cast aside their physical body, they were always with us.

The Elders of the camp would sit around the fire at night when the children and the women were abed and we would converse with those in Spirit, who would join us and tell us of the wonders that they beheld in the Spirit World. For they were as real to us as we were to each other upon the Earth plane. They called it, "The Happy Hunting Ground," for all were happy there they said. They told us of vast halls conjured up by

---

[1]Cherokee — (Member) of a tribe of North American Indians formerly occupying a large part of southern United States.

thought. Halls wherein were records of lives that were past and lives that were to be, for all were records of spirit.

They would come to us and tell us of the things that must be done, of the mistakes that we had made. They guided us, but as with you so with us, free will was allowed to take its course. Sometimes we were told of disasters that would befall, even as you are told by those in spirit who come forward to warn, to advise, to try to cast off those things that can be averted if only you will listen to those things that you are told, for as always there is free will.

We were told many many Moons before it happened, that there would be vast ships which would land on the coast on the other side of the plains where we lived. We were told how people with different coloured skins to ours would land and would set up their wigwams. And that gradually they would infiltrate into our World, our plains, our lives, bringing destruction and cruelty. But my children not all were cruel. Nevertheless those things that were told us by our forbears who came forth from spirit, all those things they told us came to pass.

We hunted buffalo. We in our turn were hunted. We had to learn cunning to deal with the ways of the white man. There had to be learned many lessons. There had to be many lives forfeited, but even so those whose lives were forfeit came back and joined us. My children there are places in Canada even now which are as they were when I was a proud Cherokee Chief. I Red Star ruled my people with love and understanding. I was their Father figure, I was the one to whom they turned with all their problems. I was the one who sat with the Elders around the camp fire and handed all these problems over to our forbears in spirit. And together we sat and thrashed out these matters, and we were guided, and we took note of the words that were said.

We were told also by those from the Happy Hunting Ground of the wonders that there would be upon the Earth plane, wonders that we would never see in the physical body, wonders which were to come. And I say to you my children that there are yet some of these wonders to come forth. There are yet to be marvellous happenings upon this planet Earth, all is not to be disaster. There will be wonders far beyond the understanding of most men, for they who do not have the awareness, are under the impression that all things that are **to be** are already upon Mother Earth, for to them there is but one sphere. But I can say to you that Mother Earth is but one sphere amongst many. There will be a great happening in the not too distant future which will set the vibrations ringing. The vibrations that are known as the vibrations of television and radio, for they are vibrations as most things, and there will be great astonishment.

I Red Star, am happy that I have been here to speak with you. I am afraid that this visit is not of long duration for I am afraid that the energy is not strong enough for me to continue. But I know that you have the understanding of these matters, and so I will go. But before I do I say to you, listen to those things that are told to you in your quiet moments, for your Guides are with each one of you, and as they are Guides so they endeavour to help you. Listen to the words that are spoken, listen to that inner ear, and you will learn and you will progress.

I must go now. I say to you, pursue your paths of spiritual awareness. Do not falter, do not turn aside. I ask for the Blessings of Father God to be given to each one of you. I ask that His protection envelop you, each one. God bless you.

The Search for Spirituality

* * *

SPIRITUAL PROGRESSION

Greetings my children, this is Thomas. Once again I come to you, for this is the last meeting before the anniversary of the birth of Christ upon the Earth plane. The anniversary of the beginning of Christendom. The anniversary of the true realisation that life is everlasting. That there is no death, just a shedding of the physical body. Even as was demonstrated by the Master, Jesus the Nazarene.

Before that time there were many prophets; those who took upon themselves the crown of prophecy. Some were false prophets and some were indeed of truth, for they had themselves returned to the Earth plane in order to spread the truth. Now there are again false prophets, false prophets who endeavour to inveigle people into beliefs other than those of truth. There are those who declare that when the end of the World cometh nigh, "We will be the only ones to survive for we are chosen." But that is not so and it will soon be proved, for there will be those of truth, of darkness, of misplaced belief, who will all perish together.

They will perish because the time will be right, and they will return to the World of Spirit, and there are those who are of truth who will progress and be given a greater understanding. False prophets will have lessons to learn and the so called chosen ones will indeed have lessons to learn, for the majority of them are taking care of the self, of me. They do not say **I am**, but it is the **me**, and that of course is on a very material level.

The birth of Christ has been made into a legend. But it is a charming legend and one which is respected, for it brings a certain understanding and it sets a pattern, and that is good. For the child in the manger Jesus the Nazarene, is indeed the Son of God, and God is His Father. But so my daughters and my sons, so are you. All are children of God and all contain the Divine spark, even as your physical bodies contain part of your Earth parents, for genetics work that way. As you were nurtured in your Mothers womb and as her blood fed you, so indeed did those genetic particles also form part of your physical body. Remember, you chose to return to the Earth plane. Nobody is forced to return to the Earth plane, and all choose the task and all choose the time, for all desire to progress. And with these experiences upon the Earth plane so also are there experiences in the World of Spirit.

It is understood that many have difficulty in believing the word of those in Spirit when we say there is much work done, there is much learning. But indeed there is, for there are hospitals even as there are hospitals upon the Earth plane. But the hospitals in the World of Spirit are not quite like that, for remember in the World of Spirit it is the spiritual, it is the spirit that needs to be in hospital, not the physical as on the Earth plane, and the spirit can be badly damaged by experiences that have occurred whilst in the physical body. It is the work of many in the World of Spirit to try to mend, to repair the damage that has be done. And when once the realisation and the desire to carry on with true understanding and love is given, then the Spirit can progress.

There are those of course who have no intention of progressing. There are those who have made a nice comfortable world for themselves whilst on the Earth plane. They are quite content to stay near the Earth plane, and sometimes it takes a great deal of effort on their part to achieve upliftment. Virtually my children, it is a case as a child stamping its foot and saying, "I don't want to go there," and this really is what happens. They do not want to progress, they do not want to leave that to which they are accustomed. Gradually of course all things change, and gradually those surroundings which held them to the Earth plane were changed and they become lost, and then even they have to attend the hospital to achieve an understanding. That does not mean to say that they automatically go into another dimension, for many lessons have to be learned. But it is possible that through the love and understanding of those who tend them, that they can be uplifted and brought to a true realisation of the work that must be done and the progression that must be made.

When the spirit that is encased in a child's body is freed, it may surprise you to know that even in a few short years they could achieve more than some who are on the Earth plane for many years, for it is the love that they give forth and the help that they give, the joy, that helps them to progress. Jesus Christ was born in a very lowly place so legend says. He was born in a stable surrounded by animals, a lowly place indeed. But it was of course a symbol of simplicity, of humility. And it is that humility which surrounded Jesus the Nazarene through the Earth years, for he was never desirous of riches, never desirous of fine clothes, never desirous of rich food. He was a simple man who walked in humility, who gave forth love; who gave forth compassion; who gave forth tolerance; who gave forth healing; who demonstrated those spiritual powers which made Him a well known figure. He was borne up, so to speak, and all exclaimed that, "He was the Son of God." You too are children of God, and therefore you too must show compassion and humility, tolerance and healing.

You already have the understanding that you are a Group of healers and teachers, for as you work so you speak and spread the truth. The teachings that you receive in this Group are teachings that enable you to hold a conversation, to speak of those things you have been told, to plant seed to develop, to help others. As has already been pointed out all healing is not a matter of laying on of hands. Some healing is of greater value if learned from books and from the teachings of others who themselves have qualified in a particular field, although they may not be of spiritual knowledge. Although you learn even as they teach, you have that special quality, the spiritual understanding, and it is that understanding applied to that which you have learned, which will bring forth a greater healing.

So now I will go, but I will leave you the thoughts of the birth of Jesus the Nazarene. And so my children rejoice this Christmas-tide. Rejoice in the birth of Jesus the Nazarene. May the Love and the Light of God surround you all at all times, and indeed it does. God bless you, God bless you.

* * * * *

Greetings to you all. I am one of the Brothers of Fire. I come to speak with you, for I am of the World of Spirit. I come to speak with you for I bring much strength.

I and my brothers work together in the World of Spirit. We go first to one and then to the other where the need is. We have been to the one through whom I am speaking when she underwent a great test, a great initiation, and we will come to each of you when you undergo a test or initiation of much value. There will come a time when you will be put to the test even as my channel, for it must be so if you are to progress in the manner for which you have returned to achieve.

I and my brothers travel to many countries on the Earth plane, but of course you have the understanding that it is not difficult to travel when one is in spirit. We have recently been to one in the country known as America, where there has been a great test upon one in the form of a woman. She was very much doubted. The words that she spoke were not believed, until she came to the state of mind that she herself did not believe those things which were given to her from the World of Spirit. She was surrounded by those of darkness who wished to destroy those teachings which were of truth. Her test was to withstand the darkness, to overcome, and she did, for I and my brothers gave to her strength. We did not and we do not, and we may not in any way influence, but we give strength, even as we gave strength to the one through whom I speak. And we will give strength to you, and you know that we are with you for I have told you so, and I speak in truth. There will be a time when each one of you will have a test of great value.

There are many happenings upon the Earth plane at the present time and there are many happenings also in the World of Spirit, for are we not all linked together and does not that which affects the Earth plane also affect the World of Spirit? Of course it does, for it must be so for we walk side by side. But we in the World of Spirit are not affected in the same way and of course you have the understanding.

It has been said time and again that there will be great happenings upon the Earth plane, and over the next few years of Earth time there will be many changes. There will be changes in the way that people are thinking, for the time is now coming for a true decision to be made with regard to the destruction, one man to the other. And as you know there are many Groups around the Earth plane who send out thoughts of protection. There are some Groups who sit in constant prayer that there will not be war, for if war does start it will escalate and no one will say, "I have made a mistake, I am sorry." And so it must be prevented, and so the Groups sit in prayer to try to protect and to stop.

There are of course many thousands of people who would say, "That is ridiculous, that is a lot of rubbish, I do not believe." That of course is so, they do not believe and that is a great pity, for if only they believed they too could do much to assist. However when the decision is made one way or the other, then that will be the peak point, so to speak. For when that peak point is reached there will come the changes, for which ever way is chosen, the changes will take place in the minds of men, because there must be progression to a higher level.

There are already upon the Earth plane those who have chosen to return at this time. There are already those who are now in the physical body of a babe. They are the ones who have come back with the awareness uppermost and they are the ones who as children, even at an early Earth age, will spread the words of love and light. There will be those who are of many years who will ridicule and find it very difficult to understand, but those little ones will have the full conviction and will know. They will not be deterred, and the darkness will not be able to touch them for they are specially chosen. They are not in just one area, they are all around the Earth plane, and they are of differing nationalities and colours. The colour of the skin is of no value whatsoever, for all are children of God.

You are upon the Earth plane at a very difficult and yet exciting time and I would say to you, listen carefully to the words that are spoken from those teachers who come to you, for you are being given teachings and understandings of those things that will happen, for they are written thus. But there is the free will of man and this is why I say to you that there could be war where man fights man, or there could be peace for all time. If those prayers and those thoughts that are sent forth are of true value then I say to you now, there will not be a war of complete destruction. It is not envisaged, but man has free will and we in Spirit do not interfere with free will.

I and my brothers must go now for there is another Group to whom we must speak. I ask you to remember the words that I have spoken. I ask you to remember that we came to bring you strength. We do not interfere for we are not permitted so to do. I say farewell. I say God's blessings be with you always.

The Search for Spirituality

* * *

SPIRITUAL KNOWLEDGE

Allah be praised, Allah greets you. I am afraid I am not the one who was to visit you, for he is one who needs much energy and you are one missing this Earth night. It is regretted, but the one who was to speak with you will speak at another time. And so I have been given the honour of speaking with you, to tell you about some of those things which have taken place upon the Earth plane some hundreds of years ago.

Would it surprise you if I were to tell you that where there is now desert there was no sand, there was no desert? Would it surprise you if I were to tell you that in those far off times there were people upon the Earth plane who could cultivate every bit as well as you cultivate now? Would it surprise you if I were to tell you that in those far off days there was irrigation, even as there is today? Would it surprise you if I were to tell you that rivers were diverted to bring about cultivation on a far greater scale than there is upon the Earth plane now?

You would have been surprised if you had been transported back to those times when I was upon the Earth plane, for I am speaking of the time when I was on the Earth plane. We lived in dwelling places built from the skins of the animals, but those dwelling places were large for all contributed to the building of such places and all tribes lived together and shared together. We did not have vast estates or vast land owners. All had their

120

own piece of land, but all shared and so all those pieces of land were joined together. They were joined together to bring about cultivation to support all. We did not cultivate postage stamps for there were many of us and we worked hard.

There was no sand where there is now sand. It is because over the years, many many centuries, there have been wars and uprisings. There have been jealousies and there has been hatred. There has been greed and there have been those who have sought power. Nothing has changed in that way for even so today there are those who covet their neighbour's possessions.

We had amongst us one who had great spiritual knowledge. It came from Allah we said, and he could divine where there was water and he would stand upon a spot and he would say, "Dig here," and we never ever refused to dig. We would work all together to bring about the finding of that water, and it was never very far below the surface upon which he stood. And from that well which he had found we would set about cultivation, and there would be much water sent in all directions. The water that he found never ceased to flow and although the heavens forgot to send down rain, we had plenty.

We cultivated and of course there came about an oasis, a name which is not very old, just a few thousand years, for it is a word that has come out of the tongue that I spoke many years ago. We would bring about a cultivation and a setting up of crops which would grow and which we would harvest. But we did not just rely on that, for this young man who was gifted with a spiritual knowledge would go forth and find another place upon which he would stand and give the instruction to dig. So over the area which was owned by us all he found five places of water, and they were in the shape of a star.

We did not of course realise that at the time, but of course it is known now. It was indeed a star which was formed from knowledge from Heaven. And within that star there was much cultivation, and spreading out from that star there was cultivation for it spread outwards. Nothing was held contained within that star. It was shared and it became known as a place of plenty, and indeed it was a place of plenty, but as I have said there were those who came forward with greed. Although there had been much work put into this our place of beauty, it did not matter, for greed knows no bounds.

We built a Temple to our Goddess, for Allah was good and He directed that a Temple be built. It was the first time that any of us had built a Temple. To us it was a thing of beauty, for love had gone into the building of it. But now of course it would be considered nothing more than a ring of stones. But it was our Temple and we knew that when we entered into that circle of stones, when we moved to the centre, we were protected, and we could feel the love from Allah pouring down. Of course such happiness and such plenty, such simple lives innocently lived, could not be allowed to go unnoticed by those who came from afar, and one night there was a massacre, for that which we had was envied.

It is a long time ago, a very long time ago, and the sands of the desert have now blown across that place. But there are the five oasis still there, not as plentiful not as lush, but they are still there in the desert and are used. There are times when those of us who have chosen to remain in the World of Spirit, visit those oasis and marvel that the sands of the desert have blown over and buried all that which we had achieved, and there are now no signs at all. So it is even now, the sands of the desert are always blowing and covering and uncovering. I do not necessarily mean sand as such, I mean the changes that are brought about.

There are many things upon the Earth plane which have been covered. Covered because others have desire to acquire, and in the end it has proved valueless, as indeed was the case all those years ago. Do not envy your neighbour, for in the end that which you think he has is quite worthless to you, but rather think what you can find. Look for your own oasis. Bring up the water clean and pure and let it flow away from you to help those who come in contact with you to be purified and cleansed; to have their eyes opened in the clear water, the living water.

I cannot stay any longer, I must go. I am honoured to have been with you. I hope that you will read carefully between the lines, so to speak. Allah's Blessings upon you all.

Chapter XII

MEDITATION

reetings my children this is Lauda. I come to speak with you regarding the subject of meditation, for meditation can be a very important healing, a healing for oneself. Meditation is a going within. The human body is a temple for the spirit. It is also a prison, so to speak, and it depends upon the task that you decided upon before you decided to return to the Earth plane, for reincarnation is a fact, although it is disputed.

Each and every one of you has the right to your own opinions, for each and every one of you is walking your own spiritual path, and this has been emphasised before. So what one accepts, the other cannot accept and of course into this comes the fact that you are on different levels of understanding. Levels of understanding which are gradually coming forth, which are part of the treasure you hold within the temple. To sit in meditation and to walk into the temple, to go deep within, is of very much benefit.

There are some who just sit quietly and are immediately transported deep within. There are those who sit quietly and appear to get nowhere and who say that it is a waste of time. Indeed it is not a waste of time, for just by sitting quietly in harmony with yourself and Father God, (and if with a Group in harmony with those within the Group,) is a healing for yourself. While sitting you are endeavouring to clear your mind of all the daily matters that take up your time and fill your conscious mind. And it is the conscious mind that you must learn to put to one side and shut the door and bring forward the spiritual mind. It can be done, with some it is easy with some it is difficult until they learn how.

There are those upon the Earth plane who find great difficulty in even stilling the mind, unless they are led into meditation with a description of a walk in a wood or in a calm country place or by still deep waters. There are those who cannot visualise such scenes, and they are given a word to say. A word which repeated over and over again in the same tone with a rhythmic sound to it, will help them go quietly within. There are those who have to visualise a symbol of some sort, something upon which they can focus their conscious mind, but allowing the spiritual mind to take over, and some just sit quietly in the silence and go deep within.

My children meditation is something which you should all achieve. For there are times upon the Earth plane when although surrounded by all those material possessions and the material physical life upon the Earth plane, there are times when you need to sit quietly. A temple of peace a temple of solitude. A solitude which you yourselves have created, for you draw to you the aura and tightly close it up, and you are therefore completely encased.

To go within is to find a very deep sense of peace, a feeling of oneness with the Divine Spirit. An awareness of the Divine spark within you. A bringing forth, a settling down, a restoration, re-energising, complete relaxation and transport-ation. For it is those who can go deep within who can forget all things physical, who can ignore all things material. They can transport themselves to places, to those who need them. It is the power of complete oneness. It is the power of thought; it is the power of love, of compassion, and when truly obtained is of great value. There are many who through meditation have been restored to bodily health. There are those who through meditation have been restored to mental health. For whilst in deep meditation those things of the physical have become as nothing, and a cleansing has taken place.

My children the problems of the mind, the sicknesses of the mind are created by the mind of the one who suffers thus. It is **not** a karmic condition. Very often a sickness of the mind is brought about by an accident, and it is therefore something which was not intended. But very often those who suffer thus when once they turn to seeking, ask the question, "Why?" If they are in a physical state to do this, they can very often have their footsteps guided to those who can truly help them, and it has been known that through a spiritual operation a cure has been completed. There are those in the Spirit World who when upon the Earth plane were great neuro specialists, and understand the problems of the brain and its construction, of the delicate instrument that it is. It is a part of the physical body and a very important part, and according to the work, to the task that was intended to be completed, so a cure is effected.

But to return to meditation. It is not necessary to sit cross legged upon the floor to enter into a state of deep meditation, but it is a fact that there must be no irritations. When you are in the state of learning you become very sensitive to the physical problems, but when once you go deep within it is as if you were discarding the physical body. It becomes no longer of any consequence, for you are within the temple. There are some of you who will see swirling colours and then a scene will open up before you and you will take part within that scene. And then you will find that gradually as you go deeper within there will be a complete silence and you will be in tune with the Creator. You will return restored, you will return uplifted and you will return at peace.

My children if you do not already meditate I would say to you it is time that you did so. For it is through meditation that your energies can be restored; that you will become stronger channels for the healing that you will accomplish. You could say, "But if my healing is just to talk to people, I cannot see how that uses energy." But indeed it does, and in many cases it uses more energy than the laying on of hands. It is usual with the laying on of hands that the patient is already seeking, but very often the healing that is given with the spoken word is given to somebody who does not have the understanding, and who is not seeking, but is somebody who is full of a deep distress. And it is the healer in this case who has to listen, who has to project compassion and understanding. It is the healer in this case who gives off a great deal of energy. For I am sure you are of the understanding that very often when somebody talks to you, pours out their problems and their troubles they say, "I feel so much better for having spoken to you," but when you yourself go home you feel very depleted. That being the case then I would say to you, go and sit quietly in meditation for a time. Cast all the words away from you and seek the silence and solitude that is within, and you will emerge re–energised.

You see to sit in meditation is not to sit in the hope that you will be given an understanding of things that must be done, but it is to sit and to endeavour to link with the Divine Spirit. Of course the understanding is that this is not possible directly, but it is possible for a link, a chain to be forged. My children please practice meditation, practice it in your units and you will find gradually you will have a calming. That a peace will surround you and that your inner eye will be opened to many things upon the Earth plane that you have not noticed, and there will come about a greater understanding of those things that you have not understood. Meditation is indeed of great value.

I go now. May the Light and the Love of Father God protect you all, as indeed it does. God bless you, God bless you.

* * * * *

Greetings my friends, it is of much pleasure for me to come to speak with you. I was well versed in the art of meditation, for

I sat for many hours in meditation. I had many wonderful experiences. It was no problem for me to leave the physical body and to go forth in complete freedom. It was as I am now, in spirit, the spirit within that went forth.

I sat for many hours, but I sat cross legged upon the floor. I was nevertheless comfortable, and you have been told that it is very necessary that you are comfortable. For if you are not you do not go deep within, and it is therefore impossible to leave the physical body, to transport yourself to wherever you wish to go. It is not impossible it can be done, it is being done by many many people upon the Earth plane at the present time.

I will tell you, for I am allowed, of one or two of my experiences. The first time that I left my physical body I was sitting cross legged upon the floor within the Temple wherein I was taught and where my teacher stood by, for I was but a small child. I sat cross legged upon the floor and cleared from my mind all thought. It was not easy for a small boy to do but my teacher was very strict and the disciplines were very rigid, and lo and behold I was looking down upon that small boy and I was free. Not entirely free for my teacher was with me, for it was not right that I should be alone for I could be lost.

We went together to a beautiful place, a place of much light, a place that was filled with many people, a place of great beauty. And I was told that I was floating, so to speak, within a dimension of spiritual value, and that I must remember that experience and that I was to return to my body which was still sitting cross legged upon the floor, and which I recall I thought was rather cold. It was no problem for I had been taught well and when I moved I was within my physical body and nothing had changed. My teacher was there beside me and all was the same, and yet I knew, for I had brought with me that which had happened. That was my first experience of leaving behind my physical body.

When I was a young man there was a great war raging, and I desired to go to fight, for I felt that it was my duty to defend my country against invaders, and I was allowed to go. I remember that I was afraid when I came face to face with the attackers, for they were fierce men with heavy weapons which they handled as if they were blades of grass. I felt that my life would end, but it did not. I was wounded and I was left upon the ground as dead, but I was not dead. I was full of a determination to regain my strength, and therefore I waited until nightfall and then I dragged myself away into a thicket which I rolled into. It was not at all comfortable.

I do not know how long I was there and my wound was bleeding badly, and I lay upon it to try to get some sort of relief. But I had without knowing, rolled upon a herb with healing properties and it did its work in stopping the bleeding. I slept and awoke feeling refreshed. You must understand that in those days wars took place almost upon ones doorstep, for marauding tribesmen would attack, sometimes in great numbers, and it was usually those who were the attackers who came the distances, and it was the defenders who were on their own doorstep. So you see by careful manoeuvring by night I was able to return to my home, to the Temple where I received my teachings.

I received treatment and I recovered, but I was not able to go to war any more. And so I sat in meditation and transported myself, my Spirit, to the place where they were fighting. I was able to look down upon that battle and I was able to assist, for there were those from the Temple who were there, and it was quite an experience for me to be able to watch and to be able to return to my body within the Temple, and to bring back the knowledge and those things that I had seen.

There was another occasions when I was older, and as I left my body I soared towards one who waited, who bade me follow him. I was taken to a hall, a place of great beauty; a place of much light; a place of great wisdom. I was allowed to meet teachers of old. Teachers who were upon the Earth plane thousands of years ago, for my friends, there have always been scholars somewhere upon the Earth plane. There have always been those who have meditated. There is nothing new in meditation. In that vast hall I met many of those scholars of old, and it was very interesting. You will probably find it very difficult to believe that you too could go forth to those places of learning if once you really were able to go deep within.

Now I would say to you, would you like to ask me a question and I will endeavour to answer for you? I do not say I know all things for I do not, but I feel that now is the time, and I have been told this. Now is the time for you to ask a question or two, and as I say I will endeavour to answer it.

Question: *When we are told about meditation it is impressed upon us that the time should always be the same. Can you tell me why it is so important?*

Answer: Because my friend when you meditate there are those who gather around you from the World of Spirit to help you. Sometimes it is very difficult for you to clear the mind, the conscious mind. In the initial stages this is something which you alone can do, but there are those who wait to help you when the times comes, and if the time comes that you can transport yourself, at such times you must have the love of those in spirit to assist.

Also my son time is important, for to keep to a specified time is a discipline, self discipline. If you do not keep to a specified time, you will not have the discipline. It means that there may be occasions when you have to make a choice between meditation and perhaps something else which you would enjoy more. Discipline **must be learned**.

Question: *Can you tell me please why some people manage to achieve this relatively easily and others may never do so?*

Answer: Yes my friend, it is a matter of previous existence. It is a matter of bringing forth the spiritual mind. It is a matter of control, controlling the thoughts of the physical, the conscious mind. You will find that in many cases it is those who are placid within their daily lives who soon achieve meditation. Basically I would disagree with you when you say that some never achieve true meditation. I would disagree for I believe that they did not learn true discipline.

There are some people who play at meditation, they are, so to speak, on and off. They say, "I do not get anywhere." Now there are some who say this who do go within, who do manage tranquillity within, but are unaware. There are others who say, "I cannot, I do not, I am not going to bother," and then at a later time they have another go. They do not have discipline. All could achieve with discipline. Does that answer your question?

Question: *Is there a time of day that is preferential?*

Answer: No my friend, we do not suggest times. At one time yes, but now upon the Earth plane the daily life is much much faster. How many times is it said, "I do not have time to do this, and I do not have time to do that," or "How quickly the days go," for you all lead busy lives. No my friend, it is up to you to choose your own time. You know the time that is most convenient to you, the time when you will be able to have the discipline, the time when you can really sit quietly.

You my friend should sit with your lady wife, for you are a unit and you would help each other, for between you, you would forge a circle of light which would help you. You have said that you have great difficulty in stilling the mind, for immediately you start thinking of one thing and another.

I would say to you my friend, think of the sea, for I know that you enjoy working upon the sea. Think of the sea, think of the deepness of the sea, think of the waves upon the surface and think of the stillness within the depths. You will find it of benefit, and if you find your conscious mind intrudes with other thoughts, you must send them away and think back upon the sea — always the sea.

Question: *I am just starting to meditate and I see pictures. What is the difference between seeing those pictures and going completely into yourself so that you can leave your body behind? Is it just a different depth of concentration?*

Answer: It is in a way a different depth, but you see my friend you have said on several occasions that you see nothing, and now you are joyous because you do see. To see pictures and to have visions is to give you an understanding that you are indeed progressing in your meditation. You note them down and in time you will be directed back, that you may interpret. It is for you to interpret my friend. Your teachers will guide you to the interpretations, but you will gradually go deeper within if you have the disciplines. It is no use me saying to any of you, this will happen or that will happen, for it is up to you. It is up to your own discipline and it is up to you to really clear the conscious mind. You have been told that meditation is a healing for you, and indeed it is. It is also a means of teaching, a means of learning.

There are many upon the Earth plane who have a great understanding of meditation, of the going within the Temple. Their knowledge is of great value, but it is not all who can achieve the depth of meditation where you can transport yourselves. I would remind you that I spent many hours sitting in meditation, many hours, and so it will not be within the ability of you, of your physical body, of your spiritual awareness, to transport yourselves, unless you spend many hours in meditation. But the meditation that you can achieve is the one of great benefit to your physical well being, to your spiritual awareness. You are healers but there are times when you yourself require healing and this is a means, as you have already been told, of revitalisation, of re-energising, of restoring tranquillity and balance. Are there any more questions?

Question: Would you tell us the origin of your country and your religion when on the Earth plane?

Answer: I was Hindu. I lived many years ago, but when I was upon the Earth plane there were, even then, great cities of a different kind to those that are on the Earth plane now. They were cities built of stone. Cities that had water running through the streets. Cities where people knew the value of cleanliness and where the people knew the value of prayer and meditation, and had a respect for each other. Now there is little respect one for the other, and so there must come a time when there will be upheavals, but in meditation comes understanding.

I will tell you no more for I am not allowed, but I will say this. Until man respects man there will not be peace. And I will say this, that gradually the understanding will come about, and gradually, bit by bit the Earth plane will be cleansed, and respect will be restored and the golden ring of love will encircle the Earth plane. But it will not be as it is now, for there are to be changes. I will say no more. I will go.

May the Love of Father God, may the Light of that Love may the Peace of that Love envelop you each one of you, may you learn the disciplines, may you respect each other. God bless you.

Chapter XIII

ASPECTS OF CHILDHOOD

G reetings my daughter, it is I Lauda. I come to speak once again with the Group. I come to speak to you about the children, for children need much healing, and so it is good that we discuss the various aspects of childhood.

There are those who return to the Earth plane with full knowledge of matters spiritual, with a spiritual mind fully opened from the time of birth. From the time they touch the Earth plane they are aware that they are surrounded with Spirit helpers. These are shown at the beginning in the form of dancing lights, and nature people which their un-focused eyes are aware of and can watch, and gradually as the muscles strengthen, bringing the eye into position, so the sight strengthens and so they can then see the nature people very clearly.

The nature people stay with them for some time until they are aware of human relationships. Then gradually there are those in the World of Spirit, children like themselves, who come forward to join hands and to play. Children who are fully aware that they are of the World of Spirit, who fully aware that they are not of the Earth plane, and fully aware that they can touch and approach those upon the Earth plane. For it is their task to bring about an understanding to the one who has full spiritual consciousness, so to speak.

Now this is where the parents play a large part, for sometimes the parents have no knowledge whatsoever of the World of Spirit. They have no knowledge whatsoever that there are those close by who guide them or help them. They take it all for granted. That is not quite fair for they do not have the knowledge, and it is these parents who will suffocate the child who has come forward with spiritual knowledge. It is not a complete suffocation, it is a closing of the door for the time being. For later on in life that child when grown into independence, will again be given the opportunity of opening the door to the spiritual mind, and in these cases it happens round about the age of fourteen years.

There are those who are born upon the Earth plane with the spiritual mind closely shut, with complete lack of knowledge of the spiritual. Complete lack of knowledge of those in Spirit who wait to help and who stand around and watch. They are the children who will come forward to seek, for all children born upon the Earth plane, all children, will desire knowledge and will desire to seek. And gradually their paths will lead in the direction that they must take, and it is then that their free will is used, for we do not interfere with free will as you are being constantly told. A child that has come back to complete a spiritual path will be given the knowledge from within of those things they must do and those things they must not do.

Then there is the child who is born, and through the free will of somebody else the brain is damaged and therefore the thinking, the conscious mind is retarded. But although the conscious mind is retarded the spiritual mind is completely unaffected, and these children while seeming to be completely uncoordinated, are very much co-ordinated within the Spirit, for the spiritual mind is, as I have said, very active.

How often have you heard it said that so and so — I am speaking of children — although they cannot move their physical body, although they cannot move their arms or their legs, seem to be quite content and seem to be quite happy? This of course is because of the spiritual awareness. An awareness which they cannot communicate with anyone else, but an awareness which is very real to them. Of course those in Spirit close to them who are there to guide them still guide them, for they can speak, because clairaudience is not affected. It may be very hard for you to understand this but it is indeed so.

There are children who are born upon the Earth plane with malformed bones, of physical defects of one kind or another, and yet they seem to be perfectly happy. This is of course because the spiritual mind is well developed and they are given encouragement by those in Spirit who work with them. This is why those children grow into people who achieve much. And people will say, "They have a strong will," but indeed it is that they listen to the spirit mind, to clairaudience, and talk with those in Spirit who come to them, who teach them. They have the knowledge of those things that must be accomplished, and although the physical body is deformed or is apparently of little use, the spiritual mind is as alive as anyone's.

There is the occasion where a child is born and immediately departs. You upon the Earth plane say it has just touched the Earth or it never touched the Earth, if it is born without apparent life. But the Spirit within is very much alive and the touching of the Earth for just a brief moment brings about a teaching; brings about a learning. But it also brings about a teaching for those who have been chosen to nurture that child. You see it is a teaching.

It may seem very hard to you that such a thing should happen, that the one perhaps who desperately wished to have a child should indeed bear one, only to find it gone in a few brief moments, but that visit has achieved something. It has achieved progression for the one who has departed, has returned to the World of Spirit. And it has achieved a teaching for the one who is left behind or those who grieve, for it brings about an understanding of the anguish that can be felt, at the despair that can be felt, the sense of loss.

They are very hard lessons to learn, but they have to be learned. If they are not learned you do not have the correct understanding for other people with whom you come in contact. I would say to you my children, think back over your lives and if you feel so disposed write down the number of times that you have felt despair, or joy, or compassion, love, sadness, indeed grief, all the emotions that are felt.

Children born blind never see the beauties of the Earth plane, but they do encounter the beauties of those who come in contact with them. For there is much help and love given to those who are blind and there are those who will spend much time using their eyes for the benefit of the one who is sightless. The one who is sightless develops other senses far more acutely. The hearing develops in many cases, that they can hear the whispering of the grass and the rustling of the leaves upon the trees long before anybody else. They can hear the flutter of a butterflies wings and know that an insect of great delicacy and beauty is near. There are many compensations for all things, many compensations, if you will only seek them. All must seek if they are to find, if they are to understand, and if they are to become aware of the path upon which they have decided many years ago to walk.

Upon one of my teachings I will tell you something of the work that goes on ahead of your returning to the Earth plane. I will tell you of this, but it will not be yet. I would say to you, give out love to the children that you see who have been born not as perfect as would be wished. Give out love and understanding, but remember that in their own way they are happy, for in their own way they are walking their own spiritual path. They are aware of those around them in Spirit who tend them, who join them with love, who walk with them at all times and never leave them. It is the physical, the conscious mind that gives out pity for these people, but it is not pity that is required. It is love and understanding. And remember no matter how ugly the physical body may be, the Spirit within is truly beautiful.

Look within, by-pass the physical body and look within. Look into the eyes of those with whom you come in contact. It has been said many times that the eyes are the windows of the Soul, and indeed they are, for have you not said, "That person smiles with their lips but not with their eyes." Look at the eyes of people and see whether there is true compassion and love. You can also see the greed and the hate, for all are mirrored in the eyes. Look at the eyes of a little child, wide eyed and innocent. How many times has it been said also that the innocence of a child vanishes as it gets older, and indeed it does, for of course one has to learn.

Sometimes the lessons are not easy. Look upon each child that you meet as a work of wonderment, for each one has returned with a mission and the children that are on the Earth plane now will see many changes within their life span. Some of them will live for many years and some will pass back into Spirit when the time is right, and some will pass back into Spirit too early through the free will of somebody else. Nevertheless those children who are on the Earth plane now, those children that will be born, will all begin to have a spiritual understanding at an early age.

There are many who are waiting to be born who will have spiritual knowledge uppermost in their minds. And those who are to nurture them in the early stages have been chosen very carefully, for they too must already have the understanding of the World of Spirit and the work that must be done, and so the young ones will come forward at an early stage. Young ones I say, but young ones with wisdom within, with great spiritual knowledge, who will go forth to spread that knowledge. For it is now time to accelerate the bringing together in the brotherhood of all God's children. I say accelerate and I mean accelerate, but of course it will take time, but the pattern is forming and the desire to cast out evil, to cast aside those who wish to kill is growing. There are many children upon the Earth plane now who have been contaminated. Contaminated by the powers of darkness, contaminated to kill, to destroy, to plunder, for the sheer pleasure of this evil way of life. And until it is understood that the punishment must fit the crime then this thinking will be carried from one to the other.

There are occasions my children when it is wise to turn the other cheek, but it is not wise to turn the other cheek when the motive is sheer pleasure from the sufferings of others. To see somebody writhing in agony on the floor is not the time to turn the other cheek, for that one in their turn should be given like punishment. It would drive the devil out from within them and give an understanding of the pain and humility. The punishment should fit the crime but only if the crime is witnessed. The children who commit these crimes are led. They do not come back to the Earth plane with these wicked intentions within the conscious mind. They are taught by those who are evil.

You can see the great problem there is, but until justice is done, until punishment is given to fit the crime, then there will be great difficulty in bringing back to true awareness, these young ones who have wandered far far from their spiritual path, and it is a great pity and such a waste of time. There are many such who have returned to the World of Spirit, there are many such who now have the understanding, but are not to be allowed to return for further progression, but will have to wait. Learning through that waiting, a patience far greater than is ever learned when upon the Earth plane. My children when you see a child within a conveyance who cannot walk, look into its eyes and you will see within a great spiritual awareness.

I go. May the Love and the Light of Father God surround you at all times, and it does. God bless you, God bless you.

Chapter XIV

ATLANTIS

G reetings to you all. I have spoken before within this Sanctuary but you were not here, for I spoke to my daughter of light. My name is Tara and I come from far off days. I was upon Atlantis in the days when thoughts of love were all powerful. I will tell you something of Atlantis, a beautiful continent that was destroyed through the greed and the lust of others.

It was a continent of great beauty where the buildings were raised by the power of thought. Where, as I have already said thought was all powerful as indeed thought is still all powerful. And it was because of this that the thoughts of man, woman and child must be directed to those of love and light. Upon Atlantis in those far off days we were of thought. We were transported from one place to the other by the power of thought. But there were of course rules which had to be obeyed, for as you will understand there were no locks upon the doors, for thought cannot remain locked behind a door when once the understanding is there.

We had those of great understanding and there were those who ruled, for there had to be those who could control because in any community there must be one who takes the responsibility, who has the understanding of those things that must be done. For of course without that one there is always chaos. There are those who come forth to lead and there are those who come forth to follow. There are those who gradually learn how to lead and there are those who will accept that understanding, and that is how it was upon Atlantis. It was love and understanding, an understanding that there must be a leader.

Of course there has to come a time when somebody comes forth who is not content with that, and so it was upon Atlantis, for within all there are given the various temptations. There were many upon Atlantis who could have given way to such temptations, but because they were of love they fought those temptations and sent them away, for temptation is thought also. It is those who clasp to these thoughts of jealousy that gradually become contaminated, and from that contamination the disease spreads. And so it was upon Atlantis. Oh yes, of course they were very small beginnings, so small that they were ignored, they were thought to be of no consequence. It was a great pity that we did not realise just how insidious those dark thoughts can be.

One day there was a great upheaval and our buildings toppled, for the darkness had overpowered. I am of course making this a very short understanding, for of course it did not happen in one day. But because of this disaster we lost our continent, it sank beneath the waves. It has lain at the bottom of the sea for many many Earth years. There are now upon the Earth plane many who were upon Atlantis at that time, who have waited within the World of Spirit until this time upon the Earth plane. There are those who were upon Atlantis who have returned to the Earth plane and to other planets to learn lessons, to be cleansed as far as they were able to be cleansed.

They have returned on several occasions and they too are returning to the Earth plane at this time, for this is the time of great changes. I must qualify — I am not speaking of tomorrow or next year or the year after, but I am speaking of this time, this

Age that is just beginning. It is an Age when communication will once again be by thought. I say communication, I do not say transportation. Communication will be by thought, and even now as I have said, is the beginning.

There are those who are even now being given the lessons of telepathy communication, and over a period of time it will become more pronounced. When there are understandings of this happening, I will call it a happening although it is not new, there is nothing new upon the Earth plane — nothing, but when it is known and understood, then there will really be great forces at work. For those who were upon Atlantis have the understanding of that which must be done, they have the understanding of those things which will be achieved.

I cannot tell you what will happen for it will happen when the time is right and there must be no anticipation, for you have already been given the understanding of the upheavals that there will be upon Mother Earth. Those upheavals are to do with Mother Earth, and Atlantis will rise again from the bottom of the sea. And when this does happen there will be another chance for those who were upon Atlantis, to rectify that which happened. **One more chance**, and *only* **one more chance**.

There are within this little Sanctuary those who were upon Atlantis at the time of destruction. I have come to say to you, learn your lessons well for you are to pass on to others the knowledge that you are given, that others may be given the key to their path. It is a time of great expectation. It is a time of great awakening. It is a time of great excitement if you will let yourself be part of that excitement and understanding. Oh yes, Atlantis will rise from the bed of the sea, but she will not rise with the beauty with which she disappeared. But in time that purity will be returned for it is written thus and therefore it will be so.

I will say to you carry within your mind, count within your mind those people with whom you are now coming into contact, with whom you are linking in your daily lives. I am not saying that you will meet every day, but count those people who are now entering your daily lives with whom you feel you have a certain closeness, although you know you have never met before. Begin to count, and you will know that the bond between you which may be quite beyond your comprehension and understanding, is a bond which goes back to Atlantis. It is not a story it is fact. Oh yes it is fact. It is the beginning, the beginning of the knowledge that you have held within the spiritual mind for a very very long time. It is a fact.

You, those of you who sit in meditation, will find that during that meditation when you have the true understanding of reaching the inner space, will be given the knowledge of what happened upon Atlantis, for you will be given the knowledge yourselves. You will have the understanding and the true knowledge of your part, your own part, your individual part. It will be given to you for it must be given to you, for it is essential that you truly know, because from that truth you can speak in truth.

I will go — remember count those that you meet from now on with whom you feel a bond beyond your understanding. May the Light and the Love of Father god surround you at all times. God bless you, God bless you.

Chapter XV

MOTHER EARTH

G reetings my daughter, greetings to you all, this is Lauda. I come to address you once again. At this time of the Earth year, there is a great awakening, a great upsurge of life. Those little creatures who have slept away the Winter darkness are now beginning to stir. The trees that have slept away the Winter darkness are now beginning to feel the life force rushing up to seek out every branch, every twig, every leaf bud.

The flowers and the plants that come to life at this time of the year to produce the beauty of their flower heads are already blossoming, and by their colours lifting the hearts of those who see them. What a great beauty there is to stand and look at. The daffodils dancing in the light breeze. To visualise the golden colour well after the flowers have passed into sleep again.

Visualise also the beauties that are to come, the beauties of a bluebell wood where the blue stretches as far as the eye can see, the blue of healing, for can you say that when you walk through a bluebell wood that you feel angry or aggressive? Of course not, for that anger and that aggression vanish and the healing takes place within you, the beauty and the peace overcome you and you feel at rest. You may not be aware that you are receiving healing, indeed there are many hundreds of people who pass through a bluebell wood who are not aware that they are receiving healing, but the tranquillity of the scene is carried away in their mind and they dwell upon it many times when going about their daily chores, and the healing continues.

At this time of the year there are many young born to start the new year with joy and hope, the young creatures of the field. The rabbits, the badgers, the stoats, the lambs, the young calves, the young piglets, the young of the cat family, the young of the canine family. Birds are hatched from the egg which has been produced through the love of those who nurture it, and babies are born to those upon the Earth plane who also have expressed a union. A union that was planned from the moment of creation, a union of all species that has to be if the work is to go on upon the Earth plane. For Mother Earth cannot achieve all on her own.

The birds cannot achieve all on their own. The young creatures cannot achieve all on their own and neither can the babies achieve all on their own. All are interdependent. The animals and the birds, the creatures of the Earth are dependent upon Mother Earth. For from Mother Earth springs the food which they require, the food which they themselves do nothing to produce, but which is supplied for them in many various ways. The medicines are supplied, medicines which have been handed down in knowledge from one creature to another, for mother teaches child.

The plants upon the Earth only grow in those areas which suit them, for where one will grow in abundance another will wither and die, and so it is repeated all around the Earth plane. There are some plants and insects and creatures who can stand a great deal of heat, who populate those areas of heat, who have been given the understanding of how to protect themselves from the heat. And when the blessed rains fall they come forth unscathed to replenish themselves from that which has been supplied from the heavens. So my children, it is with you, it is with the children, the babies and with all those who populate the Earth plane. For you see, as babies you are born and nurtured and carried securely within a mothers womb until the time when all those elements within the physical body have been brought together to produce life. A physical body in which Spirit can venture forth, a physical body which protects and a physical body of great value. Without the physical body, without the senses that accompany that body, without the brain, the conscious mind, there would be no progression.

Within the womb of the one who has been chosen, the Spirit lies, conscious of all that goes on around. Conscious of the emotions, not conscious of physical hurt of physical conditions, but conscious of the spiritual. The sensitivity of the mother is transferred to the Spirit within the womb. The fear of the mother is planted, the love of the mother is planted. The happiness that she experiences in her daily life is transferred to that within her, and thus it is that once the Spirit emerges in its protection of a physical body, it comes not only with all knowledge that has been gathered through previous lives, but with the knowledge also of a sensitivity that the mother has transferred.

The physical body carries the likeness of the one who has nurtured or the one with whom she joined in unity. In some cases this unity has been but brief, but the unity has been sufficient to put into the physical body the characteristics of both. It is a word that is now called genetics, and this of course is why there are so many differing types of the same sensitivity. Different features, different heights, different colouring, but the sensitivity within is nevertheless very similar. Of course one must also add the ingredient of the genetics of previous generations, and so there will be characteristics carried through, for many generations have linked up in unity upon that line of reincarnation.

Now this time of the year as I have already said, is a time of the surging life. The surging life that comes from Mother Earth into all creatures, all creatures, all living plants, into all things that are connected with Mother Earth. In this upsurge of life there will be many happenings for there is an awareness of those things that must be done. The awareness that unless there is action upon the Earth plane; unless those who have been given the awareness, albeit they may not understand the true source of that awareness, but all are endeavouring to bring about unity upon the Earth plane. A unity between man and beast and all living things upon the Earth plane. Think of those who are called conservationists. They cry out because animals are needlessly slaughtered. They cry out because of the destruction of trees and vegetation. They cry out because this destruction destroys the little creatures who have become used to the habitat, who return time and time again to the place from which they have always been born, going back over many hundreds of years.

It is the instinct within, the force, the understanding of Father God that that area to which they return is the one that is suitable for the nurturing of their young. And really what is happening is a great upsurge of life, of the life force. A great upsurge, to prevent Mother Earth from becoming too off balance. To bring her back into balance. To balance the life upon the Earth plane. To bring about a balance in the vibrations around the Earth plane. To bring about a balance in the purity of the air that the life upon the Earth plane breathes. There are many upon the Earth plane who say that, "Those who endeavour to preserve are show offs creating a lot of fuss about nothing." Believe me my children, it is not so, for there is a great need for balance upon the Earth plane, a great need. If this balance is not brought about, Mother Earth herself is going to endeavour to do it. It must be done.

Think of a pair of scales, scales into which you put weights. If those weights are not carefully balanced then one side goes down lower than the other, and when the balance is corrected all is even. It must be so upon the Earth plane, all must be even. If it is not then Mother Earth becomes one sided or top heavy.

Call it what you will, but nevertheless the result is the same — off balance. Mother Earth can correct this to a certain extent herself and this she will do.

There is going to be a great pull upon Mother Earth from a formation of planets who also share the Universe with Mother Earth, for the Universe my children is not just Mother Earth. There are many planets in the Universe and upon them there is life. Life created as you were created. Life of an understanding as you have an understanding. I am now speaking of course of the spiritual. There are those planets like Mother Earth who move one way or the other in their allotted place in the Universe, and the time is coming when there will be much pull upon Mother Earth. There will be planets in line drawing closer to Mother Earth, and if she is off balance all will be affected. She is off balance at the moment and it must be corrected.

Now my children I wish to give you the understanding that in this great upsurge of life at this time upon the Earth plane, the upsurge of life force, the upsurge of knowledge, the upsurge of awareness, there is also an upsurge of greed. The upsurge of greed does not necessarily mean those who rule other countries, the greed the desire of possession of other continents. The greed that desires to have hedges and shrub-land destroyed in order that a few more inches of land may be acquired to grow a few more grains of corn is just as devastating, just as dangerous. It is just the same greed. It goes under different names. But when you consider that all around the Earth plane this thinking of man is causing great destruction upon the balance, upon the vegetation and the life that produces a balance, then I would say to you, join in thought and prayer. All greed in whichever box it is placed, is every bit as dangerous in its own particular way. "Thou shalt not covet," is indeed of truth.

May the Love and the Light of Father God protect you all, and indeed it does. God bless you my children, God bless you.

PART TWO

Out of weakness shall
Come strength,
Out of striving, Peace.
Out of darkness, Light,
Out of God shall come all
Our needs.

Chapter I

THE SEARCH FOR SPIRITUALITY
SPIRITUAL PROGRESSION

Greetings to you all, this is Lauda. The time known as Easter-tide has now passed and all step forward in a greater understandings. An understanding that indeed Jesus Christ returned to the World of Spirit from whence He had come, His mission fulfilled, the understanding given, the seeds sown. And it was up to those who had been chosen as His disciples to carry on the work, to make use of the teachings that had been given to them. To go forth across the Earth plane spreading the understanding that there was indeed a World of Spirit. That there was no final death where the body was laid to rest forever; the body which is seen upon the Earth plane; the body which has within it the spark of The Creator and the everlasting Spirit.

A knowledge which many many thousands do not have or do not accept. It is their belief that when once the heart stops beating that it is the end of all things, but indeed it is just the beginning. The beginning of further progression, the beginning of retracing ones steps. In some cases to go through another life upon the Earth plane with the exact same intention, but this time with the knowledge that the task must be completed if there is to be further progression. The time is now coming when you within this Group will start to go forth. Will start to plant the seeds, to give the understandings through the healing that you will give. The understanding that life is everlasting and the thoughts of today reflect upon the everlasting life.

You will say, "I already plant seeds," and indeed you do and have done for some time. But now the need is greater and you will find more and more people who will be willing to discuss with you, things which you know. A casual word will start the ball rolling, for the casual word will be the indication that there is knowledge which can be given. And you will find that more and more people with whom you come into contact have already had a spiritual experience of one kind or another. In some cases it will be astral travel of which they are aware and which is implanted upon their conscious mind. It is an indication of what can be, and those people need to talk about it for in some cases there is fear. But a word that is said by you can, as I have already said start the ball rolling.

You will find that you will have a greater understanding, a greater patience with those people who have physical illness. For there are those who have a very low pain level and to them the merest scratch is of major importance; the slightest headache becomes a raging inferno. It is difficult to listen with sympathy to these people when you know of those who suffer greatly and complain not, but those with a low pain level need your sympathy and understanding also. They need to have their thoughts guided away from such a minor happening, and to these people you can talk about mind over matter. You can talk about casting out the pain by convincing themselves that it is of no importance, as indeed it is not.

All within the physical body suffer pain. It has to be so, for Jesus the Nazarene suffered pain. Indeed He suffered great pain, pain of the physical body and pain of the mind. He understood the meaning of the word temptation. He knew hunger and thirst. He knew rejection. He knew hate and jealousy. He was defiled. He was degraded. He learnt humility, tolerance and compassion. He gave forth a great love, a great love of healing. He would travel miles in order to take healing to one who was sick, and yet it was quite possible for Him to just think of that person and they would be healed. Today it is known as absent healing.

But there are those who need to see, who need to be touched to be convinced. There are those who had to know that their healing was directed by Jesus the Nazarene. It had to be so for otherwise there would not have been the understanding when the disciples went forth. For they too were great healers and they too endeavoured to follow in the footsteps of Jesus the Nazarene. They too knew the meaning of thirst and hunger. They had no possessions, they relied upon those with whom they came in contact to supply them with food and drink. They never ate to excess, they could not for there were days when they had no food whatsoever. But in the sleep state the food of God was sent to them to uplift them and nourish them, to enable them to carry on their way the message that had to be given.

All these things are possible upon the Earth plane now, and indeed all things are happening now upon the Earth plane, and there is a greater awakening, a greater understanding. There have always been those upon the Earth plane with the understanding of communion with Spirit. Who had the understanding that life was everlasting; that death was but the rejection of the physical body, but that the spirit progressed forward. There are those who had that understanding thousands of years before Jesus the Nazarene walked upon the Earth plane. They knew the meaning of healing. They knew the meaning of using herbs. Herbs which are grown upon the Earth plane, berries, roots etc., all with healing abilities for certain types of illness. But now of course, due to civilisation which has spread all around the Earth plane, there are diseases and illnesses which were completely unknown thousands of years ago. Illnesses which should not be, but which are. The physical body can stand just so much, for it is made up of thousands of nerve cells, of bone, of oxygen. It is a machine of great precision, and if one part becomes clogged then there are many other parts which stop functioning.

Upon the Earth plane now it is the mind which is becoming clogged with unnecessary wants. There have always been those upon the Earth plane who were filled with greed, but never to the extent of now. For the Earth plane has become very small and those with a desire for power envisage controlling the whole of the Earth plane; to be the rulers of the Earth in its entirety. They do not envisage just ruling in one small area which was of the past. The Roman Empire expanded very far around the Earth plane but it was in small pockets so to speak. There were many many thousands of miles which they did not traverse. But now everywhere can be traversed, whether by sea, by air or across the lands, and those with a desire for power set their sights very high. And it is those with this greed who can cause great destruction upon the Earth plane.

There are upon the Earth plane now many people of many colours and creeds who join in unity. They join in unity to bring about peace. It is true that they can work within a small area only, but there are many such groups who link up, and together through the linking much work can be done, much healing of the mind can be given. It is regretted that so many young people upon the Earth plane are having their minds filled with the desire to overcome. To overcome in greed, to destroy for joy, to injure and to kill for the sheer delight of doing so. They are at the very bottom of their spiritual lives and they do not yet have the awareness of the path they may follow, for it is only the conscious mind which is alive. But to those young ones there will come the realisation of the futility of throwing stones and damaging and causing harm, for it is just bravado. The time is coming when they must be given the realisation that they must do unto others as they would be done by.

When you take into consideration the number of young people that there are upon the Earth plane at this present time, those of destruction are of a very small minority. You may wonder at this but it is so. There are many many young people who are coming forth in the understanding that to give forth love, to help others, is of a greater upliftment than destruction and skulking in corners. They are learning to walk forward with their heads held high, proud in their achievements. And to those in time, there will be born young ones with an even greater outgoing of love, and gradually those of destruction will be driven into corners. There will always be those of destruction, for they have their path to live out, and each life upon the Earth plane should be further progression upon the Spiritual path.

If progression is not made upon the Earth plane, then there are problems in the World of Spirit, for they are held within a dimension of low level. All have to be tested in this way, but when once the test is over it should not be repeated and if it is, then they are contained in an earthly dimension. It has been said that within the World of Spirit there are problems also, for these people go forward and mix in the World of Spirit as they do upon the Earth plane. But this is not entirely correct for it is only the Earth dimensions that contain those of evil intent. Within the World of Spirit there is a greater control, a control of the University so to speak. Those who reach the heights within the World of Spirit are above all things. They can enter any dimension unharmed, to teach, to give lessons. They do not remain, but return to the dimension that they have attained. Those upon the Earth dimensions cannot ascend to the heights, and so you see the difference. Upon the Earth plane those who could be contained in the earthly dimensions can attain the heights upon the Earth plane. I am sure you understand the difference.

And so of course it is of great value to progress upon your Spiritual path, to take note of the teachings which are given to you. To go forth knowing that there are those things that must be said to bring an understanding to those with whom you come in contact. You have the understanding that one must be very careful to wait, to plant a word here and there, to see if a seed has been sown. But sometimes it is best to stand by and watch, for the opportunity will come. And through the healing these opportunities do come, for people who are seeking healing whether they have a knowledge of the World of Spirit or not, have a knowledge of Jesus the Nazarene, and that within the Bible there were many healings. And it is this which brings them to you, for they are seeking. Oh yes, the time has come for you to go forth to plant the seeds and to let those with whom you plant the seed reap the harvest.

I will go now. May the Love and the Light of Father God surround you all at all times, and indeed it does. God Bless you all.

The Search for Spirituality
* * *
THE SPIRITUAL PATH

Good evening. My name is Steven Winthrop. Don't suppose you have heard of me. Nice to be with you. When upon the Earth plane I wish I had the knowledge that you have. I could have used it so much. Could have spoken to many people. Could have done a bit of good. Wasted my time a bit I think. I don't really have regrets, for I did achieve much in my particular way.

There was a time when I was encouraged, for I did have an experience as a boy. I remember it well, and of course now I have the understanding, but at that time I had no knowledge and I did not pursue, and it was a great pity.

I remember I was in bed. I remember I was reading a book about Sherlock Holmes and Nelson. That gives you some idea of the times. I was suddenly aware that in my room there was a Roman standing. I thought it was a figment of my imagination, didn't feel frightened. He stood there and he told me that there would come a time when I would have a choice. A choice of great importance, a choice of paths. And that when the time came he would be there to help me to choose the path that I would tread, then he vanished. I thought I was seeing things, imagination, forgot about it.

Sorry now, because of course he was talking about the spiritual path. I never did walk it, not consciously. Pleased to say I did without knowing, but wished that I had the information and the knowledge that you have.

[1]Ramsay MacDonald you know was psychic, but then of course being Welsh he would be, for they nearly all are if they are of true Welsh stock. Goes back for generations. He never let on, but a lot of the marvellous decisions he made were after he had been in conversation with the one who was his guide. There were others also, and I can tell you this, that in Parliament at this time there are those who do not make decisions themselves, but are guided to the decisions that they do make.

What a place Parliament is now. What a circus ground! No dignity, no dignity whatsoever. Shouting and raving. Oh, in my time of course we used to lift our voices up and shout, but not like they do now. When we opened our mouths we had something to say and if we were in disagreement we were in disagreement each one because we **were** in disagreement. Not because we had been told beforehand to watch the cheer leader, so to speak, which is what happens now.

What a lot of rubbish they talk, and where are they getting themselves? They are achieving nothing. But I can tell you this my friends, that sitting in that Parliament at the present time there is one who will be a leader, and a good leader at that. It is not that person who calls himself Benn something or other, or something or other Benn. I don't know, but he is a disaster. Disaster for his Country, utter and complete disaster. He is not the one who will rise as leader. But there is one; decisive, thoughtful, with knowledge and with patriotism, that is what is lacking now.

Everybody thinks of themselves. Nobody thinks of the good of the Country. For the good of the Country is for all — all of you in this land. There must be decisions made, in fact there are decisions made, but they are not held long enough because

---

[1]James Ramsay MacDonald, (1866–1937). British Labour politician; prime minister in Labour Government 1924 and 1929–31.

somebody says they do not like them. A do-gooder. What a curse do-gooders are when it comes to Parliament. Decisions must be made and they must be stood by. It must be remembered that England, the British Isles are the British Isles and they are not part of the United States. They are not part of the Continent of Europe. They are not a part of Russia. They are the British Isles.

Things go on now that are supposed to be progress. What progress are you making? Honest men would sweat and toil late hours to achieve something for small pay. Now they want no working time and big pay, and why is this? Because there are too many voices being listened to. Because there is not a good leader. Because there have been too many who have been allowed to make their own rules, each for each one, not for each other.

The time is coming when there must be more consideration one for the other and not so much for self. More teamwork, more good fellowship. Oh! Parliament, there are some who are very good, but there are a lot who should not be sitting there. You know, in your small way each one of you can become a very large voice. Oh! I am not suggesting that you stand for Parliament, but I am suggesting that those things that are happening within this Country, those things which are happening that you do not like, that you voice more often to your Member of Parliament the way that you feel.

It is the voice of the people that Parliament is supposed to speak, and if the people do not let their Member of Parliament know what they are thinking, then all you are going to get within your Parliament is the thinking of your Member himself. By the voices that are heard, so can judgements be made. Let your voice be heard, let your point of view be put forward.

Don't put up with the things that you do not like. Don't think, "What can I do?" Voice your thoughts, because your thoughts are as powerful as the next mans. They used to call me a windbag. Afraid I was, but at least I listened to those people who came to me and I made notes and I shouted loud. Not for myself but for them, for the people of this Country, the people who are really concerned, not those who are only desirous of being disruptive. And at the present time it is their voice which is the loudest. Think I've said enough. Will go. Thank you for listening to me. God be with you.

The Search for Spirituality

* * *

LEVELS OF UNDERSTANDING

Greetings my daughter, greetings to you all, this is Thomas. The time is coming when each one of you will be advised of the healing channel you are to be, indeed that you are. The time is coming when you will be able to ask questions and receive answers. The time is coming when there will be one who will manifest.

The time is coming when you will depart, when this Group will cease and it will be closed. A time wherein you should have learned those things which have been taught. It is according to each one of your progression, whether you know the full understanding of those teachings, for of course within each teaching there are different levels of understanding. And as you progress so you will see the different levels and have a greater understanding of those things which have been told you.

It is good that the words are written down. It is good that you can refer to them. It is hoped that you do refer to them, that you read back and try to see within the different levels of understanding. Perhaps you will read a teaching that has been given wherein you thought there was one certain meaning, and re-reading it, because of your advanced knowledge now, you find a different meaning, a different understanding, a different teaching entirely. There have been those who have spoken with you regarding their own lives upon the Earth plane. It is not by accident that they have come to you, for all has been planned. Oh yes, there have been times when there has been a hasty re-arrangement, but then that is well within your understanding.

There will come those who will also tell you of their lives upon the Earth plane. There are those who have led lives of great interest, for from beginning to end their life has been one long lesson to others. Lives of dedication, complete dedication. Lives in which they have not said, "I do not have the time", for there are many who work not for themselves or for their own pleasures, but who work entirely in service to others, giving every moment of their precious Earth life in service to others.

There is always time to do God's work if you really wish to do it. There is always time to be of service if you really have the understanding. For those things of which you say, "I do not have time," are usually of service, and the things for which you make time are things of pleasure. Not always, but nearly always.

The present Earth world is wrapped around the material. Everything is of material value only. The more possessions one can gather around, the more machinery that one can use, are really time saving things. Time saved for what? Time saved for going out and enjoying oneself. Time saved, but is it? Is it saved or squandered? Is it used as it should be used? Are you using time, your precious time in this Earth life, are you using time to do those things that you chose to do before you returned to the Earth plane? Or have you too, become involved too much with the material? Have you too, become too much involved with obtaining more possessions?

What is life upon the Earth plane if one does not feel the upliftment and the Love of God around one? What is life upon the Earth plane if with head bent you hurry along and do not have time to see the beauty of the sky, of the flowers, of the distant hills, of the angry seas? Do not have time to notice the person in distress, do not have time to notice the one who is lonely, the one who is lost? Those who are so involved with their own thinking that they do not have time to see the other persons point of view and thus bring harmony into a home in which there is disharmony.

Look around you. Look around you, use those eyes which are windows. Use those eyes to see what is going on upon this Earth plane, and as you have been told before, do not hurry by, but stop and listen. And if there is something with which you do not agree, and if it is something which is likely to involve other people, write a letter. Voice your thoughts, let your voice be heard. For if one speaks with a voice of love and truth, one sends out light, whether it be to Earth plane, or whether it be to those upon the Earth plane. If it is of love and light, if it is of truth and concern, let that voice be raised. It is those voices which will bring about a greater change upon the Earth plane. It is those voices which will help to still the darkness that is creeping even wider.

Let your voices be heard, for you are of understanding. Let your thoughts go forth, for you are of understanding. And let your love be used in the work that is going on all over the Earth plane to bring protection to this Earth, to this planet.

I have said enough and so I will say, may the Love and the Light of Father God protect you at all times, and indeed it does. God bless you.

The Search for Spirituality

* * *

SPIRITUAL AWARENESS

Greetings my daughter, greetings to you all, this is Thomas. The time is coming when there is to be a manifestation within this Sanctuary, for the energies are indeed building up. We have promised that this will happen and indeed it will happen, providing of course that you maintain the seven at each and every meeting.

The time is coming now upon the Earth plane when there must be many such manifestations within the groups that have been prepared. It is necessary that the true understanding is given that we in the World of Spirit are not very far away, that we can enter your world, but that you only enter our world when of spirit. I can hear you protesting that you have the understanding that in the sleep state the spirit penetrates. It is of course the spirit that penetrates, and so once again I repeat that we can enter your world but you cannot enter our world in the physical form that you now have.

To walk side by side with those in the World of Spirit who come forward to help, to advise you, to guide you, to comfort indeed and to surround you with love, is a path that is chosen. For those things that must be will be, and those things that must not be must be averted. And one way or the other they will be averted if they are kept within control, within a limit. The control is maintained by the thoughts that you send forth, by the love and the light with which you surround areas of danger. And by that means the danger can be contained and indeed dispersed, if those thoughts are of true sincerity.

There will come a time when all men will understand this and will realise that by his thoughts, so he governs his Earth life. But at the moment of course there are those who are only conscious of a physical life, and the voice within, the consciousness, is smothered. While they are doing one thing that can mean more possessions upon the Earth plane, more symbols of affluence if you like, the more they stifle the consciousness. Many do those things to obtain material possessions which are not of truth and which are not of service to mankind.

I will hasten to add that there are many upon the Earth plane who are of service to mankind, and are yet acquiring possessions themselves. Such as a craftsman who sets up a small business, because he loves the craft with which he is engaged. Because of the love that he puts into his work there is much demand for those things that are produced, and he will in his turn employ three or four other people. He will of course choose only craftsmen who in their turn will put love into their work, the joy of creation, the joy of creating something that will give pleasure to another. Of course these crafts must be paid for, and so it can be that there will come moneys in great measure, and they will be able to purchase more properties. But that is not the way to becoming a dictator or a ruler or one of greed, for whilst love goes into the work, then love is spread through that work.

What a difference to the man that you would call a tycoon. A man who is utterly ruthless, a man who enters into business intending to step upon anyone who is in his way. A man who destroys. He creates for himself a great deal of money, but such is his greed that he invests this money in one thing and another, and it can be that through his attitudes and thoughts, his destructive thoughts will in the end destroy him and unfortunately those around him who love him. There are those who seek power merely to dominate, merely to be able to rule, (if one likes to use that word), many peoples. One who wishes to strut up and down like a peacock, but without the gorgeous finery of a peacock, for that finery is of God's creation. They strut up and down commanding and demanding, but they live in fear of their lives. Many of them become nervous wrecks, for while they are on the peak, so to speak, when their power seems to be at its highest, and when they have their eyes upon ruling the world, because this does happen, it is then they are reduced to nothing.

And so we come back again to the knowledge that we within the World of Spirit, walk side by side with you upon the physical plane. That together we go forward. We have knowledge of those things which are written. You do not, but we can advise you and we can guide you, and we can help you to overcome those things which are holding you back. And we can give you the understandings of those things that must be done. Whether you accept or not is your free will. You have this understanding. We do not waste your time upon the Earth plane, for it is precious and there is much to be done in what to us is a very short time. Step by step the understanding must go forward, until at last the realisation will be to all men that they must work one for the other. That all are brothers, that all are equal. There must of course be those who are leaders, advisors; but quite a different meaning to the leaders who wish to dominate.

Life upon the Earth plane will not be nearly so complicated if the teachings and the knowledge that are given are learned and used. For it has reached a peak of great complication one way and another, because all are not pulling together in the understanding and the knowledge that this Earth plane is a school room of knowledge, a school room of great spiritual value. Whether you have spiritual awareness or whether you do not, there are still lessons to be learned. Within this Group you have had lessons, lessons of life upon the Earth plane. Lessons of great value and lessons if used correctly, can be of great progression.

The time is now coming when the teachings that you have received will be used, for you will have the words written. The time is coming when there will be those who will be directed towards you who will have an understanding and to whom you can show these teachings. They will be of great value to you as you read back, and to others as you talk to them. For believe me the awareness, the spiritual awareness is beginning to blossom within many. It blossoms particularly within the young, for within their lifetime upon the Earth plane they can accomplish much, even as you are accomplishing much, and will accomplish even more.

I will go now. May the Love and the Light of Father God surround you all at all times, and indeed it does. God bless you all.

Chapter II

HEALING
HELPING THE SICK

ood evening. I must apologise that I am slow and take
time to speak to you. It is not often that I speak in this
way and I do find difficulty, but I must hasten to add
that it is with great pleasure that I speak to you. You
are a group of healers and I too was a healer when upon the
Earth plane.

I was a surgeon in the hospital of Dublin, a land that is
much racked with problems at this time, but I have not come to
speak about these. I was also a surgeon for a time to Her
Majesty, Queen Victoria, a lady of many diverse pains. A lady
of great strength of character, and a lady who was herself of
spiritual knowledge. A knowledge that was ridiculed, and all
thought her a crank, but indeed she was not.

I come to speak to you because I want to give you some idea
of situations that can arise when dealing with those who are
sick. Sick in mind or sick in body or both. One has to have a
great understanding of personalities and characters of people,
for no two people are alike. Those with whom you are
confronted who seem docile can turn into animals when the
time arises. And therefore you must learn to judge those who
stand before you, to assess their characters in order that you can
complete or accomplish a healing.

Too many doctors of this present day world of yours are concerned with numbers and count their patients as sheep, and send them through the same gate with the same tablets and the same advice. This must not be for all are different and what suits one does not suit another. Oh no, you do not treat your patients as if they were sheep, but each one as an individual. For each one is an individual and each one holds within them that which is of their own. You may have two patients one after the other who both have a headache. One is a headache of anxiety, one is the headache of a tumour. You cannot treat them both the same, they must have individual treatment.

And so it is with the healing that you will conduct. Each one is an individual and the only way you are going to find that out is by talking to them. There is a practice upon the Earth plane at the present time, a practice of healing which is virtually done by numbers, and it is not correct. You cannot give each patient a quarter of an hour, ten minutes, five minutes, half an hour; because some will take ten minutes, some will taken an hour, and you must be prepared to spend that hour with the ones who need your attention.

When I was upon the Earth plane there was much research going on, even so today. But it was a research of a different nature. It was a research of fighting germ with germ. Putting that germ with that one which would make a negative situation, but a positive healing. Now it is a case of research, to find which drug can overcome a certain situation, and then to supply another drug which can overcome the situation that has been caused, and it is not correct. It is **not** correct. To bring about a healing is to bring happiness to a life that sometimes has reached despair. It is a very worthwhile path that you are to tread. It is a path of restoration, for you will restore back to health and happiness those who come to you. Providing you follow those teachings that are being given to you.

We are not visiting you for fun. We like to speak it is true, but we do not waste our time or your time, for there are many such groups, as you have already been told, and there are many teachings. I would say to you, from now on start to assess the people you meet, those with whom you are speaking. Try to assess their temperament if you can. Teach yourselves to have a discerning eye and a discerning ear, to make a note of the anxiety in the voice, for that is important.

You will find that many will come to you who give you the impression that it is all one great joke. But listen to their voice and look into their eyes and you will see the anxiety that is there that they are trying to veil, for they are afraid to hear that which you might say. Of course you know that their fears are unfounded for that which they fear to hear you would not say, that is part of your training.

As a surgeon in the hospital in Dublin, the Royal Dublin Hospital, I performed an operation on a young woman who they said was dead. She was brought in as dead, but I knew otherwise and I operated on her. She had had an accident, a horse had kicked her in the stomach. It had caused great damage to the abdomen, and an operation was performed which took a long time. There were three times when I thought that the Spirit had left the body, but no. She was taken back to her bed in the ward and she lay there lifeless it seemed, under careful attention, constant watch. I visited her several times and on the third day she returned to full life.

She said when she was able to speak, that she had been carried away by six people in long white robes. That they had taken her carefully and had looked after her. That she had been fed a sweet substance which had filled her veins with life. And on the third day she was carried gently back and deposited upon the bed. She said it was an experience of great love. They could not explain it but it is something I will always remember, for of course I have the understanding now that it wasn't I who performed the operation, it was the helpers around me that I could not see. She turned in time into one of the greatest nurses, a nurse who brought such compassion and love wherever she went, for she knew the value of life and she knew the value of love. It may seem a trivial story to you, but indeed it was not, for it is an indication to one within this room at this present time that he too was left for dead. But it could not be, for he too has work to do and that time was not right. He was sent back to do that which has to be done.

My name was Spencer when upon the Earth plane last. It can be researched. I do not waste your time. Remember, teach yourselves to judge that which your patients keep hidden. Look into the eyes. Listen to the words that are said to you and then give your healing. I will go now. The Light from Father God shines down upon you all. God bless you and good night.

Healing

* * *

INNER KNOWLEDGE

I greet you. You have been healers before upon the Earth plane and you will be healers again, for now is the time that you are needed. Needed I say. On a previous occasion upon the Earth plane you were all together as healers. You worked together but you used not only the light that was sent from the Creator, but you used also great love and compassion within each one of you. You all suffered privation through your devotion to duty, if one can say to be chosen as a healer is a duty. It is an honour, not a duty.

Within each one of you there will come forward knowledge which is stored away within the inner being. Knowledge which through meditation you will bring forth. Knowledge which will become known and which you will use. All the flood gates of knowledge will open and you will find yourselves saying and doing things of which you have no knowledge at the present time, for the knowledge is to be brought forth.

You have said one to the other, "We have not been told the healing gift that we have." But the healing gift is not in pockets of information, it is a gift of healing. It is a knowledge that you learn from your own experiences. It is a knowledge that you have from your experiences upon this Earth life, *this* Earth life. The knowledge that is going to enable wondrous healings. But it is the knowledge of your senses within the physical body that you now occupy, those senses you will use. Plus of course much that is within that you will seek, that you will find when in meditation.

Can any one of you in this room at this time say, "My life has run smoothly, I have had no problems; I have had no sorrows; I have not been degraded; I have not been humiliated; I have not suffered grief; I have not suffered fear?" Can anyone say that? Indeed you cannot. You have an understanding of these feelings and therefore you can put yourselves in the place of any who come to you. And I say to you that there will be directed toward you those who will need your attention, your love, your compassion.

Each one of you individually has that which will be needed by those who come to you. There are those who have a great affinity with the animal kingdom. Who could pacify the fiercest beast, if you would send forth love and calming towards that creature. You would stand your ground and show no fear and they would advance towards you, for your love would be received. The thought has gone out, "I do not think I would wait to see," but you would. You would know within, for you have already calmed the fiercest creatures. You have played with lions, you have walked with tigers, but not in this Earth life.

It is not easy to pacify a baby or a young child who is caught up in a mighty grief of fear, but there is one amongst you who has that ability. You can pick up a crying child, hold it close and it is at peace. You have done that before and within you that knowledge will come forth. There is one amongst you who has the gift of words. The ability to use the right words at the right time. The ability to bring about a calming of those who are in near hysteria.

There is one amongst you who is a leader, one who will guide, one who will lead. Taking by the hand those who are seeking and lead them to the spot where they will receive help. You have said, "The power of thought is all powerful," and so it

is, and the power of thought directed outwards to those who
suffer, this sort of healing sent out with love, is indeed all
powerful.

There was an occasion I recall when there was one of great
value in a distant land who lay dying upon a bed of skins. He
was one of great value, not because of the possessions that he
had but because of the wisdom within. The wisdom which
caused strong powerful men to sit at his feet for hours, listening
to the words that he spoke. And it came to the ears of one of
great wisdom. He did not set forth to take gifts, he did not set
forth to take his physician. No, he called together the wise men
of his Province. He bade them sit around him in silence, all
sitting upon the ground with the hands palms down upon the
ground, with their legs stretched out all meeting, and feet
placed one against the other touching.

There they sat and concentrated upon the wise man many
many miles away — a great distance. And they concentrated
their love and the desire that he should rise from his bed of
skins, for there was much wisdom that he had not imparted.
They sat thus for two days and two nights concentrating upon
that wise man, and on the second day he sat up. The life had
returned to his eyes and he said, "I have been lifted from my
bed of skins, I have floated far up in the skies. I have been taken
to a place of great beauty where silent ones tended me. I have
indeed been to see the Creator, but I did not quite reach." He
had been lifted by the thoughts of love for his well being. That is
how great the thoughts of love can be, and you in your turn can
do just that, each one of you in your own individual way. When
you concentrate upon one who comes to you, you too will lift
them towards the Creator and they will be filled with the peace
and the light.

When I next come to you I will bring with me a visitor who
will stand in your midst. It will happen, it is promised thus. You
still have many teachings, but you know that the time of this
Group is limited. It is not a Group that will go on and on and

on, for we cannot waste time. We do not come to entertain, we come to teach. We come to teach, that you may have the knowledge and the understanding that you too can teach. And more important of all that you will bring about healings of mind, of body and of soul. That is what this Group is all about.

I have waited to speak with you, it is good, it has been accomplished. I will return, but not alone. The Light and the Love of the Father God surround you all at all times. His blessings are with you all, all of you.

Healing

* * *

HEALING ENERGIES

The wisdoms of the world be made known to you. The wisdoms of the past, the wisdoms of the present and the wisdoms of the future. I come at last to address you, I come from the past, I am the present. Teachings of healing have been given through the ages, for within the innermost sanctums of the temples there have been teachings of healings. Here again there is another teaching of healing.

In the innermost rooms of the secret temples that have been at all times upon the Earth plane, the knowledge has been given that there is only one teaching, and that is the teaching that comes from God. And thus there is but one healing, and that is the Power that comes from God. For God was The Creator and all things are known to Him, for He, as The Creator is aware of all things. Therefore the Healings that come from Him, utilise all those things that were created by Him, for He has arranged within the plan of things that energies are forthcoming which are directed to those places which are in need.

In past times the innermost sanctums of the temples directed and guided those energies to those places where they were required, to bring about those things which had to be brought about. And thus you have the scientists of your present day just beginning to realise, just understanding, that the theories that they have created over the years are not correct.

The words have been said that by the power of thought vast stones and rocks have been lifted on high, and these words have been doubted. But it is fact, for as you have been told this very earth evening, the power of thought is all powerful. There are still places upon this present Earth plane wherein there is much mystic knowledge. I say mystic for it is still kept hidden. But it will come forth, for the time is now that the secrets are exposed to the light, that people are made aware of those things which can be achieved.

You my friends as a healing Group will be aware of the energies that are within you. The energies that you can give forth to those who are in need. Unlike those of the temples of ancient times you will not be able to bring into use energies such as they manipulated, but within each one of you there are energies which can be utilised and which will be of great value. There will come a time when you will feel these energies flowing through you. Some of you have already had this experience; it is fact, it is not fiction.

In ancient times there was much wisdom, but that wisdom was held by a comparative few. The wisdoms now must be spread, for there must be a turn around within the pattern of things, and the knowledge must become one that can be utilised by all. I have walked the Earth plane on several occasions for that is how it had to be, but I have not returned in a physical body for many aeons of time. I choose to return occasionally to give teachings that are necessary.

Within the sacred temples is great knowledge, and if you look upon yourselves each one of you, as a sacred temple, you will realise that within each one of you there is great knowledge. A knowledge which can be brought forth. A knowledge which can be increased by the use of the energies which are around you. Energies which you can draw towards yourselves. Energies which you will see yourselves create. Energies which will bring about a peace where before there has been pain. Whether the pain is caused through a physical condition or a mental condition it is nevertheless pain. For within the human body there are many nerve centres which absorb and distribute that which is felt, that which comes from the physical brain which is connected to these centres.

For you as healers the task must be one of bringing about a balance between the spiritual and the physical. A utilising of the energies which will be directed through you. An understanding of those things which you can do and an understanding also that if the thought pattern is not correct, then you can cause harm. I do not wish to put a fear into your mind, for the thought pattern of true love or sincerity is one that will not cause damage.

Do not take too lightly this gift which is being brought to be used now. It is better not to attempt to use it at all if you do not use it with the correct thoughts within your mind. The thoughts that you send forth affect the vibrations, the energies that surround you; and so I say to you as in the mystic temples of the past so be it with you. To direct the energies and the power that comes from The Creator with love in your hearts, with a desire to serve within you, can bring about healings and understandings of rare value. Make no mistake I have the understanding.

There is to come to you one who will stand before you. One who you will see who will converse with you, one to whom you will be able to converse. I tell you this for it will be so. The energy within this Sanctuary is dropping, and so I will say to you, treat yourselves each one of you, as a sacred temple. Look upon yourselves as a place such as that, and each one of you will find the energies flowing towards you and each one of you will be aware.

I return from whence I came. I give unto you wisdom. I give unto you love. I give unto you the inner tranquillity, and so it will be.

Chapter III

THOUGHTS OF LOVE
BROTHERHOOD OF MAN

G reetings, this is Thomas, greetings to you all. My children, all round the Earth plane there will be many plans going ahead, plans which have been guided by we in the World of Spirit. Each one to his allotted task, a task which we choose even as you choose the task when returning to the Earth plane.

Each task in the World of Spirit is according to the understanding and thus you will see how both worlds go side by side, each from progression of their own spiritual path. When you return to the World of Spirit it can be of great interest, particularly when you have the understanding upon the Earth plane such as you now have, the spiritual awakening and the understanding.

It has been said by many upon the Earth plane that when you pass through the veil, so to speak, you are rushed to a place where you can see all those things which you have done and all those things which you should not have done, and your life passes before you in frightening truth. To a certain extent this is so, but of course this may not happen at once. Because you do not come through the veil in a great haste to start to go along your spiritual path in the World of Spirit, for there are matters which must be sorted out.

Some of you come through the veil in great haste because of an accident. It may be caused through your own free will or by the free will of others. These matters must be attended to before anything else, because it is essential that you have full understanding of what has passed, of what has caused your projection in such haste into the World of Spirit. When this full knowledge and understanding has been received, and with harmony and love around them, they can then be shown those records. There is no case for giving out orders of merit. It is simply a case of the progression you have made.

All around the Earth plane there are groups such as this. Small groups held within private sanctuaries, many held in secret. It has to be so, for the laws of their land forbid it. It is a great pity this, but nevertheless the understanding is spread. For the world has become smaller as you have been told on a previous occasion, and therefore those things which happen in a far distant land are not really very far away. The knowledge leaks through, so to speak, and there are many who in secret, question; have teachings and have great spiritual knowledge, contrary to the rules of those lands where the knowledge is forbidden.

It is quite impossible to detect those who have secret meetings; those who have the knowledge of the truth; those who have the awareness that they walk side by side with those in Spirit, for they look no different to any of their neighbours. As indeed you do not differ from your neighbours. You carry on your daily lives in just the same way, and the knowledge that is within you is discussed with those who are either seeking or who also have the knowledge.

And so it is in distant lands. There are meetings held in secret where great spiritual upliftment is achieved, and those people go forward along their spiritual paths. And they give out love and they give out the light, and others are drawn in by the radiance that they send forth. And so even in secret places the great truth and brotherhood is spread. And so you see my children, Father God is not sitting idle watching the destruction upon the Earth plane, watching the darkness that is operating within certain areas.

If you could see from a distance the Earth plane laid out flat, and if you could see the areas of great darkness, you would find that really those areas although of danger, are comparatively small, for they are contained at the present time within groups. When I say groups I do not mean groups of five or six people, I mean groups maybe of six or seven hundred people. But when that is taken and compared with all those upon the Earth plane who have awakened to the knowledge that there must be a brotherhood of man, (for there has to be an Earth plane if there is to be a future for the descendants of those who are now upon the Earth plane), the areas of darkness are comparatively insignificant, I will say.

Now in comparison with the insignificance of those groups, there is of course a very significant factor of those things which chemists and scientists are busy discovering. And I would like to say to you, that if you could read my words, the word 'discovering' is in inverted commas. For nothing is new upon the Earth plane, it is but another cycle.

The continent of South America was at one time very fully populated. There was much going on. But because of the stupidity of those who thought they knew it all, the continent became for a time dead, and when I use that word I mean dead, for there was a great cleansing. It was not empty. Oh no, for there was life always, but the death was brought about by the greed and the desires of many.

There will be no death again and there will be no death of Mother Earth, for the groups of evil, in time are being contained. And although one or two, so to speak, set forth to spread the evil, they too will be contained, for the knowledge that is now being spread is one of love. Love for the birds. Love for the fish in the deep waters. Love for the trees. Love for the animal kingdom. LOVE — that is the key word — LOVE — for the love that is sent forth by each one of you has far more value than you realise, far more value.

I will draw this teaching to a close and I will say, may the Love and the Light of Father God surround you at all times, and indeed it does. God bless you all.

Thoughts of Love

* * *

HARMONY AND LOVE

Greetings my daughter, greetings to you all, this is Thomas. It is my pleasure to come to you to deliver the first part of this your meeting. It is always a pleasure to be within this little Sanctuary, to be with you all where there is so much harmony and so much love given forth.

There are many plans afoot now within the World of Spirit, plans to bring about a greater understanding upon the Earth plane between the many races, the many countries. Some who are apparently living together in close harmony and some heartily hating their neighbours. If you think a while you can understand the great problem there is, for all must be brought together in harmony and love.

You can understand how long a process this will be if prayers of love and light are not sent forth to shorten the time. For those things which are written will be brought about, one way or another. The Earth plane is now a silent planet, thinking is slow, and those upon the Earth plane who have come back to learn lessons are indeed learning lessons, for there are those upon the Earth plane who have returned for a great cleansing. A cleansing of the thought patterns within.

You have already been told that there are many Spheres within the Universe, and the Earth plane is a Sphere that is way behind all other Spheres in understanding and progression. As

183

yet there is no bringing together in true harmony, of the countries upon the planet.

There is always someone who is desirous of power and greed, who is desirous to be dominant, who is desirous to rule the world. Some say it is in the name of their country. That they wish to raise their country to a higher status. But what is the use of that, for if it is not brought about by love and true compassion and a desire to help all mankind, it will crumble. Nothing will be achieved, many lives will be lost, and the next generation will come forth, and within them will be nurtured the hatred, and so it goes on.

It is time that those upon the Earth plane who nurture children, have the realisation that now there are those returning to the physical bodies who know there must be brought about a unity and an experience and understanding of love, pure love. There are many young people now upon the Earth plane who in their way, endeavour to send forth love and understanding, when unfortunately they mix up the love. I am not saying all, but the word love is bandied around quite freely. But the love they mean is the love of the physical body. Free love it is called upon the Earth plane.

The love of Father God is also free but oh! in what a different way, what a different meaning. One has to learn to control the desires of the physical body. It is all part of training, for to let the desires of the physical body over-rule the mind is to put up a block, to bring about a waste of time. There are many upon the Earth plane who would say it is not a waste of time, but indeed it is, for you have all returned for spiritual progression, for a desire to progress forward to the wonderful day of perfection.

There are those upon the Earth plane now who are mastering telepathic communication. There are many who are being guided by we in Spirit, to bring forth this sensitive area, for in time there will be no need for electronic communication for communication will be through vibrations and thought patterns. As it was in the past so it shall be in the future. Most of the [1]Spheres that surround the Universe already communicate in this way, and that is why great interest is shown regarding the Earth plane. We have vastly progressed and have no knowledge other than that which is obtained from the Earth plane of the thinking, of the communications here upon this planet.

It is like your explorers going back to the days of the ancient Egyptians. Great interest is shown in the teachings and the buildings and the way of life of that time. Believe me my children, the Earth plane is just as ancient to some of those in the Spheres of the Universe and therefore it is natural that one has, I believe you call them objects, appearing in your skies. They approach the Earth plane with their highly sophisticated knowledge, not to do harm but merely as a means of exploration.

It has been said that there has been seen a flying saucer, and then one or two people have disappeared. This is quite true, but they have not been harmed. They have been removed for investigation. Not an investigation of the knowledge that they have within as a means of divulging secrets, but as an investigation of thought patterns, of skin textures, of their way of life. They are treated very kindly. In fact they are welcomed and are indeed honoured guests. And it is because they in their turn learn much, that they do not desire to return to the Earth plane, and so of course they become missing persons. But do not grieve for them for they are not harmed and stay of their own free will.

Now is the time upon the planet Earth when the thought patterns must turn towards thoughts of cleansing. As indeed you already have the understanding to send forth thoughts of love and light to the area of the 'tinder box', and to send forth

---

[1]Spheres — (Celestial) — Spheres inhabited by beings far in advance of earth consciousness. A world said to be of light and harmony.

thoughts of love and light to Mother Earth that she may be brought on balance. By these thoughts that go forth, there is much being done and much being saved. And although the predictions regarding those happenings upon Mother Earth are true — are of truth — indeed they are, they can to a certain extent be toned down by the love that is sent forth. There must be changes upon Mother Earth. There must be changes, for now is the time.

There will be climatic changes for she will move in an endeavour to restore balance. There are those who have said that Mother Earth will go even further off balance, but this is not so. There will be changes, there must be changes for it is written thus. And there will be many whose Earth life will be given up, but that is so that they may return more quickly at a later time. Nothing is wasted, nothing. All experience is a learning and a teaching, nothing is wasted. You yourselves know that during the course of your Earth lives there have been many happenings, some very happy and some very sad and some of a great puzzlement. But you have learned from those experiences. There are some things which you say, "If I had my time again I would not do such and such," and there are other things which you say, "I would love that to happen again." It is all part of learning, and stored within your conscious mind are happenings which will come forward and you will say, "Oh I had quite forgotten that" or, "Fancy me remembering that." You see nothing is wasted.

And so it must be that the teachings that you are receiving within this Group are noted and re-read in order that they may not be wasted. In order that they may help you to help others in the future by the words that you will speak. The teachings that you are receiving will help you along your way of healing, for you are all healers as indeed you have been told on many occasions. But it is entirely up to you whether you use that which has been given to you. That is your choice. That is your decision. That is your free will.

The teachings that you are receiving are teachings of great value, but because you are receiving these teachings it does not mean that you can sit back and let things happen around you. To take note of teachings is to act upon them. Is to act on those things that you can accept and to put to one side those things that you cannot accept. If you cannot accept, it is usually a sign that they are beyond your orbit and there will come a time when you still might not accept, but will have a greater understanding, the realisation that maybe the time is not right. I am of course speaking of the teachings that you are receiving within this Group. I must hasten to add that I am not speaking of writings in other books of knowledge. That is quite different, for there are many things that are written which with the knowledge you now have you could not accept, merely because you have a greater understanding yourself. There is a difference in the words that I have spoken.

Now I will go, and as has become the pattern now I ask you please to remain silent. The discussion should take place when all has been said. The Love and the Light of Father God surrounds you all, at all times, and you are truly protected. God bless you.

Chapter IV

WISDOM FROM WITHIN
AWARENESS

G reetings to you all, this is Thomas. Welcome back into this Group of healing, this Group of healing knowledge. Whilst you have been absent from this little Sanctuary there has been much work done, there has been much accomplished.

My children, the time is now coming when you will all be made aware of those things which you individually must do. Indeed those things which you are even now accomplishing, some with knowledge some without. For there are those things which you carry out in your daily lives which you take as a matter of course, which you accept as part of life. And indeed they are part of life but they are also those things which are guided, and all along the lines of healing.

You are already aware that all peoples upon the Earth plane have the ability, so to speak, to give forth healing. It only needs the understanding within themselves to give forth compassion and love, to give forth sympathy, and they are following in the footsteps of Jesus the Nazarene.

There are of course many peoples upon the Earth plane who go their own way heeding not that which they could be doing, thinking only of themselves their own ambition and their greed for power. They are of course progressing one might say, in the material sense, but alas not progressing in the way that matters, upon their spiritual paths. Some have an awakening some do not.

But the concern at the moment is for the Group within this little Sanctuary. For you are under my charge so to speak, although each of you have your own guides and each of you will meet your guides in time, if not actually to see but to hear. You know, each one of you, how to listen to the voice within. Call it conscience if you like. Some hear clairaudiently, some just have the knowledge that this is right or that is wrong, but it is all of course part of the knowledge within.

During this absence from the little Sanctuary there has been illness and upsets physically, and it is hoped that through prayer you will once again be placed upon the path of health. There are times my children, when even the medical profession can misunderstand, and there are times it must be admitted, when those in Spirit comment upon something of which they have little knowledge. There are times when this does happen and it is because there are those who take upon themselves a knowledge which is not really theirs'. I do not propose to go deeper into that for we have already discussed this at an earlier meeting.

Ahead of you now will come a time of action and you will find that you will all have involvement within your lives of spiritual matters. You will find people coming to you, for this is the way it must be. Those who come to you are guided to *you* and should not be passed on without thought on your own part. There will be those who will need to be given an understanding of the World of Spirit, for they will be ready to accept such knowledge; and there will be those who it will be better to be quite matter of fact with when speaking to them, or to listen carefully to what they have to say. There will be those who will need a healing and you will feel within your hands a tingling sensation, which is an indication that healing is being sent forth. That you are being used as a channel for healing.

I say welcome back to you all. I do not propose to speak any longer, for this meeting will be a short one as after a holiday of rest or complete shutdown the one through whom I speak should not be over tired.

May the Love and the Light of Father God be with you at all times, and indeed it is. God bless you.

Wisdom from Within

* * *

RELIGION

Blessings be yours. I bring you greetings from the Universe, I bring you greetings from all knowledge. Within this small gathering there is much knowledge. Much wisdom is held within each one of you, for you were chosen to be in this place at this time. You also chose to be in this place at this time — it is no accident. You have all been together, you have all worked together at previous times both upon this sphere, this Earth planet, and upon other Spheres within the Universe. And when you leave behind the physical body in which you are now held, you will meet again and again until the work is completed. You have much wisdom between you, within you and around you.

You have already been told that planet Earth is slow, and so it is, for there are those who return to the planet Earth to learn the same lessons again and again. The time is now when that waste of time must cease. When there must be a great upsurge of knowledge and a going forward. That is why you have chosen to return at this time, and that is why you are sitting here within this Sanctuary.

You are having teachings of great wisdom from those of great wisdom who do not waste their time or yours. It is up to you to take note of the teachings, for within them is the realisation of all that must be accomplished. It is up to you whether you allow the free will that is given to you each Earth life to interfere. It is up to you whether you take heed of the words that are spoken and the teachings that you receive.

Upon the Earth plane now there are great divisions of thought. There are great tussles going on between groups of many thousands of people upon the Earth plane. There is a great dividing, great derision and great division, and all brought about under the word 'religion'. It is a waste of time, for all should unite to bring about that which is of unity and peace upon the Earth plane. The time is coming when there will be decisions made for you, for remember those things which are as written **will be**.

You have been told on a previous occasion of a false prophet who will come forth. Who will come forth with a lying tongue to cause complete disruption under the guise of complete unity. You have already been warned of that one, and you have already been advised of the action you should take, each one of you. You are requested to remember that advice and you are requested to act upon it. It may be beyond your comprehension of the effect of your actions, of the light which you will direct towards that one, but it will be of great magnitude and you will bring about an avoidance, a containing, a segregation of great value.

There is soon to be an uprising within a country of great distress at the moment. There will be an uprising and many lives will be lost. But it will be a symbol to many others that each one of you upon the Earth plane has the right to decide how you will live that Earth life. The choice is yours through the free will that is given to you. It is to be a time of awakening, an awakening of the knowledge of those things that must be done for mankind and not for oneself. It will be the beginning of an opening out that must begin soon. For the time of great spiritual awareness is rapidly approaching, and there must be those prepared so that they can accept and understand those things that are happening around them. With the awareness within blossoming forth, so it can be rebounded from them, and so can the true knowledge and awareness that without true love upon the Earth plane it is doomed. That awareness is already becoming manifest, for do you not find that as you discuss with other people outside your orbit, do you not find there is a great understanding, an understanding which was not there a few years ago?

I do not propose to speak for very long for there is another who wishes to speak with you. I come to give you further wisdoms. The knowledge that within **you** is much wisdom, and it is wisdom which you **will** bring forth. For when in the sleep state you are taken to those places of great knowledge and as yet you do not bring those teachings back into your conscious mind. But the time will come when you will, and as you sit in meditation, gradually there will unfold before you wisdoms from within.

I will go now. It is with love that I come to you and I give you that love as I leave you. Within each one of you there is great love. Do not be afraid to let it come forth, do not be afraid to share. God's Blessings be yours. I go.

Chapter V

NATURAL RESOURCES

G reetings and strength to all of you. My name is Itulka and I lived in ancient times. I lived upon this land that you call England, but it was not an island when I lived here for the parts known as Cornwall, Devonshire and Dorset were joined to the part of the continent which is now Brittany. It was not of course known as England. We had no knowledge of the size of the Earth plane for we knew only a comparatively small area.

Through the centre of our land there ran a river. It was not a very wide river but it was a very strong river. And that river eventually was split asunder in the upheavals that followed long after I had left the Earth plane. Seas rushed forth and there came about a channel of water now known as the English Channel.

We were not such a primitive race as is believed, indeed our dynasty has not as yet been discovered apart from a few prehistoric bones, as they are known. But believe me my friends there was life, a life as civilised as that of Egypt. One day divers will go down to the bottom of those deep waters and there will be discoveries of those things which are at the bottom of those waters. Part of the civilisation will come forth, a civilisation which I knew.

We knew all about tin mines. We used a metal of great strength which we brought forth from the bowels of the earth. For though I come from ancient times there were ancient times before me, before my people, before the dynasty of which I was part. There are tin mines which will be opened up within that area known as Cornwall, and there will be discovered within those mines a metal of great value, a metal of great strength. It will be discovered as if by accident, but those who discover it will be guided there. It will happen in the not too distant future, for there is a need to seek even further the treasures that are buried within the earth.

The treasure that is known as oil will be drained away by senseless drilling and bringing forth, but there is another power another energy which will take its place. The treasures that are within the earth have been formulated through many many thousands of years and drills will discover these energies, and their use will be made for the preservation of Man. For though there have been told of calamities that will happen, so my friends there will be great triumphs.

When I was upon the Earth plane we too knew the meaning of machinery but we did not make flying machines. We used our machinery for the betterment of our life upon the Earth plane. We used our machinery to bring forth the goodness from the land. To harness the energy from the stars and the solar system. We looked heavenwards for our inspirations. We had learned men who could identify and utilise the energies which are sent forth. You have now upon the Earth plane solar panels which are being used in a domestic situation. We too heated our water from the rays of the Sun, but also there is considerable energy that can be harnessed and utilised, energy which is sent forth at night. And one day this too will be utilised upon the Earth plane yet again.

The time is coming when there will be much rejoicing because there will be the harnessing of energies of a different nature from those that are at the moment being used upon the

Earth plane. There are those who spread forth the word of doom saying that all the civilisation that you know now will collapse, and that once again you will return to primitive life. But that is not so, for now upon the Earth plane there are those who are returning with knowledge of experiences of past conditions, even as I have, and that knowledge will be used. Yes, there are to be changes upon the planet Earth as there always have been over a period of time. It will not be the end of Mother Earth for it is not to be so.

You my friends have this knowledge and you my friends will experience yourselves, part of a minor upheaval, a very minor upheaval. But it will be an indication to you that these words that I speak now are of truth. When I was upon the Earth plane there was much sunshine, for this land that you call England was quite a warm area, I think is the right expression. It was not desert but it was of considerably more warmth than now. But due to upheavals and movement of Mother Earth the situation has been changed, and yet again it will change.

My friends there is much ahead, there is much joy ahead, all is not gloom. For each one of you there is much joy ahead, for you will have the satisfaction within yourselves of knowing that within each one of you an energy of considerable strength is being sent. An energy that if tested, would cause some considerable comment, for it is an energy beyond comprehension. For it is an energy that comes from spaces beyond Mother Earth. It is the energy that flows through the God Power. An energy which you are all now strong enough to receive and to pass to others.

God's Blessings be with you.

Chapter VI

THE TRUTH

reetings my daughter, this is Lauda. Once again I come to speak and join in the teachings that are given to this Group and to each one of you I say greetings. There is much turmoil in the minds of men at this present time upon the Earth plane. Turmoil of awakening; some misguided, for it is a turmoil that is stirred by those who seek to make mischief. But the turmoil that I am going to talk about is the turmoil within the minds of men as to the truth, the real truth. There are many upon the Earth plane who have sincere faith in the knowledge that Father God is indeed The Creator. But there are those who through the doctrines that have been taught through the many many years, have been split into pockets of misunderstanding, pockets of misrepresentation if you wish, for their the information is not complete.

Over the many many years the teachings have been changed, the understandings have altered. This has been done because at that particular time it did not suit those who were seeking power to tell the real truth. It suited the occasion to create a hell, where all went with damnation on their souls if they did not comply with the rules which had been compiled by those who sought power. These beliefs have spread to other groups and those tyrants have arisen, tyrants over large groups of many hundreds of people, tyrants over small groups. Tyrants over families, holding them together in fear of the damnation that does not exist, those who would tread their spiritual paths according to those things which were guided individually.

All upon the Earth plane must be brought together in one big family. Not necessarily to conduct themselves in the same way, but all must have the real truth that God the Creator is all-loving. That God the Creator does not judge His children and sort them out one this way and one that way. His children choose their own paths, and it is through their own efforts that they reach the different levels of learning and progression. The most learned philosopher upon the Earth plane, when he leaves the physical body of this life behind and enters the World of Spirit, does not necessarily proceed to a higher dimension, for the vibrations around him may not warrant this. Yet the lowliest soul may reach higher dimensions because the vibrations around them are of true love. And the understanding of the under-dog, who in many cases has been rejected by all society, recognises the value of the Spirit as against the free will because of the wisdom within. It sounds complicated but it is not really, for it is the knowledge that is within you and the love that is sent forth.

There are those who bury their noses in great books and are learned, and yet they know nothing. There are those who are considered to be difficult, who cause problems upon the Earth plane because they are rebels against the standards which have been set. The standards which have been compiled by those who are in power to bring into line, so to speak, more peoples with whom they come in contact. But there are those who rebel, who wish to say those things that they feel must be said, and that is good. It is only when a mighty mob is aroused to support that belief that problems arise. You see it is the motive behind the thought, the motive that goes with the thought, the motive that sometimes takes control. There are those upon the Earth plane who have a way with words, and something which is said with love can be twisted and altered and defaced and turned into something completely of untruth, and that is the problem. How does one decide what is truth and what is not?

This is why it is best not to act hastily upon those things which are told you; to keep a still tongue until you have pondered upon the words that have been spoken. And your own reasoning and understanding will come to the fore if you will only stop to consider. It is best to keep a still tongue than to add another spark of fuel to the fire. One seeks to comfort on occasions, those who seem to be at different parts of the scale, so to speak. Quarrels which arise through a simple incident, quarrels which arise through misunderstanding, and the strange part about it is that disharmony can be caused through love. But of course I speak of the love of the Earth plane, the physical love and not the all enveloping love that is the understanding of those who know the truth. It is best sometimes to stand to one side, to listen and to assess rather than to plunge head-long into the dispute.

Upon the Earth plane at the present time there are many disputes and it is easy to join in. But to join in, and to become involved can lead you away from those things that you should be doing. It can be a waste of time. You know, for you have been told on many occasions, that this is a Group of healing. Do not be side tracked, by becoming involved in other activities which will lead you away, which will take your precious time, for time upon the Earth plane is infinitesimal. Each Earth life will take away that precious time and therefore cause delays to those things which must be done. Time is very precious and time for this Group is very precious, for the teachings must be completed and you must all be given the awareness of those things which you can and must do. There are those who wait to speak with you and there are those happenings which must take place, for they are to be to you a culmination of discipline.

I go now. May the Love and the Light of Father God protect you at all times, and indeed it does. God bless you all.

Chapter VII

MYSTICISM

Good evening. To save you wondering who I am I will announce myself and then you can concentrate on the words that I speak rather than who I am. My name is [1]Doyle. I have written many books upon the subject of Spiritualism and I occasionally come to one or the other to speak. I do not waste my time, I say what I have to say and then I depart, for there is much work to be done.

I have said on many occasions that there is not enough thought, not enough consideration and not enough understanding given to the problems that surround the mysticism, of the word 'Spiritualist'. Nothing seems to be done to clear away the mysticism. There is much time spent on demonstrations to give proof that there is life after death, that the life as it is lived upon the Earth plane at this time is the only life. That when age or illness or accident takes away that life, that is the end. There are the words spoken about going to Heaven, but how much understanding is there about Heaven?

Ask people that you meet, "What is your conception of Heaven?" They will shrug and say that they, "Don't know," or,

---

[1]Doyle — Sir Arthur Conan (1859–1930). British Novelist, famous for his 'Sherlock Holmes' series of detective stories.

"Its a place where you can have a good time," or this sort of nonsense. They take those things that are said, accept the words and then forget. Comfortable in the knowledge that if they look after their old mum that's where they will go. What a pity the mysticism isn't taken away. What a pity that the demonstrations still go on. What a pity that the Great Truth is not spoken about sensibly.

My friends, upon the Earth plane, this old world that I knew and loved, there are those who have had 'experiences', as they are called, but it is occasions when the knowledge is being imparted. If only there would be meetings and discussion groups, drawing together these people that have had experiences and who already have the awareness. If only they could talk about it. Cut out the nonsense and get down to the truth. It is a truth, a truth of great beauty, that all work together.

There is so much to be done and so much to learn. There is so much knowledge that can be gathered. There are Psychic Societies, and what do they do? Year after year after year they carry out the same experiments. They marvel at the energies and the various conceptions that occur, but they don't really do anything. I must correct that, they have done very little. But in the Americas now there are different experiments taking place. Different research is going on, and at last there is real thinking and real investigation.

It is of little use if those investigations are not made public, but kept within their own records, placed upon their own computer and kept hidden. It is time that publications were put forth, not for the few but for the many. It is time that these findings were made public. Sensibly it **is** time for the knowledge to be made public. There is so much energy and there is so much useful information that can be given. Information which should be made a note of, information which should not be filed away.

Oh my friends it makes me cross, although indeed I should not be cross. I and others like me have written many words, but there are many who read these words who do not understand and who do not investigate. There are but a few who investigate and try to search out for themselves those things which are as far as possible made public; the wealth of information that is available; the wealth of information regarding energies that abounds. Energies that come from nowhere, so to speak, that can be directed and utilised. The information is not sought. There will come a time my friends, when those energies will be utilised. It could be now, but until Man listens to the words that are said through those who are used as channels, until note is taken and investigations made, the turmoil will continue upon the Earth plane.

I recounted in one of my books an investigation which was conducted with others, an investigation which had surprising results; results of great value if they were utilised. We went from one Ministry to another and in the end doors were shut in our faces, for we were considered unbalanced. What a pity! What a waste of time. There must be and there will be an end to the mysticism, for reality is not a mystery. And I am talking about reality, a reality so vast that there is no ending to it. A reality which cannot be explained, And yet it can be explained. For there are those who work unseen, there are those who work diligently to bring about awareness and an understanding of the other world. The other world that is teeming with knowledge. The other world that must be discussed, must be found, must be utilised.

Do not waste time. Do not waste time with the mysticism, for there is none. The days of hiding behind locked doors has finished. Open up the doors and let the light stream in. Let the knowledge go forth — not the floating tables. Energies must be used for the good of mankind, for the good of the Universe, the whole Universe. The Cosmos is teeming with energy, it must be used; it is waiting to be used. You my friends sit together and discuss openly one with the other and with others that you meet, this knowledge that you have, this understanding, this truth. You are but a small Group, but surprisingly it is possible for you to reach as many people as my books. For you can speak the words and they can be listened to. My books have to be read, it can take time.

So speak my friends, the words that will convey to others this knowledge. Explain to others that there is a whole world that works for the good of Mankind, for the good of the Universe. Speak those words my friends, and bring about mighty healing. A healing that can cure this disease of mysticism, for it is a disease that must now cease.

I too must cease. I have said what I had to say. I do not waste time. I will now depart, and so I say, good evening to you and God bless you.

Chapter VIII

PHOBIAS

G reetings to you all, this is Thomas. I speak to you today not so much upon healing as upon suffering, for sometimes it is very difficult if you have not suffered yourself, to put yourself in the place of the person who is suffering, truly suffering. There are those upon the Earth plane of course who make mountains out of molehills for they love to have the attention. They love to feel that they are being fussed and they love to feel that although comparatively small, they can seem large by the demands they make upon other people. I do not propose to talk about those people for they have many lessons to learn, but I do propose to talk about those who truly suffer, for there are many upon the Earth plane who do truly suffer one way and another.

There is the torment that is brought about by one's own mind. The torment that is brought about by the imagination. The torment that is brought about by the belief that these things are happening or those things are happening, which indeed are not but are purely figments of the imagination. This torment is brought about by the desire to be loved. It is a torment which is brought about by the desire to be loved by everyone with whom they come into contact, and of course this cannot be. One can give out love to all with whom one comes into contact, but one cannot expect love in return. To give forth love and not to expect a return of that love is indeed of great value.

The torment that is brought about by those who desire to be loved is as I have said imaginary. For they imagine that people are talking about them or making comments about them, when in fact they have not been noticed. The suffering of the mind is indeed truly horrific to many people upon the Earth plane now. Fears build up, phobias they are called now. And these phobias are forever increasing one way or another, for they too are of the imagination and yet they are very real to those people who are enduring.

When one is in good health, when one is on balance and all within the physical body and the spiritual body are in unity, it is very difficult to understand these phobias and there are so many, so very many now. The most common being the phobia, the fear of going out, to walk along the street, to go into a shop. A great fear overwhelms and that person for a time virtually becomes paralysed because the fear overcomes all physical reaction. And the body is virtually paralysed, for the brain is numb. If you go into a store or a shop or if you are walking along the pavement and you feel that somebody is in trouble, do go to them. Do not feel that you are interfering or that you are being nosy. Just go to them, for nine times out of ten the very fact that you, maybe a total stranger are concerned, will help them to get themselves out of that situation.

There is a phobia regarding animals. Cats, dogs, sheep, horses; they too can be quite terrifying. To many people the feel of the fur of a cat sets up a great fear within them. A repulsion, a distaste; and the whole body goes cold and they go immobile. Here again the brain has become numb. There is a phobia regarding heights, but that is understandable, for from a height one can look down and the phobia is that the person wishes to throw themselves over to escape from that vision. There is of course but one answer to that, and that is to walk away, not to place oneself in that situation. But there are occasions when it cannot be avoided and then of course the head must be averted. That is a very common phobia, one which goes back through the centuries.

There was a monk in Tibet working upon a Temple, the walls of which had been built in complete alignment with the walls of the mountain on which it was perched. It is still there, it is a Temple which is camouflaged very cleverly to look like nothing more than another crag of the mountain. It is a Temple wherein many Ancients dwell, where many teachings are given. Within this Temple there is one who is very ancient, but of course at one time he was much younger. He had a hand with the building of the Temple and he had a phobia for heights. He was deliberately sent to work upon the highest point of the monastery. A monastery of great love, a monastery which is now the Temple of the Ancients. He was perched upon this very high point and he looked down and wanted to cast himself off, and he cried in fear. Suddenly there was a great calming, for he had looked away from those heights. He had looked away and was able to climb down quite steadily, un-afraid. He had removed from his vision that which frightened him. He had looked the other way and realised that he was just a few feet above the ground, and so this can always be done.

There is a phobia of spiders and insects. Have an understanding of those people with phobias, send out love and sympathy to them. Do not ridicule for they are in a situation of great fear which is very real to them. There is the suffering brought about by illness, by the diseases which are ever increasing upon the Earth plane. There are those who can take out and look at those diseases, so to speak, and there are those who hide them away in a locked box. They must be encouraged to bring forth, to unlock the box, talk about them naturally and normally. You can give them understanding, you can give them courage, for it is not sympathy that they need, but courage to face that disease. And immediately it will be halved because it will be shared with you. And as the mind quietens so will the disease. There is the suffering brought about by an accident, where the body is broken, where the Spirit is broken. But the body is of course in hands other than yours. But the will to live must be restored, and that is where your understanding can help. You have the knowledge of absent healing and you know that in silent prayer, just by holding the hand of the patient, you can bring a great healing force to bear upon that person. There are occasions when miraculous healings can occur, or healings that have needed a time of several months can be reduced to several weeks through the prayer and understanding that you send forth.

There is the suffering that is brought about between parents and children. A suffering where love, the love of the parent for the child, is rejected. Where the child desires to spread its wings and leave the nest. There are those who cannot bear to part with those they have nurtured, they suffer, truly suffer. And you can help here also, for they can talk to you and you can say a gentle word here and there, trying to bring about the realisation that from the time of birth that child will eventually leave the nest, as indeed do all young things. Indeed in some cases the young one is virtually deserted by the parents, and of course this happens also upon the Earth plane between parents and children. In this case it is the understanding, your willingness to sit and listen, to let the person get the matter off their chest, which will help.

My children there is now another suffering upon the Earth plane, the conflict of the young. The darkness is invading, and I must tell you here and now that that darkness is spreading and will continue to escalate until Mother Earth begins to cause a distraction. Pillaging, burning, looting, killing, it is not new, it has been going on for many thousands of years. It is Man's way of trying to dominate. At one time it was the need for power, to seek land and territories from others. To knock down the weaker, to assert one's authority and ways, to dominate with the will, and now upon the Earth plane it is the young ones.

Through the ages there have been young ones who have been hotheads, who have brought about havoc in small areas, and so it is now. But because of the larger populations upon the Earth plane there is greater involvement with more people, with more damage. And because of the means of passing the news on, so it becomes wider knowledge. And so there are those who become affected from a distance apart, who once upon a time would not have had the knowledge, and there would have been no disturbance.

The vibrations around the Earth plane are used in ways which it would be best if they were not used. But it is the will of Man and there can be no interference. However at times there are disturbances which are arranged. The energies of these young people must be used in the right way. They must be directed in the right way, for the energy must not be wasted. But this of course is beyond you. I digress.

There are many amongst the young people who bitterly regret and feel degraded at the things that they have done. They have learned a lesson and they will not repeat. But of course there are always others to take their place. Whilst one is being carried along in a mob, one is blind and one is deaf to all those things which one should make a particular note of, and so with the young.

There will come a time when you will hear the full story from somebody who has been involved in a riot, and their minds will be greatly disturbed, for that is the way of it, and they will greatly suffer, and that also is the way of it. You see my children, there is much for you to do, much for you to understand, and there is a great need for the love which you can send forth. For love sent forth freely, undemandingly, is of far greater value than you realise, for you build around you a vibration of great value.

I will go now. May the Love and the Light of Father God surround you at all times, and indeed it does. God bless you.

Chapter IX

THE PATHWAY TO PERFECTION

Greetings this is Lauda. The time is now coming when there will be great changes upon the Earth plane. Changes within the minds of men, changes of the thought pattern. There will also be changes upon the face of the planet Earth for everything is coming to a peak.

You have the understanding that within the solar system there are those planets which are drawing closer together, drawing in a line, drawing into the vicinity of one of the other. Not of course a touching vicinity but nevertheless within the same orbital values. All this bringing together all this building up is not by accident but by design. The design of the Creator, part of The Plan. For there is to be a great cleansing, and with that cleansing will come a step forward in the evolution of the pathway to perfection.

Within the minds of men, nay indeed within the minds of children, there are disruptive elements. Elements which must find expression, elements which must be destroyed, elements which must be removed from the minds of those young people. But in order for a disease to be removed there must be an understanding of that disease, and with that understanding will come the cure; and it will be so. Of course this is a very gradual process, but nevertheless the peak is nearly at its highest and those young people who are going through this experience will learn by it. And when they in their turn are the parents of children, they will ensure that those children do not carry out the extremes that they have been carrying out themselves, for it is the turning point. The tide has reached the highest point upon the rocks and it will now begin to find its own level and it will recede, bringing with it a great cleansing. And this is how it will be.

Mother Earth is also reaching boiling point, is also reaching the peak. And in order for her to find the highest water level, so to speak, she will indeed cast the waters high upon the land. There will be mountainous waves such as have never been registered before, but with them will come a great cleansing. Volcanoes as they are called will erupt, spewing out the poisonous matter within, and this too will bring a great cleansing within Mother Earth.

It means of course that there will be many upheavals. It means of course that many people will sacrifice their lives. But nevertheless their spirits remain undamaged, and they will return to the Earth plane bringing with them deep within, the knowledge of those things which have happened. Bringing with them the knowledge also of the cleansing and of those things which must be done.

And so the time that you have chosen to return to the Earth plane is one of great upheaval and one of greater understanding, a time of cleansing. And you are part of the vanguard because of course you are not alone. There are many thousands, who like yourselves have chosen this path — the path of preparation. The path whereby you give an understanding to many others who in their turn will also give an understanding. You have had the understanding given to you in a previous teaching, *'from one can come thirty — a hundred or more understandings,'* and so the word spreads that there is a purpose to life. That it is not just a case of acquiring material goods, of acquiring a status as it is called.

All men are equal. Whatever their possessions all men are equal, for they are created. The physical body is composed of dust, so to speak, and when that physical life is ended it returns to dust. And it is because of that, that all men are equal, for it is inevitable. It is the spirit within that is not of equality. It is the knowledge that Jesus the Nazarene was a Master who set foot upon the Earth plane, in order to give the understanding that the physical body can be discarded. But the spirit within is eternal life and is ongoing, taking with it the lessons that are learned upon each visit to the Earth plane. The physical body is a temple for the spirit within, and it is the temple which returns to the classroom. That sounds rather peculiar, but I know that you have the understanding. It is the spirit within the temple that is of prime importance and it is the way you learn your lessons that enables the spirit to progress.

All is not plain sailing, for it is not intended to be thus. If you sailed through one physical body to join yet another physical body and learned nothing, there is no purpose. You are not perfection and you make mistakes, and this is how it must be. Sometimes you can progress in one life and the next time you return to the Earth plane it could well be that you are overcome by material things, and then you have a lesson to learn again. But I will say this to you my children, that each one of you have learned your lessons well and each one of you is now stepping forward, for you have chosen a time of great difficulty; a time of great mental stress; a time of great material awareness; a time of great awakening.

I would ask you to think back to thirty years ago, for I know you can all recollect thirty years ago. Upon the Earth plane at that time there was a recovery. A time when although the battle had been won you were not surrounded with riches, but knew the meaning of restriction. But although you were going through a time of restriction, a time of re–awakening, there was a great deal of love around the Earth plane. And then came a time of plenty, plenty for some, but I say this to you for you were in that area of plenty, instead of there being great rejoicing and a sharing, there was greed and a hoarding. It was a case of never mind about you for I have plenty, and that is all I am concerned about. And gradually of course there has come about a great discontent, and if only those who are complaining now were to look around them, they have far more possessions, far more privileges than you had thirty years ago, and yet there is this great discontent.

There must be a time of cleansing, there must be a time of restoration. A restoration of thought to the true values, to the true reasons of this present life upon the Earth plane. Those who have evil intent, the true evil intent which is the lust for power, the lust for domination, the greed for possessions, not only personal possessions but the desire to possess all lands upon the Earth plane, to dominate, to in fact create themselves a God upon the Earth plane, will not be allowed. There cannot be domination, a God-like domination upon the Earth plane, for there is only one God the Father, The Creator, the Giver of all things, the ever loving God. There cannot be a God who demands, who seeks subservience from those around Him. It will not be allowed.

There is one who is endeavouring to rise to this exalted position and he will meet a truly bloody death, and he will reach a truly devastating level. It will happen, but not yet. But in the meantime there are those around the Earth plane who are seeking this domination, who are seeking to rule all lands. But they are destined to fail, for it is Mother Earth who will take into her own hands the holding back of this thing which is planned. By her actions there will be but one thought and that is the thought of personal survival, for those who seek to dominate are those who will seek personal survival, and they cannot of course be victorious.

You my children are the vanguard. You will not see the happenings that I have been speaking of. You will not see those happenings whilst in your present physical body. You are the vanguard; those who are spreading an understanding to those of younger years, who in turn will spread the understanding to those who will choose them as parents in the future. And you can see, gradually the army of love and understanding will widen and spread in generations to come. That is how it must be and you yourselves will return with the knowledge within you. You will return into the next physical body with the knowledge of what has to be done, clearly to the fore. And it will not be a case my children of waiting for fifty years, it will not be a case of waiting forty years. It will be foremost in your minds from the time you draw your first breath upon the Earth plane at that time. And at that time there will be many thousands, and I do mean thousands, upon the Earth plane who will be in various stages of understanding. And thus the great cleansing is commencing now with vanguards such as yourselves. Yours is a very precious life this time upon the Earth plane, a life of great value in The Plan of The Creator Father God.

May the Love and the Light of Father God surround you all at all times, and indeed it does. God bless you all.

Chapter X

THE VALUE OF TEACHINGS

I bring you greetings. I bring you love. I bring you understanding. I bring you teachings. I come from the mountains, I travelled the seas, I studied the moon and I studied the stars, and from these studies I was able to sail the seas of the world.

I was not an educated man for as I have said I came from the mountains. I lived with my parents in a cabin of logs. The stars and the moon fascinated me. I used to go to the monastery as a boy and I was very fortunate for there was one there, Father Berne, who was very knowledgeable, a great reader, a great scholar, a philosopher, and he used to teach me. He soon discovered my interest in the stars, the night skies, and he taught me much.

He encouraged within me a sense of adventure. He told me of lands across vast seas and aroused within me, I who lived in the mountains, a love of those seas. And so it was inevitable that in time I found my way down to the coastline, that of France. There I saw sights of great wonderment to me for there were vast wooden ships. By the standards of your present day world they would be small, but to me they were vast for they held cannon and many men, and there were huge sails and many windows, and it was to me a wonderment.

I sailed as a cabin boy on one of those vessels. It was a vessel which plied its trade to the Mediterranean. A journey of many days for we went around the Bay of Biscay and what is known as Gibraltar and to Malta, and we passed islands which were bleak and deserted. We went to the north of Africa where there were small ports where we would collect silks and spices, camel skins, jewellery, precious stones and such like.

We would spend much time going from port to port and it was in this way that I found myself in Spain. I found myself suddenly caught up with a huge armada. There were many vessels and their guns bristled and it was obvious that there was to be a mighty war, a mighty battle upon the sea. I had no intention of becoming involved, but I was on shore with some of my friends and we were shanghaied, I think the word is, and taken aboard a man-of-war. We were kept aboard, not allowed any freedom whatsoever and eventually the great Armada set sail, and we were then set to work. There was no mercy shown, for our masters did not believe in mercy. We were there to do their bidding. To make sure that the mighty vessels sailed, that nothing went wrong. For Philip was King of Spain and he had little love for England, and that is where we were due. It was the intention of course that he break the back of the pride of England and master them. But it was not to be of course, for his intentions could not be allowed. The time was wrong.

The vessel upon which I was a captive worker was sunk and I was rescued by a British man-of-war. I was treated as a prisoner at first and was not allowed to sit idle there. But I was befriended by a sailor who took great interest in my knowledge of navigation that I had learned in the mountains from my friend the Monk. He took me under his wing and eventually we were taken to a port in England and he smuggled me ashore, and I found myself in Plymouth. He took me to his home which was not very grand, but it was a home and I was given kindness. And through the love that I was shown there I looked upon that place as my home.

I listened to the old sailor talking with friends who had sailed the sea on many occasions. I frequented taverns, for that was the thing to do. And I listened for I had little money to spend, money which I earned from doing various work around the harbour, for there was always work upon those great ships to be done. Gradually I acquired quite an education of seafaring matters, and then I heard of a vessel which was setting sail under a great sea faring man, and the purpose was to go around the World. Perhaps I should correct that and say, to go as far as the seas stretched, (for that was the intention), until land was reached. I considered myself very fortunate that I was taken as a hand upon that vessel, for it was to be a great adventure. It was to be of navigational value, and it was to be of great teachings for those who were to follow.

And so in due course we set sail. We had no idea when we set sail of the hardship that we would encounter, the fear, the hunger that we would know. We left with a well stocked vessel with water and food of a kind. We knew that the food would not be plentiful for it had to be rationed right from the outset, but we had no idea of the might of that water.

As we set sail we felt as if we were within a castle set upon firm foundations. But upon that water we were little more than a cork, and when the winds blew and the mighty waves crashed on the decks we were truly afraid. For the first time we had come face to face with the might of the elements and there was no firm footing beneath us. It pitched and tossed in an alarming way and there were occasions when it seemed as if we were doomed for a watery grave.

But no, we lost the masts and the sails, not all of them of course, but when the mighty mast crashed to the deck we lost our strength and we had to rely on secondary sails. But that did not daunt us for we all worked together to improvise and to re-establish that which we could re-establish. There were those who fished, and the seas at that time were plentifully stocked, and one way and another we survived until we saw land ahead.

We looked at it, a black speck in the distance, and it was indeed a blessed sight. But as we approached we realised that this was no Garden of Eden, for it was bleak, a very bleak coastline. Slowly and painfully we made our way towards that black speck, drawing closer to the shore, and a party went ashore to see if we could find fresh water. They were gone for several days and we feared for their lives. But they eventually returned and with them there came people, three people to be exact, fair of skin. They had been set ashore by a pirate ship, for they had been captured and placed upon this desolate land to die. But they had found fresh water and food. They had trapped animals and they had survived. There was improvised a means of carrying water and a party was sent forth to bring fresh water in order that we could proceed further down the coastline, because this place was not for us.

And so after many days, when we had rested and work had been carried out upon our vessel, we set forth once again. And we eventually came to an island where the sea ran into a bay and we sailed into this place and found it rather beautiful. We stayed there for some time and those aboard who had been given the task, went forth to collect various samples, (I think you would say now upon the Earth plane), but they were specimens of the various life in that place. They were taken aboard the ship. And then there came the task ahead of us of sailing back whence we had come. It was then that the knowledge that I had been given all those years ago by the Monk on the mountain became of vital importance, for from that knowledge I was able to navigate the vessel at night time, to keep it on course.

Eventually we returned to England, much older, much wiser and with much information on board our vessel. We were hailed as explorers, for there had been much information gathered of territories, of sizes of land. Much information gathered which was later to be used by sailors upon the Earth plane who were to follow.

My name was Nathaneal Shoewright. It probably means nothing to you, but if you searched in the navigational archives you would find out more about that journey, for I have but touched on the fringes. I would say to you, teachings are never wasted and there are times when the smallest teaching becomes of paramount importance to someone, and those things which perhaps you suffer are allied to the suffering of others. You learn as you go through life, for that is the reason for this life. To learn, to remember, to use and in your turn to teach. Use the teachings that you are given, they will be of value to many. Adieu.

Chapter XI

MEDITATION
THE ACT

G reetings. Tonight we are going to do something different. We are going to have meditation. First of all let me tell you my name, it is Pu Ti Yung, and I was a son of Siam.

Tonight we will have meditation for there are one or two of you who have problems, and it is hoped that you will follow, if you agree with the teachings that you will have. But first of all I will explain that through the meditation one goes as one says *within*. One finds the peace that is safely locked away. One loses all awareness of the physical life around you and you come back refreshed and with peace in your heart.

First of all the way that you are seated is important. I would ask you to put your feet and your knees together and to sit bolt upright. Now I will ask you to gently relax so that you are comfortable. Let your shoulders drop, and in that position, if you are seated correctly, you can forget the physical body for it is but a casing, a temple. I wish that you place your hands palms downwards upon your knees. It is important that you are balanced and comfortable.

There are many schools of thought. There are those who give pictures, there are those who tell you to concentrate on a special thing, but tonight I would like you to follow those things which I tell you for it is good to know different ways, different thinkings, for the result at the end is the same.

I wish you to visualise yourselves at the top of a high mountain. I wish you to be aware of the space, the vast space that is all around you. And now I wish you to set forth into that space as a bird does. I wish you to feel the silence. I wish you to feel the air around you and I wish you to quietly float upon the different air currents that rise all around you — quietly — quietly. And now I wish you to be aware of the stillness around you, the silence, the peace. Quietly asleep. I will waken you in a short time. (The Group go into meditation). Ssss — Ssss — Softly — Softly — Softly — return to the knowledge that you are seated within this Sanctuary and you have not moved a single muscle.

In Si Ting which was the Province where I lived, meditation was considered an every day part of our lives, a very important part. For within each one of us there is so much knowledge and so much help, so much advice that can be reached, can be sought and can be given. It is knowledge of great value but it is not knowledge that is freely given.

Remember you are progressing in the awareness that each one of you is on a separate Spiritual path. And so therefore each one of you holds within knowledge of previous happenings, of previous lives wherever they may have been in the Universe. Knowledge which you can bring forth when in true meditation. There are always small beginnings. To commence with there are problems because the physical world, the material happenings that go on all around you, hem you in and do not allow for the expansion that is needed.

Therefore there are disappointments to begin with, for to be told to sit as I have told you, to have instruction as I have given, then immediate results are expected. It is not always possible, for here again things hasten slowly when you are involved in a busy working life. Life upon the Earth plane now is a hopping from one thing to the other. Not necessarily physical hopping but mental hopping, and this of course causes considerable tensions within the area of the brain. The tension points between the head and the spine are very very sensitive and it is very difficult to let go. And so I wish you to follow an exercise which will relieve the tensions in the neck. It will free the movement of the neck.

And so I would ask you to gently drop your chin upon your chest, completely drop it. Now I wish you to take a breath, a deep breath, and at the same time slowly lifting your head, holding the breath, and then to bring your head forward again slowly releasing that breath. — Again. — As you bring your head back you can feel tensions on the top of the neck and either side of the shoulders. — Again. — Bring forward, letting the breath out.

Now turn your head to the left as far as it will go without any strain, and from that position start to take in a breath, moving slowly until your head is round to the right as far as it will go comfortably. Hold and let the breath out, at the same time bringing your head back to the left side. I am sure you can hear noises as you release the tensions in the back of your neck as you move your head. Now I wish you to move your head in a circular manner taking in a breath as you go. Starting from the left and bringing your head round slowly back to the left, letting the breath out slowly, and then round again. You can hear the sounds at the back of the head.

I would suggest that you do these exercises at least four times before sitting in meditation. It will release the tensions and give you freedom in your neck. And you will find that you do not hunch yourself so much when you are in a position of tension or stress. If you do these exercises at least twice a day you will receive great benefit. It will loosen the tensions and free the neck and it will also relieve the pressures on the psychic centres in the head.

Now I want you to feel here (hand put on stomach). Here is the centre, for it is roughly the same distance from head to stomach as from stomach to feet, give or take a little. It depends on the length of the leg, but if the leg is long it usually balances up. Here is the centre and I want you to place your hands upon the centre. I want you to take a deep breath, a really deep breath, and in taking that deep breath I want you to feel that your abdomen extends out, for your breath must go right down. It extends not because you push it with your muscles but because you have taken in a deep breath which has gone down to here (indicates bottom of stomach). Now take a deep breath. Hold it for the count of seven and then slowly let it out. Another one — and again.

Here within this area is a spiritual point of considerable value. A spiritual point which sits in the middle. It is the point, it is the centre, it is the [1]Chakra of absorption. It is to here that all stress flies, and it is this area which you must protect when you are in fear; when you are worried; when there are vibrations around you which tense you. It all flies to here and that is why there are so many illnesses which stem from the stomach, for they go down and they go up. An unprotected Chakra can absorb too much.

If you are in a situation of fear I would ask you to sit comfortably as I have advised, and to just quietly cross your hands so, across the solar plexus Chakra. To just sit quietly for about ten minutes relaxed, and you will find that the problems, whatever they may be, will be eased. I am not going to say they will completely vanish because your own physical mind will still be busy, but you will find that by protecting your Solar Plexus you will ward off within the etheric that which is flying straight to you to be dispersed over the body.

I do not feel that we can do a demonstration. You can try, but I do not feel that unless you are in a state of worry or tension or stress, whatever it may be within your physical life, I

---

[1]Chakra of absorption — The Solar Chakra — sometimes called the Solar Centre, is located at the level of the solar plexus. This chakra is the seat of the element of fire in our nature.

do not feel that you will really understand the benefit until such a situation arises. But then do sit quietly and protect the solar plexus. It does work, it does help.

You see, meditation covers all sorts of fields really. It is to bring forth the wonderful treasures that are within. It is to forget the physical body and to go forth to bring back those things which are stored within. To go forth to receive teachings, and these are of great value. You can meditate merely by just sitting relaxed quietly. You can bring about a protection by crossing your hands so. It is all to ease your physical body, to enable absorption of that which is within the etheric body which is waiting to be absorbed. But if you are too tense you can sometimes stop the help that is all around you.

It has been a great joy for me to be with you and I hope that I may be permitted to return at a later time, for I would very much like to come back and talk again with you and to discuss the progress which I am sure you will make. I would like to say, The Creator of all things be with you, each one of you.

Meditation

* * *

TEMPLE OF LOVE

Greetings my daughter. Greetings to you all, this is Thomas. It is my task now to give you the first part of your Group teachings. It is my task, for we are now building up the energies within this Sanctuary in order that those of greater power may be able to reach you. We are lifting you in order that they may reach you.

This is the thirtieth meeting of the Group. You are over half way now and of course you have this understanding. There will come a time when you will look back upon these Group meetings and realise just how much you have learned, and just how great an understanding has been given to you, and just how great a difference it has made to your earth lives. That is of course if you read the words that have been written and the words that will be written to complete your book of teachings.

I want to take you for a brief time to the country of India. I want to take you to a Palace of whiteness, a Palace of material, a Palace of great beauty and delicacy. It is a [1]Palace of Love, for it is a shrine which was built to a loved one. She was of great beauty and her grieving husband knew not how to capture her beauty. So he built a Palace of whiteness to signify her beauty,

---

[1]Palace of Love — Taj Mahal — a marble mausoleum of great splendour and beauty at Agra, India, built (1631–45) by the Mogul Emperor Shah-Jahan in memory of his favourite wife.

her purity; his love; the devotion they had one for the other. For they were twin souls. I want to take you within that place to where her body lies. To where he thinks she will join him eventually.

He did not realise that she was with him. He did not realise that she stood beside him, helpless to help him with his grief. Helpless to take his hand. Helpless to give her love in the way that he was desirous of. But she surrounded him with love just the same. They are together now and he has a greater understanding. And together they stand in that place either side of the casket which contains her body, preserved forever so long as the air does not reach it.

One could say, "What a waste of money." But that of course is material thinking. For with that Palace that he built for love, a deep and everlasting love, there have been many who have visited and have come away with a great peace within them. In fact it is now a place of healing. A place where peace and tranquillity can be absorbed. Where one can go and sit in a corner quietly and shut out all those who are milling around, and really find within the healing peace. The tranquillity of mind that comes with a closeness to Spirit.

I speak of this place for it is a shining example. With the moonlight shining upon it, it is like a vision, a vision of ethereal beauty. Something that cannot really be there, but is. And so it is my children, in your daily lives. The visions that you will receive through sitting quietly in meditation will be of such wonderment that you will feel that they cannot really be there, that it is just imagination. But no, to go within, to find the source of all love, to reach the peace, is not imagination, it is there and it is very real.

There are those amongst you who say you cannot find the time to meditate. But you can find the time to do other things. You can receive a telephone call with a request to do something. To go and meet somebody; to go and visit somebody; to go and collect something. And you stop whatever you are doing to do that deed. Then what is so different with meditation? If you can find time to do one thing why cannot you find time to do another?

You will find that if you set a time for meditation, sometimes you will forget that time, but gradually within your conscious mind you will record that time and know that that is when you must go and sit quietly. You will receive much benefit, for you will receive a calming within yourselves. You will receive a healing, because by sitting in meditation you slow down the physical body. You will receive teachings, you will receive knowledge that is held within.

Is it not worth it? If it is not then is it worth it sitting within this Group? You sit here at a certain time upon a certain day. You have learned the disciplines to do this, and through that discipline there will come the true teachings, the true understandings and the wonderful manifestations. If you sit quietly in meditation then there too you will receive teachings. And there too you will receive understandings; and there too you will receive your own personal guidance of those things which you should do. Those things which are written and those things which it is up to you to decide to do, or otherwise.

I had not intended to speak for long, for now my children it is the second part of these Group meetings that are of the utmost importance. I come now to prepare the way. I come to bring within you a calming and a tranquillity that the energies within this Sanctuary may truly build up. That you may be uplifted. That you may receive those teachings which are of great value. And so I will go.

May the Love and the Light of Father God surround you all at all times, and indeed it does. God bless you all.

Meditation

* * *

ALLOCATION OF TIME

This message was received after the normal teachings as the Group was holding a discussion regarding giving up time. This discussion was interrupted.

Thank you my children, I have been listening. I have been listening with great interest for you have turned yourselves right the way round, perhaps without realising it, but you have. You have been speaking of your family as being your dedication, so to speak, your full responsibility. And that is true, for what greater responsibility is there than to be accepted as a parent. To bring forth into the world, a troubled world, a young one, a young physical being, one who may be an old soul within, but nevertheless has to be trained in the ways of the Earth plane. You are of service because you have brought that young one upon the Earth plane. You have responsibilities towards that family, but nevertheless you have responsibilities towards yourself. The conclusion that you came to after your discussion.

It is possible, in fact it is necessary that you find time for yourselves. As has been stated one hour a day is not very long. But one hour a day can be of greater value than all the other twenty three. For that is the hour that you devote to your own physical forgetfulness, to bring forth the Spirit within; to seek the knowledge that can be given to you in that hour. A knowledge that perhaps cannot be given to you clairaudiently. A knowledge that perhaps cannot be given to you because you do not have the gift of clairvoyance. But **all** can meditate and go within and bring forth those treasures. Make no mistake you can bring them forth, for you have all been on this Earth plane before, and you have all been to other Spheres for there is much training, much teaching, much progression. Make no mistake that knowledge which is held within in that one hour of complete oneness, complete unity, will be of far greater value to you than you realise.

You are all now of the understanding, you all know the value of meditation. For if you have not sat under instruction you have read books or you have discussed. To sit quietly with a still mind will bring forth those treasures. But a mind that cannot discard the problems of the physical is a mind that greatly needs a rest. Within that one hour you can receive great revitalisation. Within that one hour you can receive great inspiration, and within that one hour you can receive knowledge of great value.

There are those of you who know the necessity to record those things that you are given in meditation, those treasures that you bring forth. And I would say to all of you, record. Record the Earth day and record those things that you see, no matter how minor. Somebody will say "I only see colours." But that is of value. Record them and gradually you will see a pattern developing. And if perhaps in one or two Earth years time you look back upon your first recordings, you will be amazed at what they will tell you.

The discussion was good, it was lively and it is good that you all joined in, for we listen and it helps us. We can hear and we can see and we too record. Thank you for letting me be with you. God bless you. Before I go I will tell you my name, for the thought has gone forth "I wonder who it was?" My name was Sharpe when I was upon the Earth plane. I was a teacher. I was a teacher at a Cathedral school at Winchester. Thank you.

Meditation

* * *

TRANQUILLITY

Greetings my daughter, greetings to you all this is Thomas. Today within this Sanctuary there will come one who has much wisdom to impart. There will come one who will utilise a great deal of energy, and it is as promised.

My children, all around the Earth plane there is a great need for the thought patterns of love that can be sent forth, and indeed are being sent forth. But they must ever increase for there is a massing within the centre of the land, a place which has been called 'the tinder box'. There is a massing together there of forces of darkness within the minds of man.

There have over many centuries, been great turmoil's within that area but they have been confined to comparatively small knowledge for the means of communication were not as now. But now there is darkness massing in the minds of men bent upon destruction, for in that area there is great greed, because from within Mother Earth there gushes forth [1]precious energy. An energy which is being utilised for many reasons for many purposes, but an energy which has not an everlasting source. It

---

[1]Precious energy — Crude oil — inflammable mineral oil — found in many places in the upper strata of the earth, particularly in the Middle East, containing large numbers of different hydrocarbons and used especially as a source of oils for heating and mechanical power. [Latin & Greek: petra - rock, Latin: oleum - oil]

is not as the waters, the everlasting springs. It is an energy which has come about over the centuries; millions of years of the settlings and eruptions and the settlings and the decayings and so forth. But I do not need to tell you this for you have the knowledge. This great testing of the minds of those who are of ancient knowledge, this great testing may be overpowered if the darkness becomes too strong.

So you are asked to concentrate upon this area; the area known upon the Earth plane as the Middle East. You are asked to concentrate a healing upon this area — a healing of thought, for the thought patterns are absorbed and utilised. You are asked my children to sit quietly and to concentrate upon that area. You are asked to visualise masses of people. You are asked to visualise them in their native costume, (I will use that expression), but not to visualise them in small groups, but as a vast mass stretching as far as the eye can see. You are asked to project thoughts of peace, thoughts of tranquillity and thoughts of love to that area. I ask you now to do this, for this time is very important. *(At this point the Group sat in silence, sending out thoughts of tranquillity and love, as requested.)*

From this Sanctuary there has gone forth far greater power than you realise, and there are many such groups who are being requested to send forth their thoughts of healing love to that area. You have already been told on many occasions now, the power of thought is very valuable and very potent, and I would like you all to remember this and to be careful when you are directing thoughts towards one individual, for you are now becoming of much strength, each one of you.

During your earth life there is of course the free will which you know about, and it is the free will which brings about petty irritations. It is very necessary that now you reach a stage of tranquillity, — a state which within your normal daily lives it is not always possible to maintain — a state of tranquillity which you can reach as you sit quietly within your own dwelling house. A state of peace, of harmony. It is this state which you must reach in order that the full healing abilities, gifts, energies, call them what you will, can be utilised by you. For through this tranquillity you become a clear channel. Whether it is to be healing through speech – through touch – to animals – absent healing – by colour – by vibration – by love, you must be a clear channel, for if your mind is clogged with too many petty happenings within your daily life you cannot reach that high vibration which is necessary, a clear channel.

At our previous meeting you were given instruction on meditation by one of considerable knowledge. He will visit you again at a later time. It is necessary that you carry out meditation as instructed by him, and to visualise as instructed will help you to reach a vibration of tranquillity. A bringing together of a true balance within the physical body and within the spiritual body; a balancing of all things.

We are now reaching the time within this Group when the teachings must be of greater depth, when the understandings must be reached and when the knowledge must be imparted. A knowledge which will be of value to each one of you in your own individual ways as you walk your own separate spiritual paths. And although the knowledge to each one of you is the same, each one of you will use it differently.

There is also to be a time of individual instruction for each one of you. All these things **must be** if we are to achieve that which has to be achieved. Each one of you must be given the knowledge that is written and each one of you must be given the understanding how to utilise, and you yourselves must have the disciplines to utilise. Disciplines — disciplines — disciplines, this word keeps arising, but it is very essential to have disciplines in all facets of your daily life.

My children opportunities are being given to you. Teachings are being given to you. Love surrounds you. But you are the ones who must use these teachings and take from them those things that you can accept. You are the ones who have been chosen. There has been a great bringing together, you already have this knowledge. It is up to you to follow those things which are for your spiritual advancement. You will spread out from this Sanctuary eventually like a seven pointed star, and the brilliance from that star will be tremendous if each one of you fulfils your part in the Master Plan.

You are truly blessed. Gods' Love is yours, as indeed He loves all, but you are truly blessed. God bless you and indeed my children He does.

Chapter XII

FALSE PROPHET

I draw from each one of you the energies that are necessary for me to stay with you. I draw from you, but not to your limit. I come, for the time is now that you be told of things that you are able to understand, of those things which are of importance. Things which are of now but which are connected with the past, for all are as one. I do not intend to be dramatic but that is my way, for I have to make sure that the cosmic energy is with me.

There is soon to be upon this Earth plane one who will declare himself the Messiah. One who will declare that he is Christ returned to this Earth plane. But I say to you, he is a false prophet. He is one for you to look out for. He will come at a time when there is much disorder upon this Earth plane. He will come with his lying tongue and he will bring about him a following, for such will be his strength; but he is a false prophet. There will be many who will believe, but there must be those who have the understanding that they must send forth their all powerful thoughts.

You must, each one of you, send forth your thoughts towards that one, covering him with light that the darkness he intends to bring will never grow across the Earth plane. We know that this must happen for it is written thus, for the minds of men must be cleansed. As these false prophets come towards you, you can cover them with the light, the light that will be directed through you from the higher realms. For you are all in contact with the higher realms.

The time is now coming for the turning away from this negative situation which is predominant upon the Earth plane at this present time. The time is coming when it must be dispelled. It is upon you who are now upon the Earth plane that we are turning to, for we do not wish to see this planet destroyed. Indeed it will not be destroyed for that cannot be allowed. But mark my words there can be a great destruction. You do not have the awareness that you have returned to this planet at your own request, at your own desire, at this time which is of much excitement and much enlightenment. You are not here to play games.

You are here because you have chosen a task. A task of which you are becoming ever-more aware. Look for this false prophet, he will come. Listen to his words. It will be hard to distinguish that he speaks not with love. It will be hard to distinguish that he is not a Master, returned to the Earth plane to bring about a greater understanding. He will arise, it will happen; remember my words. Send forth light towards him and keep close to him the darkness that he would spread. For believe me when he comes he will appear in an area of great chaos. That will be his way.

There will come a time before the end of your meetings within this Sanctuary that I will stand before you — there, *(finger pointed to centre of room)*, and you will see me. But that will not be just yet, for it will take considerable preparation. Each one of you here within this room, this place of much love and upliftment, have within your hands great strength. You have free will but you are being given the knowledge. You will know each one of you, that which you can do. You have the free will as to whether you do it or not. But as I look around at each one of you, I can commune with the Spirit within and I know that each one of you will complete the task that you have returned to the planet Earth to achieve. As the Sun rises, it brings with it an energy force. An energy force that you can use to revitalise within that which is of most value.

From the realms from which I have come to meet you I bring to you a promise. A promise that you will be aided in the fight that is to commence. That you will be aided and that no part of you will be depleted in any way because of the energy that you will send forth. It will be replaced, according to the Tenfold Law. It is a promise from the realms from whence I came and from whence I must return. The energy is going, for I use a great deal. The power that is yours is greater than you are aware of, for with the love and light that is poured down around each one of you, there is given a great power. You must use it. Do not let it be wasted.

And now I return, but I will come back and I will stand there. Wisdom be yours, wisdom and the knowledge how to use that wisdom. For wisdom must not be kept to oneself, but shared. I go, I go.

Chapter XIII

PAUL

Greetings. It is my pleasure to speak with you, my name is [1]Paul. It is a pleasure for me to come. I come to speak about those things that may be beyond your understanding. I come to speak about the life of the Christos. A life of great wonderment. A life of dedication. A life of knowledge from beginning to end. A life of misunderstanding, and yet of love, compassion, of suffering, and yet a life that followed a path that lead to an even greater understanding.

The Christos was a Master, make no mistake. He came from the realms of the Masters. He could have ascended even higher but He chose to descend to the Earth plane at a time when there was great chaos, even as there is now. From the time He took His first breath upon the Earth plane He had the understanding of the path that He must follow. And although He went through the Earth life in a physical body, at all times He knew those things that He had to do. And at all times He knew that which

---

[1]Paul — The story of St. Paul is interesting from the Spiritualist's point of view, as the recorded experiences provide examples of phenomena so familiar to them. He mentioned a natural body and a spirit body, and his listing of "Spiritual gifts" (Ch.12, 1st Epistle to the Corinthians), is almost a summary of modern mediumship. The vision on the way to Damascus was psychic evidence of survival.

would be the end. For the understanding had to be given, the true knowledge.

As a small boy He went into the Temple and discussed with the elders those things which were of greater knowledge than they themselves had. They who thought they knew it all. They who thought they knew the beginnings and the end. But they were but children to Him, He who was a child. The things that He told them amazed them. They disbelieved, but time proved the truth of those things they were told by that child. He learned a trade. He learned to be a carpenter, for He was within the physical body was He not, and therefore had to follow the path of a physical being upon the Earth plane? Therefore He had to live a normal life, although He was no ordinary person upon the Earth plane.

He knew He had to gather around Him a band of men who would understand, for within them they had the understanding. He had to find them and there was much searching. But as soon as He looked upon those who were to be with Him, closely connected with Him, to link with Him in thought, He looked into their eyes and knew. Theirs was no easy path, for He made no secret of those things which were to be. He made no secret of the privations they would have to face. He made no secret of the ridicule, of the hunger and the thirst. For all those things they suffered, it was no secret.

Many people came to Him when once there had been healings. People turned to Him for all manner of reasons all to do with healings, and He taught those who were with Him to become channels of healing. To have the understandings, even as He had the understandings. To be able to send forth, even as He sent forth.

He went into the wilderness to meditate, to commune with His Father, even as you can meditate and commune with the Father. He went within the inner Temple, even as you can go within the inner Temple. There are no secrets for are you not also learning to be a channel of healing.

The Christos was one of great strength, He was a channel of great power. Through Him could be directed a power that is beyond the comprehension of most people upon the Earth plane. He did not command this power for it was channelled through Him gladly. There were many who insulted Him; ridiculed Him; despised Him; were jealous of Him; hated Him. All darkness was directed towards Him, but such was His strength that He could withstand all.

There will come a time when you too, if you follow the path that should be yours, will find that there will be those who will disbelieve, who may even ridicule through ignorance. But it will not matter to you either, for you too will know that you are following the path. That you are doing those things that you intended to do; that you have accepted the task and you are following that path. It is not an easy path but if you are steadfast in the knowledge that you are of truth, that you are endeavouring to go forward, that you too can perform miracles, then you **will** perform miracles, for you will be channels of great power.

It will be so. But if you pay heed to the words of ridicule and disbelief that are said to you and turn aside, you will be as nothing. There is no halfway course. There is a gate, a door, a very solid door that you either pass through or it will close. There will be no second chance of this Earth life for you have been chosen. But the decision whether you pass through the door must be yours. The Christos passed through the door from the moment He took breath. There was no turning back. He knew that at the end of that path when He left the physical body behind with all the physical sufferings, whether they were of mind whether they were of body, He knew that it had to be. That when He left that physical body behind, He left behind with it a knowledge and an understanding. A knowledge for those who were to follow; of those things that could be done; of those things that must be done; of those things that must be achieved.

Paul

You have the knowledge, for are you not sitting here listening to the voice of one of many thousands of years ago who returned to the Earth plane to walk with the Christos, to suffer with Him. Did I not know that suffering? Did I not stand by and watch that suffering? And after He had left the physical body was I not there within that tomb to see it dissolved into dust upon the ground? I was there and I witnessed, and yet within the garden there He stood, a great life, a great knowledge, a great love. A love which is ever spreading across this Earth plane. A love which many have endeavoured to conceal, to distort. It is a love of such magnitude that after these thousands of years it is growing ever stronger.

To you I say, you know of these things. You know of the great truth and you know that you are sitting here listening to one who has no physical body. You know this is no fantasy. I am not from your imagination. I am not a dream. I am reality, the true reality. I come from the world of reality, I will return to that reality. But before doing so I would say, stand steadfast upon your paths, for you know the truth that is within and you; know those words that have been said to you are of truth. Stand fast even as the Christos stood fast, for the end is but the beginning.

Blessings be yours. Follow your paths, take heed of the things that are told you. Do not let words fall upon stony ground. Heed the teachings. Be steadfast.

Chapter XIV

RING OF FIRE

Greetings my daughter. Greetings to you all, this is Thomas. You will find the powers building up. You will find the energies around you and be aware of them, for within this Sanctuary there is building up much energy. It is necessary, very necessary.

My children, you are undoubtedly aware that the tinder box is ready to be lit. You are undoubtedly aware that this could happen by the lighting of a tiny spark, and it must be averted. For the actions of one madman can cause the death of many thousands; can cause a bloody war to spread up and down within that area. A war which could spread through the lust for power, and a war which would take many Earth years to quell. We are asking all those who sit within the groups that have been chosen across the Earth plane, we are asking that you say prayers. Sending out those thoughts of love towards that area, that the darkness may be overcome by the light; that the minds of men may be cleansed. We ask this because it is very very necessary and very urgent.

At the end of this conversation, for it is not a teaching, I will ask you to sit quietly in prayer, directing your thoughts towards that area and visualising everywhere diffused in light. Imagine many multitudes, and the light coming all around them as a

240

blanket of mist. Hold it for a moment or two, that will be sufficient. Matters upon the Earth plane are now beginning to reach a very high peak, and within the next twelve months upon the Earth plane there will be many changes. Changes upon the crust of the Earth and changes in boundaries.

It is essential that people have the understanding, it is essential that the knowledge be given that there will be changes. The next twelve months upon the Earth plane will indeed be crucial for they could be of great value. They could be of great destruction. Before these Group meetings finish you will already have had your proof of the matters of which I speak for the 'ring of fire' will commence erupting. You understand of course that this is not a case of lighting a firework, so to speak, that all will go off in quick succession. Oh no, but there will be an eruption here, an eruption there, and you will see that it follows the ring of fire.

There are those who are deeply concerned at the readings they are getting on their special instruments, and these readings are being kept secret. They are readings which tell of the unrest under the Earth's crust, so to speak, but the readings they do not receive are the ones from the Earth's crust under the oceans, for it is not easy to take readings from many fathoms down to the sea bed. There are of course ships which sail upon these regions who have very delicate instruments, but even they do not reach to the parts that I am speaking of.

Man thinks that he has conquered all things except the elements. He thinks with his electronic equipment he can have knowledge of most things. There are some things of course which he knows he can never reach, but the sea bed is not one of them. They are under the impression that they know all things, but indeed they do not. There are many who have had readings of great concern, readings which if published would set people panic stricken running hither and thither. Life goes on, for there is nothing that can be done except to stop wars, and to stop these senseless experiments with bombs and weapons of great destruction, for they interfere with the elements. This winter-tide upon the Earth plane will be different.

This winter-tide will bring about what is known as freak weather. There will be snow in areas where there has never been snow and there will be hot sun in areas where there has never been hot sun. There will be variations all across the Earth plane. It will happen, it will happen thus. And to you who are being told these things it will be an indication that these things that you are being told are of truth. It will be a proof to you that many things that happen have to happen. It is not by chance.

Many things that happen do not have to happen, and they can be averted by the prayers and the love that is sent out by groups such as this. It is not my intention to speak for long, for I wish you to sit quietly in prayer. And so before closing, I ask you now to join together in prayer. To join together quietly, to send out love and light to the tinder box, each in your own way. I do not propose to lead you but I will close when the time is right. Will you please now join together in prayer. *(The Group sat quietly in prayer).* — Amen.

Thank you for your prayers. I will go now. May the Love and the Light of Father God surround you at all times, and indeed it does. God bless you all.

Chapter XV

ENERGIES
THE PREPARATION

reetings my daughter. Greetings to you all, this is Thomas. You will find more and more opportunities to reach an understanding of those things that must be done, each one upon their own individual spiritual path. We are endeavouring to show you the way. We are endeavouring through the teachings, to give you an understanding of those things that must be done. We are endeavouring to give you an understanding, a different outlook, so to speak, a different interpretation upon the happenings around you and a different realisation. A realisation that you can and must help those who are lost whether it be through a state of health, whether it be through a loss, whether it be through tragedy. Whatever the reason you who are healers can help. Help by the words that you speak, by your actions. You will receive much upliftment, for you will know that you are indeed being of service.

There are those lessons that have to be learned, there are those lessons of much value. I know you are very tired of the word discipline, for we have repeated and repeated and repeated in an endeavour to make you realise the value of discipline, and we are pleased that now you do have discipline, a discipline of attendance at this Group. That is good for as you have the understanding of one discipline so you will recognise the need for other disciplines, and so you will progress. We do not wish to waste our time with teachings that are not heeded. We do not wish to waste words upon deaf ears.

There has been a great change within this Group over the weeks that you have been meeting together. A change within yourselves which perhaps you are unaware of. But if you sit down quietly and think back to the time of the first meeting in this Sanctuary, you will see that you really have progressed. A progression in your understanding, and a progression in your knowledge: a realisation that indeed you are going forward, you are progressing. I can hear in a discussion one or the other of you saying, "I can't say that I have been doing healing." But progression is not necessarily a progression on healing, but a progression of thinking leading towards healing. You are all healers, you have all been chosen to sit in this Group. You have all been given the teachings. And those who for one reason or another have not been able to attend, have still received the teachings through the words that have been written. But of course that is not the same as a discipline of attendance.

Tonight there is to speak with you one of high value, and you should learn much. He will need energy to penetrate to this Sanctuary. After I have finished speaking you will remain silent, for the words that I am speaking are a means of bringing forth the energies for you. You sit peacefully and relaxed and that is good. You all know the value of complete relaxation. You all know the value of quiet moments and while I am speaking you are in fact having a quiet moment. A moment of relaxation, a moment when the energies can be sent forth to build up even higher energies that are already within this Sanctuary.

So my children, I will go having set the scene, so to speak. God's blessings be with you. May the Light and the Love of His protection surround you at all times, and indeed it does. God bless you.

Energies

* * *

THE TENFOLD LAW

May the fountains of wisdom pour down upon you. May the Light of love surround you. May you be aware of those things that are within you. May you know that all things are as one. It is my joy to speak with you within this Sanctuary of love, within this place wherein the energies are built. Energies which come from the cosmic forces from the Galaxies. Energies which are centred within this Sanctuary. They have to be, for without that energy I could not be with you.

There is no 'time' in the realms from which I come, no 'time' such as you have upon the Earth plane. We do not have clocks or watches. We do not even have sun dials for it is not necessary. There is no 'time', for all time is now, all things are now. Within the Realms from which I come there is nothing of the material as you know it. Nothing of the etheric as you know it or as you have been given the understanding of such matters. All is Light and all is Love and all is energy. An energy which can control, an energy which can be directed, an energy which enables the planet Earth to be a planet.

From the Realms from which I come we see many such planets, for there are many planets within the Universe, many of which you have no knowledge whatsoever. Nevertheless they are there and are as much a world as your world. Peopled even as this planet is peopled, where the work of The Creator goes on. There are those upon those planets, greatly advanced according to your knowledge upon this planet. They have been fortunate and contamination has not reached them. The Spheres in which they live are not as solid matter as on the Earth plane.

The Earth plane is of much value to you who are here at this time, for it is a school room. A school room, nothing more and nothing less than a school room. A school room which can be of great value, of great progression, but a school room where the dunces are left behind. I use the word dunces, for there are many upon the Earth plane who have the ability to see and to work, to serve, to progress. But they are clothed in desires for material gain alone. Bringing around them destruction, bringing around them fear. Drawing to themselves all that should be cast aside.

There are Spheres to which they eventually go. Spheres which can be a very hard teaching, for they reduce themselves to another beginning. It is a pity. You see, lessons must be learned. Understandings must be brought forth. You are sitting in this Sanctuary because you have an awareness. That awareness is gradually enlarging and you have the knowledge, indeed you know, that the time has come for a great enlightenment upon the Earth plane. For a great awareness that there are those who also surround you, who cannot be seen by many. An awareness that there is work to be done and that work **must** be done if this planet is not to disappear. Do not take any fear at my words, for of course there will be no disintegration.

The planet Earth as you know it will change. That has to be, for there are conditions in the Galaxies which are changing also, and those changes inevitably cause changes in the Spheres around. As the Galaxy alters so the Spheres move. This of course brings about great changes and in the case of the Earth plane, which is very much of the material, the changes will be greater than in other Spheres. It has to be because of the solidness.

Your scientists predict many things, but your scientists also conceal many things. Like most big bodies of people upon the Earth plane they have their secrets. They give explanations for the minor happenings but conceal explanations for the major happenings. Indeed some major happenings are completely hidden from them for their instruments cannot register, and this you have already been told at a previous meeting within this Sanctuary.

Within the centre of this Sphere there is a great building together of energies. Energies that you cannot conceive. Energies which bring about balance. Energies which are vital. With the experiments that have taken place upon the Earth plane, some of which you know of and some of which are secret, there has been brought about within the centre — disturbances. We in Spirit, we in the Higher Realms from which I come, are using the energies within our control to bring about a balancing, for Mother Earth as you call her is one sided, so to speak.

Within the manipulation, many factors come into being. One of these factors is the endless destruction of the nature forces upon this Sphere, which are necessary for balance. The minerals are withdrawn and great cavities left. Great areas wherein grow trees of great strength are destroyed, bringing about a situation causing imbalance. These things must be brought to knowledge.

As indeed you have already been told the value of prayer, the value of thought. Do not treat these teachings lightly, for the value of prayer is great. The caring, the discipline of sitting in prayer, the thoughts of love, all help. For you are sending forth energies within those thoughts, energies which can be utilised. It is not just words, it is a truth. Each one of you give off energy of great intensity. The vibrations spread out and expand. Energies that are positive thinking; energies that are positive love; energies that are positive prayer come under the Tenfold Law, and expand, and the area to which those prayers are sent can be lifted. It is difficult I know, for you to understand, but there will come a time when you will understand, for you yourselves will be in Spirit having cast aside the physical body, and you will see the Tenfold Law applied to prayer.

There are those upon the Earth plane who think that to send forth a prayer is ridiculous, is a waste of time. But when they are in trouble themselves what do they do? They call out to The Creator. They themselves send forth a prayer for themselves. The prayer is heard, for it is a cry for help. It is never a waste of time to pray. In the Realms from which I come, as I have said all is light, and if there had not been great preparation I could not speak to you now, for it is not possible to project oneself in this manner without preparation.

It is of truth. You have been chosen to sit within this Sanctuary for a certain period of time to receive teachings, to be given understandings. It is of truth — it has been planned long ago. You have been told on more than one occasion you are the vanguard. You **are** the vanguard, part of a body of people across the Earth plane who are being taught those things which must be spread. Do not be shy to talk to people, for there is a greater awakening. If they turn from you what does it matter? For they will turn back at a later time to ask you questions.

But remember that unless prayers go forth to those areas of darkness, for there is darkness, many lives could be lost. But by sending forth your prayers, positive prayers, you will turn back the darkness and those who are endeavouring to send it out. It is of truth, I do not waste my time or yours and I ask you not to let the time be wasted.

It is time for me to leave you but I would say to you, please do not speak for there is one other who would speak with you. I go, pay heed to the words that I have spoken. The Creator of all things sent me and to each one of you is given His Love. There is no more that I can say.

* * * * *

To you I bring the gift of knowledge. To you I bring the wisdom's of the Universe that I hold within my hands. Within this small Group there can be much wisdom, indeed there is much wisdom, for you have been having lessons and teachings.

It has already been said on a previous occasion that according to your comprehension so will you receive different understanding from the words that have been said. And so it is in your everyday life, in the actions that you perform; the deeds that you do; the understandings that you have; the understandings that you can obtain from the words of others who come to you.

The Universe beyond this planet Earth is very vast. It is beyond, beyond, beyond. And within that Universe there is a great gathering together of energies that must be directed towards this planet Earth. There is a bringing together of forces of great strength, a passing of planets which happens from time to time, and within the passing of planets there is a reason. There will be a time of great upheaval upon this planet Earth. And it will be through the massing of the energies within the Universe and the passings that will occur, which will pull back from destruction this planet Earth. For is it not written that it is not intended that there be the destruction that some say must be.

There will be upheavals within the centre of this planet that will be brought about not only by those things that have been told, but for other reasons also. There is a great strengthening taking place. Already you have the understanding of sending out your thoughts of love and light towards the planet Earth. Within this small Group you can have no idea of the value of those thoughts, for indeed as requested, all are linked together across the Earth plane, and through those thoughts there is great energy, upliftment, a balancing being brought about within the Spheres of the Universe. There is much knowledge also of a greater intensity than upon the Earth plane, a knowledge and linking together of one Sphere to another. Not by chains or by ropes, but by strings of energy. And through these energies there is communication. Not as upon the Earth

plane, but through thought patterns alone. There is organisation, it is not chaos. It is not a case of turmoil, but of
organisation, for there are arrangements, so to speak, of times of
communication one with the other. There are vast distances
between these Spheres and yet they can be bridged instantly.

The time is coming upon this Earth plane when it must be
speeded up. That does not mean to say that your life will speed
or the life upon the Earth plane will get any faster. We are
speaking of energies and of thought patterns, of wisdom's and
of a bringing together of all peoples to the understanding, as
you have already been told this earth evening, an
understanding that all peoples are equal. The realisation will
come in time that this is so. Many things have to be achieved
before that time and one of the most important that has to be
achieved is a knowledge of love one for the other and for all.
There are many upon the Earth plane who cannot conceive such
a love, it is beyond their understanding. Indeed there are many
upon this Earth plane who do not give forth love in any shape
or form. Who do not see the beauties of this Earth plane. There
are many who live their lives in a mist. It is a mist that they
have created around themselves, a mist of self love and they
find it impossible to penetrate, for indeed they do not even
know.

You are approaching the time of the anniversary of the birth
of Christ upon the Earth plane, and after that time there will be
the commencement of another earth year. When you reach this
time at the end of that birth year, many of the predictions that
have been spoken of within this Sanctuary, which have been of
truth, will have happened. There will be a parting within this
Sanctuary for you already have the understanding that this is a
Group of much value. A Group who will go forth individually
upon your own spiritual paths, bearing with you the teachings
you have received and the understandings that will be
completed by the time you go your various way. But you will
never really part, for you will always be linked together in

thought. That is as it must be. In your daily lives there will be happenings, because you are of the teachings, and there will be those sent to you, guided if you like, who you will be able to serve because of the teachings that you have received.

There will be occasions when you will find it necessary to link with one or the other of the members of this Group. For such will be the understandings between you that you will be able to draw one from the other through the power of thought. You will be able to link up, one with the other through the power of thought, it will be so. There will also be a time upon the Earth plane, around the fifth month, when you will have proof of words that have been spoken regarding the ring of fire. There are those things that must happen, but there are those things which can be averted and will be averted through the thoughts of all of those across the Earth plane who have the understanding and the awareness that through those thoughts, much can be averted. You have already been told that in the Americas there is a false prophet. His voice is already beginning to be heard and through the darkness his words and his deeds could cause much havoc in and around the area that he pleases to call his domain. You have already been advised of that which you must do in order to 'contain' within that area.

There will also be upon the Earth plane, a stilling of the voices of those who are demanding — ever demanding. They will be faced with a choice. I am speaking of course of Ireland. You are requested to send your thoughts towards that place also, for there is a desire to set brother against brother and father against son, and it must not be. You are asked to send your thoughts towards that area, that tranquillity and peace may enter the minds of men and that a dreadful calamity be averted for all time, for within that area there are but a few who are desirous of this dreadful deed.

You will be told through your means of communication that there is much excitement because there has been seen in the sky a new star or planet, whatever they will call it. There will be much excitement because it is something different. It will be a sign, a sign sent by The Creator. A sign of which all of you sitting within these Groups will have knowledge, for you are all being told. It is a sign to those who have the understanding that Mother Earth is taking action, for all Spheres and all energies are mustering. You will know then, by the sign that will be given to you, that Mother Earth is not alone in her struggle for survival. You will find much of interest, for from the words that have been spoken to you, you will recognise the different happenings and realise that indeed you have been given teachings and knowledge of truth.

There was a time upon the Earth plane that there was a complete turn around of climatic condition. There will be climatic changes once again, but gradually and not so drastically. You have already the awareness from the words that have been spoken to you, that there will be snow in places where there has never been snow before, and there will be bright sunshine where there has never been heat before. It is all part of the plan to assist the planet Earth, for the school room must be protected. It is of great value — of great value.

From the Universe I bring you the energies, that each one of you may receive that which is within. That each one of you will soon be aware of we who come to you. That individually you will know who is by your side, and individually you will hear the words of guidance and love that are spoken to you. You are indeed loved and you are indeed of value, and from the Universe these energies are brought to you.

The Creator of all things protects you with His love. It is so. It is of truth.

Energies

* * *

ABSORBING THE ENERGIES

Good evening. It is a great pleasure for me to come and speak with you, a very great pleasure. There have been times when I have stood by groups such as this, and listened to the words that have been said. I have sat in large halls and listened to the words that have been spoken by the speaker upon the platform. I have wondered just how much understanding there has been of the words that have been said.

One looks at the faces of people and one realises that they do not understand and one feels in despair, particularly when one is upon the platform speaking. How can one make those who do not understand, see the wonders that are around? What does one do? How does one bring about an understanding of all that goes on around in another world? You of course think that I am speaking of the World of Spirit, but I am not. I am speaking of the many tribes within the continent of Africa in the time that I walked the Earth plane.

How can one make people understand that there is famine and disease, that there really is cruelty beyond understanding? How do you make those people who are fat and well fed, who have good homes and everything that they desire, realise that upon the continent of Africa there are those who are starving? There are those who do not know the meaning of warmth, clothes or of food. How does one achieve help? I will tell you.

One sets about working themselves in those areas. One sets about teaching. Teaching how to grow food, how to plant seeds, how to grow things and to make use of that which is around.

I tried to stop slavery. I tried to bring about an understanding that to take babies away from their mothers and cast them into the jungle that they may die in order that the mother may be taken into slavery, was wrong. I tried to tell them. It was difficult and many would not listen to me. Even now on that continent known as Africa, although the understanding is that all are free, indeed they are not free, for the skin is still black, and although they think they are liberated, indeed they are not, they are still in slavery. A different kind of slavery, but there are still restrictions. The restrictions are within themselves, for they do not have the knowledge and they still carry with them the thinkings of the jungle.

There will have to be many teachings on that continent to bring about a freedom, for there will always be upheavals until the thinkings of the jungle are overcome. So the teachings must still go on, to try and bring an understanding to the other peoples upon the Earth plane who are well fed and clothed, that there are great sufferings in certain areas, and until these sufferings are corrected, until all are recognised as being in need of help, there will always be problems within that area. They are not being given the opportunities to prove themselves. They are still being kept in compounds, because it is said that their understanding is low. But they are not being given the teachings to improve their understanding.

I fear that there will be great calamities in that area. Oh not calamities such as you have heard, but calamities brought about by their own lack of knowledge. I fear that the jungle thinking, as I will call it without disrespect, will become uppermost and will run riot, for they are not being given the teachings or the understanding that they should be given. I was out in that jungle country as a missionary. I am still a missionary, for am I not speaking as one? I was not of any consequence, I have not a name that you will recognise, but I was permitted to come to speak to you for it is said that I would help to bring about a balance within this Sanctuary. Thank you for listening to me, it has been a pleasure for me to speak to you. God bless you.

* * * * *

This is Thomas — I have returned to explain to you that the speaker who was with you from the Universe had brought with him great energies and it was necessary that you should sit quietly in order that each one of you may absorb those energies. The little one who has just been speaking with you is one who is used to occupy you, so to speak, while you are absorbing those energies, for they are of much value to you and will help you in your progression. So I ask that you send out your love to that one, for she takes much trouble and comes with much love to you. I hope you have the understanding. God bless you.

PART THREE

That Spark Divine within us, must reflect
The Radiance of His Smile
Shedding Love's Ray into the
Darkest corner of the fight
Only from Him, can we our vessels fill,
Then bear His Light.

Chapter I

MATERIAL POSSESSIONS

G reetings my daughter, greetings to you all, this is Thomas. The time is now drawing nigh for the celebrations of the Birthday of Christ. A birthday that is celebrated in many different ways across the Earth plane. All around the Earth plane now there are groups of people who have the understanding that Jesus Christ was of great love and was upon the Earth plane to give teachings. That He was sent from Father God in order that those teachings could be given.

The legend says that the Wise Men followed a star — wise men always follow a star. And you have been told that there will be a new star within the Universe, and that this will be a sign to you. With the coming of that star there will be many happenings upon the Earth plane. For from that star there will be great energies directed to this planet. It is a star that receives energies from the Universe which are to be directed to the Earth plane. It is all part of a pattern. The light from that star will indeed be bright, for there will be tremendous energy radiating towards the Earth plane. It will be, so to speak, the lifeline for Mother Earth.

As children you were taught a nursery rhyme. There is a great deal of truth in this nursery rhyme, for the stars that are of brightness, the stars that are of diamond brightness, the stars that have many facets are of great value, even as a diamond is considered to be of great value upon the Earth plane.

> Twinkle, Twinkle, little star,
> How I wonder what you are.
> Up above the world so high,
> Like a diamond in the sky.

The facets of a diamond when properly cared for, when properly treated, when properly understood, send out multi-colours of every hue. Radiating and flashing in all directions, sending out in their way energies, bringing happiness to many and bringing out darkness in others. Other colours are always there and the energies are always there, for a diamond is indeed of the mineral kingdom.

A star too sends forth multi-colours which are not visible from the Earth plane, but which are visible through the mighty telescopes that are faced up towards the heavens to capture all those things that are within the night sky. The star sends forth much brightness, many colours — like a diamond it has many facets for it too is mineral. It is of the mineral kingdom even as a diamond and yet it is suspended up in the heavens, so to speak. But then also are all Spheres held by energies within the Universe. They are not there by accident, they are of great value and all are within the Universe to be of service, one to the other in differing ways. Whether a Sphere be within the Universe, whether it be within a physical body upon the Earth plane, all things should be of service one to the other.

Within the animal kingdom there could be complete balance. I do not say there is, for Man has interfered through the many many centuries, but the plan was that there would be complete balance. Within the animal kingdom they themselves would have brought about balance, for through the stages they would supply food, one for the other, thus keeping down the population. It is the natural way, but Man through his so–called progression; through the knowledge that he has invented — I will use that word — has brought about a multiplication in some places and complete annihilation in others.

As the Earth progressed through the evolutions that had to be, so all things that had been placed upon the Earth plane progress. For by the thinkings, by the developments, by the understandings, there should have been a balancing out and an understanding of those things which had to be done. The animal kingdom has deteriorated greatly, for there have been vast slaughters, wanton killings, unnecessary destruction. And these are still going on, and the animals upon the Earth plane are becoming smaller and smaller, for they are being squeezed out of their own environment. They adapt and they are helped in this way, but they have their rightful place upon the Earth plane and this should be respected. There are animals on many of the Spheres in the Universe. They are animal kingdoms vastly different from that upon the Earth plane, and the animals have their given place. They fulfil a function, even as you within the physical body fulfil a function.

You know that your function upon the Earth plane at this particular time is that of healers. You know that you chose to be upon the Earth plane at this time of stress, a time that was within the understanding that there would be upheavals. For Man is reaching a peak, a peak of self destruction one against the other, instead of being as brothers and living in love one with the other. He is breaking down within himself all those things that are of value.

There is a great negation upon the Earth plane. There is a quotation that "When you die you cannot take it with you," and this is true. When you pass into the World of Spirit those things which are of value upon the Earth plane are not of value to anyone in the World of Spirit except yourself. They are only of value to you. And you will find that it is those things that are surrounded with love that will be of value. The monies that are accumulated upon the Earth plane are of no value whatsoever in the World of Spirit. It is the love that you have sent forth, it is the service that you have given that are of value.

There has been a rescue, a rescue where there were two sisters. Two sisters who were reluctant to leave the Earth plane, one being held back by her stronger sister. They were earthbound because they loved the house in which they lived upon the Earth plane, and they loved the possessions that they had within it. Many of these had been handed to them by their parents of whom they were very fond, and whom they very much loved. And therefore there was a great reluctance to leave this house and its contents upon the Earth plane.

It must be remembered that when once you leave the physical body then you automatically go upon a higher vibration — one step away from the Earth plane if you are earthbound. It must be a different vibration for otherwise you would not be able to move and there would be complete chaos upon the Earth plane. Because of their devotion to this house and their reluctance to leave, they caused great disharmony between the two sisters who now live within that dwelling house. There have been other people living in this house, but they did not concern the earthbound sisters so much as the two present sisters, for now it was like four ladies living in the same house, so to speak, and they were all very similar in disposition.

There had to be a rescue and there was a rescue, a word that is used upon the Earth plane. We say, 'a guiding through'. They were guided through by the love that was sent forth and they are now in a house in the World of Spirit which is a replica of the one they loved so dearly, and the furniture within is as they had. It is a transition period, it is a time of calming, it is a time of understanding and of rest. From there they will go forward to work and they will of course progress along their spiritual path.

I tell you this that you may have the understanding of the difference between the possessions which are acquired through greed and through negation and the possessions that are acquired through the love that you send out to somebody else.

It is those possessions that are with you in the World of Spirit in the time of transition.

I will close now for there is one of great value who will speak with you. May the Love and the Light of Father God be with you all at all times. May His protection surround you and indeed it does. God bless you, God bless you all.

* * * * *

Hello, I've come to speak to you because I want you to know that although on the Earth plane I was considered silly and frivolous, I had great spiritual awareness which nobody understood.

I took my own life because although I was surrounded with all luxuries, I was so unhappy. Possessions mean nothing if you are just empty within, for nobody understands what you are trying to say and all they want you to do is stand around looking pretty. The intellectual capabilities are ignored, and although my husband was a man of great intellectual ability, he did not understand me. He did not try to understand me.

There has been a long time of waiting, but now I am allowed to come and speak to groups, and distance means nothing when you are in spirit. We are told where we may go to speak, for we are told that those to whom we will speak will have an understanding. I do not know your names, I don't know whether you know mine, but I was called Marilyn Monroe when I was in pictures, when I was in the film industry. That was not my real name of course.

It is a place of very high tensions and the film industry can tear you to pieces, for all the time you are at the mercy of others really. When you are making a film you have to follow the instructions of the Director, and there are many things that go wrong and there are many things that you would like to do differently. But you are not allowed to and this builds up within you a frustration.

When I was filming I would go home like a wet rag and the tensions would build up and there was no real outlet, and so you give vent by screaming, and that is what I did. It was just a way of letting go, of releasing the safety valve really. The magazines would show me lying at ease here there and everywhere, but it was really not like that. It seemed as if we just lazed around, but for those pictures to be in the magazines, it was a case of an appointment at a certain time, of being once again told to do that or do the other. All in the name of publicity. All in order that the film would be widely circulated.

If only I could have spoken freely to someone. I did have a friend to whom I could speak, but he was killed in a car crash, and that really was my death too. When you see film stars now they have a much more relaxed life, for there are not so many pressures. There are pressures of course and things build up during the making of a film, particularly when on location. But now there are long periods of holiday or rest, and so things are not so bad. But you can tell those who are frustrated, for they all take to drugs one way or another, and those who lead a balanced life are those who are the happy ones.

Making a lot of money does not really count. It is better to have a life of true balance, of true understanding and of truth. I hope I haven't bored you. Good-bye.

Chapter II

THE AGE OF MOSES

With the palms of my hands uppermost to show that I come in friendship, I greet you. I come to speak with you, it is my pleasure so to do. I come to tell you of some of those things which are of the past and yet are teachings of the present and for the future. I come to speak of ancient times. I come to speak of times before the Nazarene walked upon the Earth plane. I come to tell you of the times of Moses, for it was in those times that there were great upheavals and wickedness in the minds of men, even as there is today upon the Earth plane.

In the times of Moses there was a great driving out of people from their dwelling places by those of great strength, who moved in to take away that which belonged to others. In those times also there was great spiritual knowledge and awareness. There were great writings, there were famines. But there was one who stood forth as a mighty leader. He was guided by a voice above, a voice which thundered in his ears at times, and which told him of those things which had to be completed if there was to be a future upon the Earth plane for Man. And even now as then there is the voice that thunders, that there will be destruction upon the Earth plane, destruction of Man. But those were ancient times, the times of Moses and yet there has been no destruction, not complete destruction as was foretold then. There will not be complete destruction for the time is not right.

In the time of Moses voices were lifted on high to the mighty God. Voices must once again be lifted on high to the mighty God, for through the power of prayer as then so now. I say to you the power of prayer will bring about seeming miracles. I say to you that through the ages there have always been those groups around the Earth plane who have knelt together and prayed. There are still those places where lives are given up completely to a discipline of complete prayer.

Jesus the Nazarene walked upon the Earth plane spanning the time when it was needed, when spiritual awareness was needed. He came to bring the teachings that were necessary at that time. He came to bring the teachings that have been carried through all these years. And only now is there a true sweeping out, I will say, an expansion of that knowledge. It is through that expansion that Man will enter a new phase. The next phase of progression.

There is a great escalation in the knowledge that is now being received by those upon the Earth plane within a physical body, from those who work within the World of Spirit. There is a great upsurge, and within the next two decades upon the Earth plane there will be a greater awareness spreading all around the Earth plane than there has been since Christ was upon the Earth. There is to be a great escalation and you will become aware of this by those to whom you speak; those that you meet; those things that you observe and those things that are written. You will notice that there is an acceptance of things that have not been accepted by many people.

Within the next two decades there will be great changes in the understandings that are given forth from the Churches on the Earth plane, whatever denomination, whatever understanding they may have at the present time. There will be a great merging together. It is being guided thus for there are those who are returning to the Earth plane who will enter the Churches as teachers and through their words will come about this great awareness and acceptance. An understanding of things which have not been accepted, of things which have been denied and of things that have been said to cause fear, in order to keep the understanding of those peoples who attend, to a level almost amounting to fear. That is to go. Within the next two decades there will be many changes. There will be changes upon the face of Mother Earth, but most important will be the changes within the minds of Man, with the understanding and the acceptance of those things, that because of fear are not understood at the moment. There is to be a great sharing of knowledge.

There will also become known some of the secrets of the times of Moses, for there is a linking now with that time. There will be discovered ancient documents. Documents of stone upon which the words of ancient times are written. There are three people upon the Earth plane who will be brought together to help to decipher these writings. They are people who have returned to a physical body who have the knowledge within; who have the interest and much teaching and wisdom of these ancient times. They will be brought together to decipher the writings upon stone, for they were the documents of those times.

There is also to be found within the deserts a temple. Not the hidden Temple of [1]Isis, for the time is not right for that to be discovered. The secrets that are there are for a future time. But there will be discovered, through the rushing of water, a building that has been buried beneath the safety of the sands. And within that building there will be found teachings for this present time upon the Earth plane. Remember it will be through the rushing of water.

---

[1]Isis — (Egyptian mythology) Sister and wife of OSIRIS, and mother of HORUS, regarded as a nature — goddess.

There is also to be some great concern, for there are to be reports all around the Earth plane of the sightings of unidentified flying objects, as they are known upon the Earth plane. There will be rumours of enemy approach from other planets and in some instances, in a certain part of the Earth plane, there will be fear and indeed panic. It is regretted but it is through ignorance that this will be caused. These unidentified objects come in peace to asses the energies that are flowing around the Earth Plane, for there have been reports to other spheres that the atmosphere around the Earth plane is becoming poisoned.

There have been reports that the Sun's rays will not be able to penetrate to the Earth plane and that all upon the planet will die because of this. It is made up in the minds of men, it is not as written. Never will the Earth plane be allowed to be encased with an atmosphere so thick that it will keep away the rays of the Sun, It will not be allowed. It will always be on the move and ever broken, until Man learns that through his folly and ignorance he can cause harm but not destruction. The damage that he will do will be within comparatively small areas.

I say to you my children that, these things that are foretold, that I say to you, are of truth. Remember, the unidentified objects that will be seen and reported from all parts of the Earth plane in quick succession will not be an invading enemy force from another Sphere, but friends who come to help to assess. To take away information to other Spheres where the energy forces will be directed through the star that you have already been told about. To act as a lifeline for Mother earth at a time when the balance will need that extra energy. At the time that Moses was upon the Earth plane there was a time also when the balance of Mother Earth was affected. As I have said there is a similarity one with the other.

Around you all within this Sanctuary there is a silver light. It is an energy which will help you to penetrate a vibration. It is an energy that will help you in your spiritual knowledge. It will be absorbed through the nerve centres of your spine, to be dispersed round your physical body, to enter the spiritual centres, to strengthen and enliven. It is the gift I bring to you from the all loving, all seeing, all compassionate God.

I bring you love and His Blessings to each one of you.

Chapter III

SPIRITUAL TEACHING
TEACHING THE YOUNG

G ood evening. I've spoke to you before, [1]Baden–Powell is the name. I spoke to you before regarding the children, the young ones that you would have within your Church. They will come you know, they are increasing. They will come and it will be necessary in time for you to arrange teachings for these young ones. It is very necessary that they have the correct teachings and are not fed with what I will term as bogey stories.

Children have very vivid imaginations and it is with that in mind, always in mind, that you should speak to them. For a few words carelessly spoken can set up within that vivid imagination all sorts of weird and wonderful things. You will find that a lot of the children that come to the Church will already have knowledge of the World of Spirit, for that is the way it is developing. That is the way it has to be because that is the only way that there can be a true knowledge of service one to the other — a spreading of the love.

It's when children share one with the other, unselfishly and lovingly, in the early stages of their life that should be nurtured,

---

[1]Baden-Powell — Robert Stephenson Smyth, 1st Baron Baden-Powell of Gilwell (1857-1941) English Soldier; defended Mafeking, 1900: founded the Boy Scout organisation, 1908.

for that is the way they must be all their lives. Not to give away all things that they hold dear of course, but to share one with the other, a giving and a taking, a helping hand etc. It has been said and it is the plan within many of the churches, that there is an afternoon service held, when parents are encouraged to take their children. The clairvoyance that the adults have is of no interest to children. They do not understand, they become fidgety and that is the time when they could have their own teachings on a level that they can understand. In a gentle manner, something to absorb them; something to interest them; something that they will remember; something for them. That is a good plan and it is one that I suggest you bear in mind.

The children will look forward to going down to your Sanctuary. It will be their play room or school room or whatever you like to call it. They will enjoy going down and listening to stories or whatever you plan to do. But whatever you plan to do, it must be a teaching for them on the level that they understand. There is no need on a hot summers day for them to be confined within the four walls, for you have a garden and it can be used, and it should be used. And if there are complaints from those within the Church because of the children's voices, they must be told that there is happiness in the laughter of a child, and it is something that is to be. But of course as you understand, the children's parents will be there and they will not object.

There is coming a time now when there is to be a change round in the churches, in the understanding, in the way the service is conducted. It is gradually being introduced and it is to be the new way. But of course as with most things it has to be done slowly and gradually. There should be services held from time to time with no clairvoyance, but where afterwards there could be a discussion where you have a speaker, or where you have a medium. One who is of true value, who will give an address. The service will continue afterwards and then close and then there could be a discussion of the address or of spiritual matters. It would be a change and it is something that will happen, for it is already being introduced in a few places.

It is an entirely new concept and it will remove, at times, those who come seeking nothing but clairvoyance. It will give those who are seeking knowledge and opportunity, an opportunity which at the moment is not given to them in a lot of churches. It is an opportunity, they are within the Church, they have already made the journey to the Church and they have free will to get up and leave if they wish to, but you will find that many will stay and they can then have teachings from the medium. Mediums who are now being trained to have knowledge. Mediums who themselves are seeking knowledge, who are not content just to stand and give clairvoyance, but who wish also to give teachings.

It is something which will be of great value if you look upon it over a period of time − a gradual introducing, and there will be acceptance. It will mean of course a longer Sunday evening if you have the meeting on a Sunday, if you hold the service on a Sunday. But it does not always have to be on a Sunday. There are other days in the week when services can be held in that manner. It is a good thing too, to revert back to the children to give them an opportunity to have a discussion group. You could do this on an occasion when they are taken away from the clairvoyance, and with skill you can get the children talking about their own experiences. Have they seen fairies? Do they have a little friend that they play with who nobody else can see? This sort of thing. And you will be surprised at the number of children who speaking in truth, really do have these experiences. And because they are with other children and they all have the understanding, it is something that they know and not something that they think or imagine.

The library within the Church could be increased to include a small modest children's section. Though there are books there for children, there are many more upon the market that have been written for children with spiritual knowledge, and a modest library could be arranged, to which the children could go and select their own books, apart from the books that are for the other members. There should be more knowledge passed from one church to another. There should be more communication between one church and another. This does happen in some areas, but it would be nice to link your Church up with a church perhaps in another area of the country. Not within your town but in another area where you could interchange ideas and visits and get to know each other.

There are many ideas that other people have within their churches which could be used in many places. There will come a time when people will enquire from you and ask to come and see your Church. To see what you do, how you teach the children, and it could be made into a very pleasant and social occasion. All social occasions do not have to be within your own Church, for your own members. Expand — open up your arms and welcome in love those who have the same ideas and the same knowledge as you. Link up within your own country and then link up across the World.

I was surprised how quickly my Scout movement spread around the World. Those who came for teachings, who came to have the understanding of how the Scout movement commenced, the ideas, the thought behind it, went away and lit their own camp fires. And it spread around the Earth plane into some very remote places, but it was very worthwhile. And so will the knowledge that you have. And so can you send forth those to light their own camp fires, so to speak. It can be done, indeed there is one already within the Church — I must correct that and say two, for they are husband and wife — who are going to New Zealand. They will take the knowledge and the love that they have had within your Church with them to that far off land, and those things that they have learned they will talk about. And it is envisaged, although they are as yet unaware of it, that they will light a camp fire in New Zealand, and many more could do the same.

Well I have enjoyed speaking with you and I'll go now. God bless you all.

* * * * *

I bring you greetings. I come from Naples, a place of much beauty, a place of much misery, a place wherein there is much evil. A place where small children are treated as rats who live within the sewers. A place where a child is left in the gutter to fend for itself, even as the sewer rats. At least their mothers teach them how to fend for themselves, but a child is helpless until it learns to follow others. The rich pass by in their carriages and if a horse kicks a child it matters little, for that is how they are in Naples. It is a place where there is much pleasure where those who can afford, play all day and night. They over dress and over feed and would rather give to the pigs that which could feed a hundred children.

I was one of the nuns in the Convent upon the boundaries of the slums of Naples. I was given the proud name of Camellia, but a camellia within that place would have been sadly lost. I was appalled when I saw the children, for I came from a family who lived in a palace, who had plenty, who played all day and all night. It was while driving through the streets of Naples in my father's carriage that a horse reared and kicked a child and the horse man whipped the horses on. I stopped him and went back to the child who was covered in blood. He was not dead but mortally wounded. I sat in the filth and tried to comfort him and I heard another child say, "He is going to Heaven, an Angel is holding him in her arms." I realised that I was being called an Angel, and it was that incident that sent a Camellia to the slums of Naples to do that which could be done.

I became a nun, a nun who used to go forth to collect the children, to bring them back to the Convent to make sure that they were washed and clothed and fed. To give them an understanding that God loved all His children. Because I lived in a palace once, there were friends who had plenty that I turned to for help, and the food from their tables that was not required, was sent to the Convent. Some of the children in that dreadful place were taught to be clean, to be honest, to speak in truth, and to earn an honest living. But how small were the numbers compared to those who were always arriving. Who would turn up and ask if they could come too. Who wanted to be warm, who wanted to be loved.

There are many such children in Naples, and now I know there are many such children in the World. The Earth plane is full of such children. Spare a thought for them, send forth your love for them, help to uplift them. It will help, if not in a material way, it will help more than you realise. Remember the children of Naples. Remember the children everywhere who are hungry and unloved, for it is the children who must have the teachings. And if they are allowed to live as rats in a sewer, how can they receive the teachings that must be given, to bring about that which must be brought about upon this Earth plane.

I consider it an honour that I have been allowed to join you in this place. It is a Sanctuary, indeed it is a Sanctuary from which the light can be seen for great distances, and to which are drawn those who need its upliftment. Arrivederci.

Spiritual Teaching

* * *

PAUL

Greetings, greetings to you all, I have spoken to you before, my name is Paul. This is a time upon the Earth plane of great rejoicing. A great rejoicing for those who call themselves Christians, for they follow the teachings of Christ the great Christos. Teachings of wisdom, teachings which brought the understandings and the realisations that within each one upon the Earth plane there were the same gifts that He had. For He was of The Creator as you are also, and so were all men who went before him. But His teachings were the teachings that were visual — spiritual but also visual. Those who could not see, could see after He had sent towards them thoughts of love and healing.

He did not always need to touch, but He had the understandings of those who needed the assurance of caressing fingers. It was commonplace for Him to be sent a messenger stating that there was one very ill, or one who had indeed a physical body that was cold. He would make for that place and there would be immediately a return to life within that physical body. A return to health within that physical body, for that which was diseased was made whole.

He would set forth and stand upon a hillock or climb a mountain to give His teachings to the multitudes who followed Him. The words that He spoke were of wisdom, for they were teachings that all could understand according to their various understandings. After He had left there would be discussions amongst those who had listened to His words, and one would say, "Wasn't that wonderful, He said such and such a thing." "Oh no!" another would say, "You misunderstood, He said such and such a thing." And then there would be gatherings of people all discussing the words He had spoken. One would add their part and another their part, and they marvelled at the different understandings of the very same words.

There was great value in these groups who were left behind to discuss the words He had spoken, and they received words of wisdom and great teachings. Teachings which when they went their various way, they in their turn were able to impart to those who would listen. It is very important to discuss and not to just walk away. He would enter the house of one or the other who would invite Him in to give Him food, and to give Him warmth as He slept. But He never left without words of wisdom being imparted; deeds of healing if they were needed; compassion and above all love. He loved His fellow men, but remember He was within a physical body that suffered tiredness. He had a conscious mind that suffered anguish and doubt.

At times He felt completely lost, for He did not know which way to turn. He said that by thought, mountains could be moved. And so they can, for there are many mountains in your lives upon the physical plane, mountains that seem insurmountable. But you know that you must go over the top, there is no way round. And you find that you have been to the top and you have found your way down the other side and that the mountain is now behind you, for you moved it. And so did He. There is a difference. The difference being that Jesus the Nazarene knew His path. Knew the understandings, knew what had to be achieved.

You in your physical bodies at this time upon the Earth plane, have had to wait for some considerable time before you began to even have an awakening. But that does not mean to say that you will not achieve much, for the awareness has been withheld from you until the time was right. That time is now right for you, and the time is right also for Mother Earth to whom you are linked very closely. It is the awakening that you are now receiving, the understandings that are coming forth, the knowledge that you are gaining that will be utilised in the way that it should be utilised. And you will achieve much. Perhaps at this moment sitting within this Sanctuary you cannot understand the true values, but in ten years time your thinkings will not be as they are now. You will have progressed much in your knowledge and you will also have progressed much with the spiritual abilities that are yours.

Within the next ten years upon the Earth plane there will be many changes, great changes within the minds of men. Changes which you will witness and at which you will rejoice. There is to be a great cleansing for all those who are Christians. Those who follow the Nazarene, who understand the teachings. And the wisdoms that were of His time will find a great upsurge. There will be many caught up who do not have the awareness, but you have. You will witness many who will come forward with great spiritual gifts, surpassing those which have been witnessed in recent Earth years since the time of Christ. You will find that within yourselves you will begin to receive the gift of energies from the Universe. Energies that will uplift you as you sit in meditation. Energies which will sustain you. And you will yourselves see many things, for the time is coming when your own teachings will be given to each one of you during your times of meditation, when it is to be a time of much progression.

There are many babies being born upon the Earth plane at this time who have the wisdoms and who will be remarkable. It will be said their intelligence is very high for they will learn quickly and they will see those in spirit who will be near to them. They are the ones who will carry forward the next stage upon the Earth plane, the next stage of development for all those who are in a physical body. The next stage which will lead towards the race of [1]Tan, for the race of Tan will be highly intelligent. The race of Tan will have the spiritual awareness and will be using the thought patterns constructively and not destructively as now.

And so the babies that are now being born upon the Earth plane are of great intelligence and great wisdoms. Listen to the words that they will speak as small children and you will realise the wisdoms that are within. You will find yourself saying, "What a wise thing for a young child to say." Take note my friends, it will be so, and to you it will be proof and an indication that these words you have listened to this Earth night are indeed of truth.

The teachings of the Christos are spreading across the Earth plane as a forest fire spreads when the wood is dry. It will spread more within the next ten years across the Earth plane than it has done in the last two thousand years, for Man will not be held down by fear. Man will not let the Gospels be misused, for the intelligence of Man is not to be continually held down by those who seek to dominate. There will be an upsurge and you will witness it, and you will have the understandings. Remember the star.

God's Blessings be yours, Shalom.

---

[1]Tan — Brown colour of tan; bronzed colour of skin that has been exposed to sun or weather. Of the colour of tan or tanned leather, yellowish or reddish brown.

Spiritual Teaching

* * *

BEATRIX POTTER

Good evening. I don't quite know how to start. When I was upon the Earth plane I used to write books and paint pictures. I lived in the Lake District and it was there that I wrote my books. I wrote under the name of Beatrix Potter.

I come to you for you have young children, grandchildren, I beg your pardon. I just come to say, Oh dear, it sounds rather as if I'm going to force my ideas upon you, but please don't take it like that. I come to say to you that your grandchildren can learn a lot about the World of Spirit through the books and through the way that you speak. For you have already been told that the young children that are born now upon the earth plane already have spiritual awareness well to the fore.

Through talking to them about fairies and animals; animals who have homes and lead ordinary lives, a life that a child can understand; you bring to them an understanding that there is ordinary living in the World of Spirit, for the fairies become reality and the little ones can actually see them. They will see an animal and immediately associate it with that which has been said to them.

It is essential that the young ones are understood when they talk about their *friends* that they play with, when they sit upon the floor talking to someone. It is important that although **you** cannot see them, you accept that which the child is telling you and draw into your own life that which the child sees. So that when you are told that they are playing with a little girl of such and such a name, or by a little boy of such and such a name, you will accept that he or she goes with you. It is very essential that that which is of the Spirit World is accepted by the child in the early stages.

I used to see my little animals that I wrote about. They were very very real to me. Their lives and the happenings in their lives helped me a great deal in times of stress. I am very pleased that I had them with me. I am very pleased that I was able to write about them, in order that the little children can also join in that world of fantasy, which isn't really fantasy.

Good-bye and God bless you.

Spiritual Teaching

* * *

MESSENGERS OF GOD

Minarets against the skyline — between them and where I stand, the sandy wastes. Above the sun shines down relentlessly upon that desolate place. But let us soar upwards, ever upwards towards the Sun. And suddenly it is cool, it is pleasant. It is life within life, within life. We speed beyond the Sun to that secret place that is not seen from the Earth plane. That place wherein much activity takes place. That place of great strength and energy in which those who control such matters do the work that must be done.

Look down upon the Earth plane, a tiny speck below. It looks very small and very insignificant, but you know that upon that speck live many who you love. There are many there who need that which is sent from the secret place. The Universe is beyond mans vision in its vastness. For within the Universe there are Spheres which have not been seen by man. But there are some things which have been seen by those who set forth from the Earth plane upon exploration, men of intellect and men of wisdom, for as they have sped through the Universe circling the Earth plane, there has been one of your space vessels that ventured off course and they saw something of the wonders of the Universe. They were visited by those from the Universe who wished to encounter them. They have seen and spoken to those from another Sphere, those who they would say were Messengers of God. They do not speak of those things that they saw, but one day one will disclose that which they encountered. But they have realised the magnitude of God.

In the secret place there is much knowledge, and there is much work ahead to bring the Sphere known as the Earth plane to a higher vibration. To stop it from complete destruction, a destruction which will happen eventually. But there is much to be accomplished before that time, which will be as far in the distance as in the past. Man upon the Earth plane brings about his own destruction through the way that he thinks. Man upon the Earth plane does not learn the lessons that are sent to him through the millenniums of time, but just continues each Earth life without progressing very far in his knowledge of himself. He looks to his neighbour too much and not to himself.

You yourselves, each one of you are a Universe within your-self. You are all things. And until you understand yourselves you cannot understand that which happens in the Universe, apart from the tiny speck of information that is passed to you. You have no conception of the Universe. To you it is but a word, and yet within the Universe there is everything. From in that secret place at this time there is much energy being distributed around the Earth plane, to bring about a buoyancy. A buoyancy which must be, for the Earth plane is the heaviest Sphere, it is as of lead compared to the other spheres.

Oh yes there is life on the other spheres, life which is not visible to those machines that are sent forth, those toys of information. For they are but toys, toys into which are fed the information that is allowed to return to the Earth plane, nothing more. For upon the Spheres there is life, but a very different life from that upon the Earth plane, for those who people the Spheres are of light. They have progressed and earned their place upon those Spheres, all of which fulfil their own individual contribution, if you like, to the workings within the Universe. When man upon the Earth plane looks to himself, to his own thinking, to his own thoughts, and realises that he concentrates upon himself, upon those who are near to him and does not expand his thought patterns to envelop and embrace, to uplift, he will realise that there is much that can be done.

There is much that will be done from that secret place, the minarets across the skyline in the distance. The desert waste between will change. For that desert waste will become fertile and the sands of the desert will run with water. And with the flowing of the water will also flow understandings and a cleansing, for there will be those places which are fertile. Those places of plenty, plenty which is not shared, plenty which is selfishly held to a comparative few, will turn as dust. For those who have little will have plenty and those who have plenty will know what it is to have little, and thus there will come about a balancing. Thus there will come about a realisation. Thus there will come about a unity.

Think upon these words. They are not entirely as they seem. Think upon them and it could be that the true understanding will be given to you, for within yourselves you know the truth. Remember when you look at the Sun above, remember to look beyond to that secret place wherein there is much work, much planning, to avert that which could be. The Universe waits to lift the Earth plane, you can help.

Spiritual Teaching

* * *

CONAN DOYLE

My name is Doyle, I've spoken to you before, greetings. The time is coming when once again my words will be spoken from a platform. For it is time that teachings were given — that a few people were shaken up. I did quite a bit of that and caused quite a lot of consternation in some circles. Thought I was a crank, but no, from tiny acorns big oaks do grow. You do I am sure know this saying.

There are a lot of books written now, some of them are good and some of them are rubbish, for they speak only of those with ego. But some of them are of great value for they speak of experiences that many encounter and hold as secrets within because they do not understand what is happening, and are afraid to tell anyone. And by reading a book of experiences by somebody else it makes them feel better and gives them a greater understanding.

Books are of great value, for they can be read at times of quietness. And the words are imprinted upon the mind to be mulled over at various times; to be discussed with others; to be argued about and debated upon. I understand that one of you within this group will at a later time write a book. It will be a book of value. It will be a book that many will read, for it will be culled in simple language. Language that all can understand and yet not trite so that it is discarded.

It will be a book that young and old will be able to read. It will be a book that learned and ignorant can read and understand. It will be a book of much value. I propose to write another book, using of course one in a physical body. It will have volume one and two. It will be much discussed and written about. It will be argued about. But my voice **will** be heard from platforms once again, for now is the time of spiritual awareness. And now is the time that those things which would not have been accepted in the past, will now be accepted. And in three or four Earth years you will remember my words that I am speaking to you now, for there will be much publicity and you will remember, for you had, so to speak, an advance notice.

I am telling you this in order that you will remember and you will acknowledge the truth that is being spoken to you. It is nice to speak to you once again. Good evening.

Spiritual Teaching

* * *

ABRAHAM

Greetings. The [1]Children of Israel were in torment when in the land of Egypt, for they were not wanted. They were but slaves, not understood. They were waiting for One to come, the [2]Messiah they called him. They would beat their chests and wail at their ceremonies, but it was not quite as it seemed. It was considered that they were slightly mad. But no, all they were doing was a form of chanting to lift the vibrations, that those of the World of Spirit who had understanding could communicate. It was as simple as that, because the Elders were in spirit communication.

There came the time when they set forth on a journey which was guided, a journey which they followed faithfully. Those who were the leaders not knowing where they were going, but realising that they were being given hope. There were times when they were attacked. Many were killed, and there were many graves of men, women and children, and there was much heartbreak. But of course that was only a physical loss, for even

---

[1]Children of Israel — Hebrew nation or people traditionally descended from Jacob, whose 12 sons became founders of the 12 tribes. Israel was the name given to Jacob after he had wrestled with the angel (Genesis 32: 28) [And he said, Thy name shall be called no more Jacob, but Israel: for as a prince hast thou power with God and with men, and hast prevailed.]

[2]Messiah — In Old Testament, prophetic writings, the promised deliverer of the Jews; in Christian doctrine, Jesus Christ, regarded as this deliverer.

287

those who were murdered continued on the journey in spirit form, in order to be close to those they loved, to uplift them at times of despondency.

It has ever been thus with the Jews, for they are looking for a Messiah. A Messiah who is with them. A Messiah who is all around, and a Messiah who will attend the Earth plane at a time when all have understanding. He will come at a time when He will be very much needed, a time when the awareness has spread and is understood and recognised. However He will not be for the Jews alone, but for all peoples upon the Earth plane.

The Jews at the present time are fighting to establish that which is really their right *(The State of Israel)*. They are fighting to establish their right to life upon the Earth plane. They are fighting to establish a place where–in, so to speak, their roots will stay. There is much hatred directed towards the Jews. There always has been hatred towards the Jews, for their ancient religion has not been understood and their customs have been ridiculed. Why is it so? Why are they so different from others who have customs interlaced with their beliefs? Why did the Germans, a certain section, endeavour to wipe out the Jews that crossed their paths? Why were there such massacres? It solved nothing for the Germans, it solved nothing for the Romans. The answer is not to destroy; the answer is to love.

The Jews themselves are at fault, for they see no further than the boundaries they have set up. They endeavour to build around themselves a wall behind which they can hide, if you like. It is an inbred thing, it is natural, for handed down through the generations has been the knowledge of the sound of the whip, the cry of anguish. And it will remain so until it is learned that love must be sent forth. Not just for each one of your own coloured skin or understanding, but to all around the Earth plane.

The Jews are protecting that which they have now been given. There is much hatred directed towards them, as there has always been. They know the meaning of privation, they know the meaning of hard work, but they have not learned to trust. Can you blame them? For within them are generations upon generations upon generations of thought patterns. Yes you can say that they are spirit within a physical body and when they are freed and leave the physical body behind, if that of reincarnation that has been told us is of truth, then do they return as Jews in another physical body or do they go on to another country, another tribe, another belief? No, there are those who are in the physical body at this time who are called Jews who are of great wisdom. Who will go forward to another dimension, from whence they can assist those who are in a physical body and who are called Jews.

There are many many Jews who are of great wisdom, and they will return to the Earth plane to walk side by side with those in a physical body — to advise and to impart the wisdoms and knowledge that they have learned. It will be that in time each one of, you within this sanctuary will be given the name of one whom you call a guide. One who will come to walk side by side with you. One who will help to impart greater wisdoms, and the name will be that of a Jew. Each one of you in time will be aware of this, and you will know the significance. The significance that your teachings, your advice, guidance as you call it, will be of great spiritual value to you and to those with whom you communicate. It will be thus.

For your knowledge, my name is [3]Abraham. God's Blessings be with you.

3Abraham — Hebrew patriarch, from whom all Jews trace their descent (Genesis 11: 25-27: 12).

Chapter IV

PRAYER
PRAYERS FOR PEACE

G reetings my daughter, greetings to you all. The next time you sit within this little Sanctuary will be after the anniversary of the birth of Christ, and during that period there will be much merriment, much laughter and a bringing together of friends and family and that is good. But in many parts of the Earth plane there will be no such celebrations at this time, for there is not the awareness. Their celebrations are upon another day, upon another time. But they too feast and bring together families and friends in happiness. What a pity it is that the bringing together does not go on at all times during an Earth year. What a pity that at other times there is disharmony amongst friends and families, a disruption of the harmonious link.

There is time now upon the Earth plane of much looking forward to the birthday celebrations of the Christos. Symbolic of course, but nevertheless reality. Reality of a wonderful legend, reality of the beginning. For was not the beginning the following of a star by three wise men? It is this which is ongoing, the following of a star, the progression, the creation. And so it will be in the future, for the star that is to appear will be followed. It will be of great wonderment, for with it will come many changes upon the Earth Plane. Changes upon the

Earth's surface, changes within the waters and changes within the minds of men.

It will not matter what colour, what creed or where they are upon the Earth plane, there will be a bringing together of all peoples. For is not the Earth plane becoming smaller and smaller? Not physically but through the development of those machines which carry Man from one place to the other at great speed, tearing through the atmosphere, in some cases causing havoc. But they are part of the progression upon the Earth plane as it is now.

It had to be, this bringing together of those peoples of various colours, of various creeds. These pockets of individuality, so to speak, had to be opened up; there had to be a mingling. There had to be travelling from one land to another and there had to be changes in the colours of the skin, for the time is coming when all men will be of one colour. The characteristics of the features will vary too, will alter, and there will be a bringing together of the understandings and Man will realise that all things lead to The Creator.

If one imagines, and this is but imaginary, if one imagines a great Being above the Earth plane, with many many millions of strings leading down to each physical body upon the Earth plane, one would realise that all are from the same source; all are equal. That it has been because of their location upon the Earth plane that the colour of the skin has varied. There was at one time a bringing together of peoples from several Spheres, who agreed to settle upon the Earth plane to bring about habitation. And from those few people in their various allotted places upon the Earth plane there is now the population that you know.

A few years ago there was upon the Earth plane what was called a physical explosion because of the many babies that were born, because of the many souls who returned to the Earth plane. Many of them were young souls who have now developed to the degree that was required for that which must be achieved in the future of this planet. Conditions upon the Earth plane are vastly different from any other Sphere in the Universe, and therefore there has to be a preparation.

There has to be a growing through the various stages of education. I will use that word, for you already have the knowledge that the Earth plane is as a school room where one learns to lose those things that are a complete waste of time. Those things which lead to wars, one with the other; hate, envy, greed, selfishness, complete lack of consideration for your fellow man. A destroying destruction which could cause the annihilation of the planet Earth. But this I hasten to say will not be allowed.

There could be vast destruction and alterations of Mother Earth through those things which have been devised and which are misused knowledge. There could be the destruction of many thousands of people upon the Earth plane, and there could be a slow and painful crawling back to the realities that are now upon the Earth plane. To the realities that all are brothers. There are many many thousands of people upon the Earth plane who in their various tongues are sending forth prayers for peace upon the Earth plane. For peace amongst men, peace amongst countries; for peaceful understandings. These prayers are ever increasing, for there are many who just sit quietly by themselves within their room praying for peace. Many pray simply for peace of mind for themselves, but it is all part of a great calming. It is all part of a reduction of vibration. It is all part of the desire of Man.

There must not be disharmony upon the Earth plane. There must not be those who feel that they have the authority and the right to dominate others, for by their domination they will destroy themselves. Free will is not interfered with, but thoughts of darkness build up into a mighty barrier. A barrier which is as nothing against the light, and a barrier which will be dispersed. And according to the Tenfold Law, so it will be returned to those who have erected these thoughts of darkness.

I ask you to never forget in your daily lives to send forth a prayer for peace upon the Earth plane. The prayer that links up with the light and the love for Mother Earth, one is for the Planet and the other is for the minds of men.

May the love and the light of Father God be with you all at all times, and indeed it is. God bless you, God bless you all.

PRAYER

* * *

THE VALUE OF PRAYER

Greetings my daughter, this is Thomas. Greetings to you all. And so we come to the fortieth of these Group meetings. Meetings during which you have had teachings of great value. Teachings which will be passed on to those with whom you come in contact. Teachings which one day will be put into a book so that all may read. They will be chronicled just as they happened, and many will read. It will be thus.

There are many upon the Earth plane at the present time who call this a sick world. Sick because of the thoughts within the minds of men. Thoughts which are uppermost at the present time, always centred on thoughts of killing, of destruction. In Ireland there are a minority who think nothing of taking lives. In the tinder box there are those who think nothing of taking lives. But in this country of yours and all around the Earth plane there do not have to be wars, for people to take the lives of others. It is a fact, a very sad fact that with each life that they take, they put themselves back further along the spiritual path.

They do not go round in a circle as do those who do not do those things which are intended. They do not walk side by side with spirit as is intended, particularly when they have an awareness. All upon the Earth plane come to the fork in the road, and there are occasions when the wrong road is taken, but

294

it simply leads back in a circle. Round you go until you come back to the same place. But those who take lives because they have no respect for humanity, go backwards along their spiritual path — backwards ever backwards. They do not go off in a circle for they do not come back to the same spot. It means that their progression is seriously retarded, and it means that some will go back and destroy several lives of progression.

Within each one of them there is a spirit, a conscious mind and a spirit mind, and within the conscious mind they absorb all the vibrations of darkness. And although the spirit within cries out, no heed is taken until the time for reckoning. A reckoning which takes place sometimes when there is still a physical body, at other times when the physical body has been discarded. It is a great pity, for the life that they have chosen, the task that they have chosen on the Earth plane this time is a time of destruction for themselves. For they heed not those who walk with them. They heed not the warnings, because the ego envelops and smothers.

It is those who have experienced an injustice who very often decide to take toll of mankind around them, whether innocent or otherwise. The incident no matter how small, is blown up. It could be that perhaps they have been badly treated, bullied I will say, and so they take out their spite on mankind. Mostly the injustice is within their own mind, and very often it is this which leads them along the wrong path. For they seek to dominate, to get one better, and it is such a waste of time.

The realisation is being given to many people upon the Earth plane now, the realisation of the value of thought and the value of prayer. There is much value, of course, in loving thoughts that are sent out, and so loving thoughts must be sent out to those of darkness, to try to lift them clear of that which is dragging them down. Those who are seeking power to dominate their fellow men are also of darkness, and your loving thoughts should be sent towards them, to ask that they may be cleansed; that their thoughts may be for the good of their fellow

Man, their countrymen. Not for their own gain. Not because they want to strut around giving orders and dominating, but because they want to help their fellow countrymen, they want to bring about a better understanding with all men. Send thoughts to those people and lift them above the darkness, and a spiritual understanding will be given to them.

Within the Great Pyramid there is a secret chamber. A chamber of much power, much energy, where wise men of old would direct the energies that were within that place to control many things upon the Earth plane at that time. There were chambers of prayer, as within the Cathedrals, as within the Churches, as within the Sanctuaries, the Monasteries, the Convents, the Temples. Much time was spent in prayer and although there were wars, and there always have been wars, for there are always those who are seeking to dominate, the aggression was not so closely knit as it is now upon the Earth plane. You have already been told the Earth plane is considerably smaller simply because Man can travel from one place to another more quickly. News spreads more quickly, as do ideas, aggression, love and understanding.

At the moment they are all rolled together in a hotchpotch which must be sorted out, which must be straightened and where calmness must reign. All this will be sorted out in time through the strength of the prayers that are sent forth. In the knowledge that prayer is of great value and the knowledge that prayers, if of value, will be answered. There are many these days upon the Earth plane, who pray that they may have a new motor car, or pray that they may have a new house, that they may be invited to such and such a function and so forth. These prayers are of no value because they are of the material. But prayers that are of value are answered, one way or another. Not always as you would expect, but they are answered, and the end result is the same.

And so I say to you, by your own prayers, by your own efforts, by giving up your time in prayer, if but ten minutes of your Earth day, it is all of value, and will all bring about a greater love and understanding upon the Earth plane. It will also spread the spiritual awareness that must be spread, that man may act towards man as brothers and not as enemies. That one will recognise the colour of the skin has nothing to do with the spirit within. For the skin may be black or yellow, but the spirit within of true value. It will be that each one of you will come into contact with those of different coloured skin. It will be a teaching for you, for you will know that those who come to you, those who you meet, will be those that you have met before in previous lives. For there is a bringing together upon the Earth plane now, of those who have worked together before in previous incarnations.

You will find it very interesting as you progress along and as you realise that those things which have been told you are of truth. God's Blessings be yours. May His Light and His Love protect you at all times. God bless you.

PRAYER

* * *

THE POWER OF PRAYER

Greetings my daughter, greetings to you all, this is Thomas. It was intended that before I spoke with you there would have been a meeting with Helios, which has indeed taken place. The question was put to Helios regarding the Star, the new star to which energies would be directed in order that they in turn could be directed to the Earth plane. It is a teaching that was received within this Group a short while ago. Our daughter knows that there was a confirmation of this information and there was an enlarging of those things that will happen upon the Earth plane.

This is a time of a bringing together of vast energies. This is a time of explosion. There must be an explosion within the volcano in order that the gases may be removed; that the poisons can be dispersed; that there can then be peace within that volcano. And so it is upon the Earth plane at the present time. There are many volcanoes — the ring of fire will commence to spew forth that which bubbles and boils within. But there will also be an eruption and a spewing forth upon the Earth plane within the minds of men. Those who are endeavouring to bring about darkness, a destruction of Mother Earth, will themselves be removed.

Upon the Earth plane at the present time there is much preparation going forth in all directions. Preparations within the minds of men; within the minds of young people; within the minds of children; within the minds of the new born babe. Minds that you can say have not had time to need cleansing. Maybe not, maybe so, but they must be guided in the right direction, and they must be guided to do those things that must be done, because they are as written. And so it will be. Nobody will respond to instructions given if they are not of truth. And so there have to be teachings. Teachings of truth, teachings of which there can be no doubt. Teachings from which there can be a great awareness. It must be. You have already been told of the value of the young people, of the babies who are being born at this time upon the Earth plane. Statistics will show that there are more babies being born within a period of six months than in the previous six months. An increase that is not by accident but is of necessity.

Upon the Earth plane from the four corners of the Earth, there are those of great strength who muster around the Archangels waiting for the word that will be spoken only if it is necessary. But there are great energy forces mustering around the Archangels, and you in your way can add to that energy. You in your way can contribute much to saving the Earth plane from destruction. You can create around the Earth plane a great upliftment. And there can be a great reduction in those things which could happen, through the thoughts that you send forth. Through the prayers, through the energies within those prayers. It is no good sitting back and saying that "I am a healer." Yes indeed you are healers within this Group, I do not have to repeat myself, you already know this and have been told on many occasions. You can bring about great upliftment for Mother Earth, because you can bring about healings with your prayers. And as you send forth love and understanding to Mother Earth, although you are but a small part of the cog within the works, without that small part the whole machinery could come to a halt. And although you are but a small part, you are part of the Master Plan for all upon the Earth plane.

You have returned to the Earth plane to complete a task. You are being given the guidance in order that that knowledge which is within can be brought forth. That you may be aware of the task ahead of you. That you may be aware of those things that must be done. You are given the advice, it is up to you to take it. We can do no more than advise. You have a span of time upon the Earth plane in which to accomplish that which must be accomplished. A span of time that is ample to do that which must be done. If you do not utilise that time upon the task that you have chosen, then there will not be the triumph and the glory that could be.

It is all very well sitting back and waiting for something to happen, but that is not the way. Those things that are written have to be done. Those things that are written are a bringing together of awareness, an awareness that much can be accomplished by the spirit within a physical body. Much can be accomplished by the spirit in the World of Spirit, and together there can be a great fusion, and therefore there can be much triumph. Not triumph of the ego but a triumph for the spirit that is within, and for the one that is in spirit and for all those who gather around to work together in harmony and understanding.

It has been said this Earth morning that it is a very exciting time upon the Earth plane, and indeed it is, for it is a time of spiritual awareness. It is a time of going forward. It is a time when the physical body will begin to change gradually upon the Earth plane and the commencement is now, within this time. For it must be achieved that the gross body in which you live is refined considerably. Refined to accept changes within the atmosphere that will be round Mother Earth. Changes which must occur for her protection. Changes which will bring about balance, and changes which are as written.

I will go now. God's blessings be with you. May the Love and the Light protect you at all times. God bless you.

PRAYER

* * *

THE ENERGY OF PRAYER

Blessings my children. My sisters and my brothers, blessings be upon you from Our Father. I come to speak to you for the time has come for Me to do so, for you are of understanding and of love.

You have already heard the words that I once again walk the Earth plane. The time has come when there must be a great uniting in prayer in order that a great source of energy may be sent forth. The energy that will move mountains if need be, and throw them into the sea. The power of thought that can move that which is of darkness and disperse it, that there may be no more problems upon the Earth plane. That all may be lifted and the dark places closed, for the power of thy prayer is of great value.

My sisters and my brothers there are many now across the Earth plane that I visit, and gradually you will hear from others that they too have been visited, for it is my intention to let the words I speak be known. There will be many who will scoff if you mention that you have heard the words of the Nazarene. They will scoff at you as they did at the words that I spoke. But I know that the words that I spoke were of truth and from my Father, and you will know that without a doubt the words you heard were spoken by the Nazarene. You are of great love and great knowledge within. This knowledge and wisdom must come forth to be used. And gradually the understandings will come forth and the communications will be given to you from Spirit — from those who wait to serve. Even as you wait to serve, to bring about that which must be brought about upon the Earth plane.

The darkness is reaching its peak. The darkness when the minds of little children become sullied with the thoughts of murder, for this is what is happening now upon the Earth plane. But within the minds of those children also is the knowledge that those things must be done for which they returned. And so gradually there will be brought about great storms, for then it will be made clear that Man upon the Earth plane is of very little value in the physical body against the strength and the might of the Universe. There will not be destruction, just lessons to be learned. Even as the children of Israel had to learn their lessons, so lessons must be learned now.

The time is coming when many will say they have heard Him speak. There are false prophets upon the Earth plane, but that is inevitable and you have already been given an understanding regarding one such. My brothers and my sisters the time is coming, the time is now when all must unite in love and harmony. Unite from your various centres, but unite through the prayers and the thoughts that you send forth, for they are indeed used and replace energies that are being used by those of darkness. And therefore they strengthen for they are increased according to the Tenfold Law of our Father God. For that is His law. The love and the light that is sent through from each one of you is multiplied ten times ad infinitum, and you can see and understand the magnitude therein.

There is one who will tell you that I have stood before him and he has seen Me. It is so. You too will see me for I am everywhere. The Holy Spirit has entered each one of you this night. You are indeed My brothers and sisters, and from your hands will flow the healing even as it flowed from My hands. Each one of you are indeed Healers. Each one of you will know as time progresses, the extent of that which can be achieved and the extent of that which will happen, for with each one the time will vary. But with each one will come the knowledge and the realisation that this night is a very special turning point within your lives upon the Earth plane. Within each one has been planted the certainty that the Nazarene is upon the Earth plane once again. This time there will be no Crown of Thorns. This time My Father's Will be done

Chapter V

THE SEARCH FOR SPIRITUALITY
SPIRITUAL AWARENESS

G reetings my daughter, greetings to you all, this is Thomas. And so another year begins upon the Earth plane — the year 1982 — a year of great changes. A year of progression for you all if you follow those things which are advised.

In the year that is to follow upon the Earth plane you will see come about some of those things of which you already have knowledge. Some of those things which have already been told to you. The beginning of changes upon the face of Mother Earth. Within the atmosphere there are also great changes taking place, for Man does not need to fight wars to bring about destruction. Through the knowledge of the scientists there are already great changes in the atmosphere. And in order that the life giving energies may flow there must be changes, to reverse the process that the scientists have commenced.

You have been advised to sit in prayer, to send out light to Mother Earth, to send forth the love and the light that the darkness may be dispersed. Much of the darkness is in the minds of men, but much of the darkness is in the atmosphere. For gradually around the Earth plane there is building up a layer of darkness; a layer of darkness that does not enable certain life giving energies to reach the Earth plane. And therefore there must be upheavals to break through this ring of darkness. When once this has been accomplished there will be a general breakdown of that encircling condition. Scientists upon the Earth plane can be of great value, but they can also be a great danger, but they are of course necessary for they are men of wisdom. Some are over enthusiastic, some are corrupted and some are just interested in the experiments and in the knowledge that they can impart.

During this coming earth year this circle of darkness within the atmosphere will be penetrated in several places and will be kept open by the energies that will pour through. And it is because of this that there will be areas in the future that are presently sand, which will become fertile and areas of snow that will become as desert. If you picture this within your mind, if you imagine the Earth plane and you imagine encircling the Earth plane a dark circle, some distance away of course, and then you make gaps within that circle, you can see how energies being directed through will land on certain spots. It is obvious, I do not need to enlarge. Thus it will be. But in order to bring about this penetration there must be upheavals, and so the beginnings will be within this next Earth year. There will also come about within the America's, changes that you have already been told about — the beginnings. They will happen for they must.

Now for each of you this Earth year there will be a clearer spiritual awareness. Each one of you will become aware of your own helpers — the guides who stand by you. You will be able to speak with them for they have already introduced themselves. It is very necessary that you do have the understandings of those things that should be done, in order that your spiritual progression and awareness may be made clear to you.

For each one of you this could be a year that you would look back upon, a year that you will remember. As indeed the last year should be memorable, for much happened upon the Earth plane in the last year and much happened to you. You will find that those things that were promised at the commencement of these Group meetings will have taken place by the end of this Earth year, it will be so.

And now I will go. May the Love and the Light of Father God protect you at all times, and it does. God bless you, God bless you all.

* * * * *

Can I come and talk to you? I'm not anyone important, I used to sell flowers from a basket on the steps of Piccadilly. I used to sit and watch the world go by.

I came of a good family. I was well educated, but my father died. As we thought, he had spent all his money and we were left without anything. I went as a governess to the children of a Member of Parliament. It is the old story. I was disgraced because I was to have a baby and was not married. I did not know which way to turn and I was in Piccadilly and one of the ladies who sold flowers saw my distress and crossed the road and took me by the hand and sat me down on the steps beside her.

I found myself telling her all my troubles and she took me under her wing. She hadn't very much money, only what she earned from flowers, but she showed me how to do the flowers also, because in those days they really were the forerunners of the florists. There were the big florists of course who used to do up camellias for buttonholes for those who could afford them. But those who sat with their baskets of flowers, which they used to go to Covent Garden very early in the morning to buy and to arrange, would also do buttonholes, and they would do little posies, and she taught me to do this.

I never had my baby it was stillborn, but nevertheless I was shown kindness such as I had never known before, because it was true kindness, true friendship and true love, and we were so different, she and I. One day when she was sitting there with her basket and I had gone to buy some bread and cheese, a runaway horse came down Regent Street and crashed into the steps and she was killed. And so I carried on and I would sit there, for a new basket had been bought by the gentleman whose horse it was, and I would sit out there, all weathers with the others.

I got to know a lot about people and I got to make a lot of friends. I used to sit there and next to me used to sit my friend; she was in spirit, but she was with me. She was for a time what you would call earthbound, for her passing was very sudden and she could not accept. But after a time she realised, for I used to speak to her and she went, and she had lessons of under-standing and then she would come to me from time to time.

I spent the rest of my life earning my keep by doing my flowers. And I enjoyed my life from then on, for as I have said I met many people and I would talk as naturally about those in the Spirit World that I could see, as naturally as you speak about them. I had the understanding as you have it. They used to call me Mad Meg, but I wasn't mad and I wasn't simple. That was the fate of many people in those days who had spiritual awareness. They were considered odd and peculiar and not all there. Nevertheless people would come and buy my flowers and talk to me and be given an understanding. You see it isn't madness, its knowledge. Knowledge of the truth, and you have it. God bless you.

The Search for Spirituality

* * *

THE LIGHT WITHIN

Blessings upon you all. My friends it is my privilege and an honour to speak with you upon this very first day of a new Earth year, according to your calendar. It is my privilege to bring to you advice and teachings, for they can be one and the same.

You have met together within this Sanctuary for thirty eight teachings. When you commenced you were all expectant. You all wondered what would happen, but you all came seeking. There are two of you here who were not within this Sanctuary right at the beginning. But right from the start the awareness was given to you when in the sleep state, and you have the words which were spoken written for you to read, and they are familiar.

It was not by accident that you were drawn together, for you were chosen and you already have the understanding. You are yourselves lights, replicas of the Light of the World who Himself came down to walk the Earth plane. Not for the experiences and the teachings that you see, for He already had the knowledge and the teaching that you are seeking. You are learning well and within there is the knowledge which gradually will come forth.

You will look back as you progress along your spiritual paths, lights that will grow ever brighter, and you will look back and marvel. Marvel at those things which have been told you. Marvel at those things which you have experienced and marvel at the things that have been accomplished. For you **will** accomplish, you **will** learn, as indeed is already happening. But thy will is the will of God, for that is how it must be and that is how it will be as you progress along your spiritual paths, for you will know that the light that is within you will shine forth and you will know those things which must be done for you will all have your own individual guidance.

You will all be able to converse with those who walk by your side. And as you progress you will find that those who walk by your side will change, that as one comes forward so one could fade. But having once walked side by side there is always a link, and a being together. As you progress along your paths you will of course have tests and initiations, and as you pass each initiation so you will penetrate another vibration, another dimension; receive a great understanding and more wisdom. Thus the light will become brighter within each one of you.

By sitting within this Sanctuary you have taken upon yourselves a great responsibility, the responsibility of going forward. Of spreading the words that you will speak, the light, the brotherhood, the thoughts of peace. Bringing one to the other the knowledge that whatever colour the skin may be, the spirit within each one is spirit. It is but the physical case around that varies according to those who were your Earth parents and the colour of their physical body.

There will come a time many Earth years ahead, when all men will know that all are equal and all men will know that they must live together in true harmony. When all men will know that thoughts may be transmitted one to the other and that there are laws and disciplines which must control those thoughts. One can understand that if all communication and all travel is to be by thought, if it is not disciplined and controlled there could be utter chaos. And so the disciplines that you are learning now upon the Earth plane are but a forerunner of the disciplines which will be needed upon the Earth plane in the time to come.

You have already been told of the young ones who are now being born upon the Earth plane, and there are those here who have recently had a young grandchild, a new addition to the family. Both of these children are of knowledge. Both of these children are of wisdom, for they are not young spirits, but of great wisdom. Although the physical body has to learn those things that must be learned upon the Earth plane, the spirit within is of wisdom.

Both of these young ones will develop and grow and will be of high intelligence, and both of them have great spiritual knowledge which will be made apparent to their parents. This spiritual knowledge must be accepted and spoken about freely and naturally, for it will help the clearing of channels for the greater wisdoms that will come forth eventually. It is not by chance that you sit in this Sanctuary, for you must be given the knowledge of the importance of these young ones. They are all part of the Master Plan, and there are many such being born upon the Earth plane now.

You will find that from now until the closing of this Group, when this dwelling house is closed and those within have gone forth to another dwelling house, you will be given greater understandings of your own path. You all have the understanding that you are healers and you are also under the teachings of Thomas and also under the teachings of Helios. This fact has already been recognised this Earth evening for there is much wisdom here. I correct for there is one who is not under the teaching of Helios, but I say to you that you are not unknown to Helios and Helios is not unknown to you, for you have met and therefore it is right and proper that you be included.

Helios is one of great wisdom, but you do not need me to tell you that. You do not take lightly your visits to his Temple and you do not take lightly the instruction that is given to you with regard to meditation, and you do not take lightly the words that are spoken, but you remember them. You will find a greater meaning to those words as the wisdoms within you are brought forth. The time is coming when in those meditations you will be given your own individual teachings, when you will bring forth the understandings. You will recognise, accept and learn, for you will remember and you will find that the pieces of the jigsaw puzzle that is life, will fit together more readily. And you will find that gradually the full picture is beginning to appear and you will have an under-standing of that picture.

It is not by accident either that you have all been drawn to the Temple of Helios, for it was planned thus. Your life upon the Earth plane is as a jigsaw puzzle but then how much greater is The Plan for the Universe? By visualising you will realise that really your life upon the Earth plane is but one piece in the jigsaw puzzle that could be the Universe, and yet without that one piece, the Universe is not complete. And so that one piece is indeed of great value, as indeed you are. The lights that you are, the wisdom's that are within, the service that you will accomplish are all of great value. Do not underestimate yourselves or your value in the Master Plan.

God's blessings surround you. The wisdoms are within. Go in peace and bring peace to those with whom you come into contact. May the Sun shed its rays upon you. May the Moon bring you tranquillity. May God's blessing protect you.

The Search for Spirituality

* * *

TREASURES WITHIN

The gifts of the Gods I bring to you. The pearls of wisdom I lay at your feet. Use the wisdom wisely, for within each one of you there is great wisdom from lessons that you have learned over thousands of years. For you were all together in that wonderful land that was destroyed through the misdemeanours of the many.

Atlantis was of great knowledge, of great wisdom, of intense teachings, of high spiritual understandings. It was destroyed through misdemeanours of those who were in high places, who even in those times became corrupt, who whispered in dark corners and plotted for their own gain. In this Age of Aquarius there are many similarities to the time of Atlantis. There is a parallel but of different understandings, of different levels of understanding. But nevertheless there is a parallel, for there are those on this Earth plane who are corrupt. We speak of course of spiritual levels. They are corrupt because they desire to dominate all peoples upon the Earth plane and they too whisper in dark corners. But unlike Atlantis there are many now who are being prepared across the Earth plane.

Those who were upon Atlantis at that time of destruction, those who fought to save Atlantis, have now come together, are being drawn together. They have returned to a life upon the Earth plane, a life that is dedicated to spreading the knowledge and the wisdoms, to send out love, and to bring about a realisation through prayer that evil ones can be overcome. For the thoughts of the evil ones can be cast out by the individual, with the help and the guidance that is being given through those Atlanteans who have returned at this time, and are returning. They are being born within the form of babies at this moment.

At this period of time there will be continuity and more and more people will turn to those who are the leaders. Not the leaders who stand up and wave banners and flags, but the leaders who go about their business without accolades in the physical sense. Who do their work because they know they are working of service and of love and doing the Will of God. For it is His Will that cleansing will take place upon the Earth plane, in order that there can be an escalation of spiritual awareness; of the realisation that all are equal. That **all** are equal.

It is said that when you are born upon the Earth plane, you are born naked and without possessions. And when your life is spent upon the Earth plane, you leave without possessions. Physical possessions, material possessions yes; but nobody comes down to this Earth plane without vast treasures within, and when your life upon this Earth plane is finished you leave with your treasures, if you have accomplished that which had to be accomplished. And if you leave this Earth plane with your free will, the Will of God, you do indeed have vast treasures with you. Nobody can acquire treasures of that value with money, nobody.

There are those upon the Earth plane who have monies, who have the advantage, so they think, of going to Universities and acquiring knowledge. But the knowledge that you receive from the teachers from the World of Spirit are not bought with money, and it is those teachings that enable you to open up the door to the treasures that you have. It is the understandings that you have within you which enable you to go forward to do those things that must be done. Those things which you know, because you have those in Spirit who walk side by side with you, and advise in various ways. You know those things that must be done.

At the time of Atlantis, before the destruction, there was much knowledge, much awareness, and thought was the means of communication, and through the spiritual awareness one could project from one place to the other. It will happen again in time, when all the havoc has been cleansed away in the waters of truth, of light, of love. Those three together will be the means of cleansing. Will restore that which must be restored, that the spirit may go forward, that all will recognise the perfection that is around them.

Pearls of wisdom are given to you. You may interpret each in your own way. And as you progress in the work that you must do, your interpretations will change and you will indeed be of wisdom. There is within this Group much strength, and each one of you will draw on that strength and each one of you will find it replaced time and time again when you are in need.

I leave you the Light of Eternal Love for each one of you. The Light that pours direct from The Father of all, The Creator and the All Bountiful Love. God bless you, God bless you.

The Search for Spirituality

* * *

I would if I could build for you a pyramid of knowledge. I would if I could take you through the corridors and show you the wisdoms that are within each one of you. But the wisdoms that are within each one of you are for you to seek and to find. As you work in service to mankind and to God, so wisdoms will be given to you. You will be told where to seek, and the wisdoms come to you only when you are of service. For it is that way that you walk along your path of spiritual enlightenment and progression.

You have the understanding now that the [1]Great Pyramid was not built by hands of man. You have the understanding now that in ancient, ancient, ancient times the pyramid was shaped by the energy beams. That the great rocks were lifted by levitation through the thought patterns that were directed by

---

[1]Great Pyramid — One of a group of three 4th Dynasty (c2613 – c2494BC) pyramids on plateau on the West bank of the Nile near Al Jizah, known as 'the pyramids of Giza'. Northernmost and oldest was built by Khufu (Gk. Cheops) second King of the 4th Dynasty and is called the Great Pyramid. It is the largest of the three, the length each side at base averaging 775¾ft and the original height was 481¼ft.

In 1925 the only undisturbed royal tomb of the old Kingdom (c2686 – c2160BC) yet known was discovered near the upper end of the causeway of Khufu. The tomb was found at the bottom of a deep stone filled shaft, and it contained the sarcophagus and funerary equipment of Queen Hetepheres, mother of Khufu. The tomb objects attest the high artistic ability and technical perfection of the 4th Dynasty craftsmen.

those of wisdom. There are chronicles that are hidden within the Great Pyramid which have not yet been discovered, for the time is not right. These things are hidden there along with many other understandings of matters that man is seeking now. For only now, because it is their task, are those of enquiring minds beginning to uncover certain things that have been hidden for many many years within the great Temple that is within the pyramid. A Temple which is not yet uncovered and yet people pass through as they investigate. It is not discovered for it is of a different dimension to that of the physical bodies upon the Earth plane at this time.

Within that Temple there is much knowledge, much wisdom recorded, many facts and many figures of times beyond the thought of man. Within the Pyramid there is great healing, great tranquillity, and there are those who are aware of this. There is a part of the Pyramid into which those who are sick could be conveyed, and they would be healed, if the reason for their being taken there was one of love. This place will be discovered in the not too distant future. It will be discovered by what appears to be an accident, but it will be no accident but it will be the time for the door to be opened.

It is said by many that the Great Pyramid is crumbling, but it will not crumble until the treasures, the wisdoms are discovered and the time is right. When the knowledge that is within the Great Pyramid has **all** been discovered, the pyramid will vanish, it will **not** crumble. But that time is not yet, not for a very long time.

Each one of you has within you, as within the Great Pyramid, a secret place wherein are stored wisdoms. It is the centre of centres within you. It is possible for you in meditation to enter this place. It is possible for you in meditation to bring forth the wisdoms that are within that place, for as you enter the stillness so you will receive a great calming, a great peace and much wisdom. But of course it takes time and it takes disciplines. To sit quietly takes discipline, especially when your physical life, the material things around you are so demanding. But they are only demanding if you let me be, for remember it is you who has the control. It is you who are the deciding factor. It is you who is the keeper of your own Earth life, and it is you who has to decide those things that are of most value. The life around your physical body or the life of spiritual value, which is of most value? Which is everlasting, which drops away from you?

As with the Great Pyramid so with you, the wisdom's within the Great Pyramid will gradually become known step by step, and then the pyramid will vanish. And so with you, the wisdoms within will gradually become known. Your spiritual paths will unfold before you and when you have completed the task for which you returned to the Earth plane, that which is visible will drop away and that which is of Spirit will go forth to the home that awaits you.

I do not need to build a pyramid for you. I do not need to take you along the corridors of wisdom to those secret places within the Pyramid, for each one of you are your own pyramid.

* * * * *

Good evening, my name is Rosie. I used to be a dressmaker. I made dresses for many very wealthy ladies, but they did not pay me very much. I was one of the sewing seamstresses in a shop in Kensington, London.

It was a very grand salon where the ladies would come and parade with their husbands or boy friends. Where the gowns would be shown to them and they would choose. Or they would come with rolls of fine silk that had been brought to them from China, and they would want a dress made, and there would be much excitement for the material was beautiful.

I was allowed to fit the ladies. I was allowed to adjust and to alter where needed. And thus I met many beautiful ladies, although they did not notice me. But there was one lady who was very kind and she used to speak to me. She was a lady who used to come quietly without any fuss with a lady-in-waiting

317

by her side. She was [2]Princess Alexandra, who later became Queen of England. She always noticed and always spoke to me. She would sometimes give me a pair of gloves or a beaded purse or a little gift, just by way of saying thank you when she was particularly pleased. For she always used to say that the one who fitted the dress would make all the difference.

We worked below stairs in a big room which was in the cellar. It was not very nice, for it was not considered that the work girls needed very good conditions. We were below stairs and therefore not seen. When I first went there to work, I used to spend the time picking up pins and cleaning up and running hither and thither with different things. I used to go home very tired. But when I was allowed to go upstairs to help with the fitting it was like another world. The ladies and the gentlemen who came were so clean and pretty that it was a joy just to be there, and I did not mind how tired I became.

There were many who had no work. There were many who had little food, but I was lucky and I was happy to work. To work, whatever you do, is of satisfaction, but to work knowing that you are guided, that you are loved, is of great upliftment. I am of the World of Spirit and I come to say to you, for I know and understand now that there is a lot of work in the World of Spirit to help you upon the Earth plane. There is work for all to do, work in plenty if you will only do it. Thank you for listening to me. Bless you.

---

[2]Princess Alexandra — (1844–1925) — Became wife of Edward VII and queen of Great Britain, daughter of Christian IX of Denmark.

Chapter VI

DISCIPLINES

T o each of you I say greetings. To each of you I say the bountiful blessings of the Universe are being directed towards you, and those of you who have the understanding will feel those energies pouring within you to strengthen and uplift you. To guide you along your path, the path of much value that you have chosen to tread. The task that must be completed before you return once again to those realms from which you have come.

There will be given to you the understandings of those things that must be achieved by you. And gradually you will find that the guidance that is given to you, to enable you to have the understanding of the path on which you must tread to complete that which must be completed, will be unfolded before you. Gradually there will come to you the realisation that those things that you have been told at the commencement regarding the disciplines, are the key to all things, for without one the other cannot be achieved. I come to tell you this because it is urgent that you have this realisation. There must be a great going forward in understanding of knowledge of those things that must be accomplished by each one of you.

There are two of you who are already aware and are waiting for that advice which will send you forward. You have great awareness and before you there is much to face. There are two of you who are just beginning to have the understanding of those things you must do in order to commence along that path that you have chosen. There are two of you who are involved with those things of your daily life who find it difficult. I am to correct that which I have just said, for I must say there are three of you who are very much involved in your daily lives, who find it difficult to maintain discipline. It is understandable, but nevertheless there are those disciplines that you must follow, 'discipline of prayer'. For you are sitting within this Group, a group who have been chosen, a group of light, and there must be prayer to send forth the light.

There must also be discipline of meditation if you are to receive the understandings that will help you along your path. It may seem a waste of time when there is so much else to do, but it is through the disciplines of meditation and prayer that you will see your pathway clearly, for you will be advised. And so you see from the words that I speak, how you are progressing in your various ways towards that which must be accomplished. And you can see also how you are in varying stages, each following on from the other. I am not in any way reprimanding, I am merely telling you as it is.

There will be a great enlightenment before this Group is closed. You have already had a visit from a Master, the Christos. You have already been given the understanding that this group is one that is under His loving care. You already have the understanding that you are not the only group under His care, for His groups go round the Earth plane. It must be thus for it has been carefully planned. There will be a linking up with other groups, for there will be words that will be printed in papers that are circulated around the Earth plane, and there will be those things with which you will have great understanding, and you will know that you are linked. The chain is growing thicker, it is becoming of much strength for there are many peoples like yourselves, leading ordinary lives. I say this with no disrespect, leading ordinary lives, but within each one there is the knowledge of a task that must be completed whether you understand that or otherwise. There are things that are said now which but a few years ago you would have laughed at — would not have understood, indeed would not have accepted. The fact that there are those who pray for certain areas in their own town, areas of great darkness; and it has been recorded that already the light is penetrating into that area, it is indeed so. And so the prayer that you send forth will also bring about a lightening, the entry of the light to disperse the darkness.

You should now have the understanding that through groups such as this there is much energy sent forth. There are those energies that are sent to you, to stimulate and help you. And with the prayers you send forth you send forth energies and light also. It is a to-ing and fro-ing of differing energies of great power and value. There are those upon the Earth plane who have with them teachers of great value, who are restricted by the physical body, and so that body has to be strengthened. And in order to assist the teacher the energies are poured into the physical body. They have to be strengthened by gradually increasing energies, for if those energies were directed with the full force that was required, then the physical body would burn. So there has to be preparation. And when the time is right so will the teachers emerge, and their voices will be heard and their deeds will be recorded all around the Earth plane, and there will be a great upsurge of the spiritual knowledge that must be. It must be. Those of darkness will be swept aside and the tide will turn. It will be thus, it is written thus and the Will of the Creator must be. Remember the discipline of prayer.

Remember it is of great value, and it is also the key to your own path, to the task for which you have returned. You are all here to complete a task not to repay debts. The energies of the Universe be all around you at all times when you are of true discipline.

* * * * *

Greetings my daughter, greetings to you all, this is Thomas. In the realms of understanding there are many understandings. Within the realms of understanding there are many teachings, and according to understanding the teachings are received. If the understandings are of a high value the teachings will be of a high value, and if the understandings are of a lower value then those same words will be understood at a lower level.

Within man, within each one, the understandings vary. For there are those who are young spirits who need to seek, who need to enquire, who need to ask questions. Who do not always accept or understand the words that are spoken to them on the level at which they are addressed. But from within there is a great sorting out and an understanding is given at the level to which they have traversed. Each one of you within this sanctuary are at a different level of understanding, for it is not always the level from the lowest to the highest, but there are also different levels, as you would say, sideways.

Upon the Earth plane there are those who prepared what are known as graphs, and within their calculations there are moves, moves sideways and moves downwards. Within the realms of understanding you start at the bottom and move upwards or sideways. The time is now coming when there will be no downward moves, but a situation that is stationary or a situation of upliftment or sideways. For side moves of understanding are, as it were, a clarifying of a present situation. A teaching which is given at the level of understanding, a teaching which is given simplified, if you like, that can be accepted and understood before the next understanding is given. Before the next happening, before the next realisation. And so you progress upwards, but sometimes on a zigzag course.

Each one of you within this sanctuary are on a different level of understanding, a different vibration, and yet you are all progressing upwards. Sometimes there is a sideways move before the next step upwards, the next step forward, but you are nevertheless going forward along your spiritual paths. With some the disciplines are good and progress is now becoming evident. With others the disciplines are not so good and progress is slower, and with some there is no discipline and therefore there is a standstill, and that is how it must be. We will not speak any more of disciplines within this Group for you have been given the understanding over and over again, and now it is up to you, each one, to accept or dismiss disciplines. But as you accept or dismiss, so your progress will be marked.

There is a great awakening at this beginning of the Aquarian Age. There is a great spiritual awakening. There have been many plans, there have been many preparations, and now the teachers are in place. Those through whom the teachings will be given, those through whom many will receive understanding which will awaken within them the spirit that lies dormant. Dormant in so far as awareness and understanding of that which must be achieved.

There will soon be a mighty battle between those of darkness and those of light. There will be many arguments and clashes, but clashes of words and not of swords. The places are being prepared, the universal energies are waiting. The time draws nigh and you within this group, and many more like you who have been given the advice and the teachings that you have been given, will be aware of the time when light and dark confront each other. But mark my words the light will overcome the darkness. The light will penetrate and disperse and all men will come to realise that words are indeed swords, and words are indeed shields, and battles can be fought around a table without bloodshed. And those who sit around the table to discuss will raise their voices in protest or in agreement or in anger or in love, but no blood will be shed, no lives will be forfeit. The pride of some will hit the dust. The love of some will overcome and envelop, but there will be no bloodshed.

The time is coming for the conflict to begin. For the great cleansing to spread around the Earth plane, for the realisation that life is sweet, that life is of interest, that much can be learned and much can be accomplished. That respect for each other and respect of properties and countries, respect brought about by love, is of far greater value than destruction brought about by hate. One so positive the other so negative. It is the positive aspects of yourselves that must be developed. It is the positive thinking and the discarding of all things that are negative, for negation is destruction.

Within each one of you there is much knowledge and wisdom of positive intent. Do not let it remain hidden, but bring it forth to use it to help you and Mother Earth. To help your fellow brothers and sisters to bring about a great unity, a great love, a great marrying together, in order that the spiritual awareness may soar within each and every one. The young children have this awareness and many will hold back from doing those things that young people do now in the way of negation. For within them will be the understanding of positive action, of positive thinking, of positive love. Go forward as you must. Go forward sending out positive thoughts, positive actions, positive compassion and love, and help to bring about that which must be brought about — an awareness that all are brothers. Do unto others that which you would have them do unto you. Cause no pain or sorrow, be at peace towards all men. The Love and the Light of Father God surround you all at all times God bless you.

* * * * *

Greetings my daughter, greetings to you all, this is Thomas. You adorn the walls of your homes with pictures. You place those pictures into position carefully in order that you may gaze upon them, reflect upon the meaning and enjoy their beauty. Sometimes you are given a picture that to you is not really harmony, but because it has been given to you by a loved one, you place that too as an adornment upon your walls.

So it is with the various experiences of your life. You do not exactly place them upon the walls, but they are there within the inner mind, pictures of past experiences, cameos of those you have met. Some are of beauty, some were of fear, but when recalled now, the fear has gone. The experience remains to look at, as if from a distance. An experience which has become a teaching, for it is from experiences of happenings within those experiences of life, that lead you forward in progression and understanding.

To sit quietly to meditate is not easy. But it has never been easy for it is not intended thus. Disciplines must be learned, and sometimes it means giving up much in order to sit quietly in meditation. But this is not a disadvantage, it is a great advantage for those things that you will recall. The treasures that you will bring forth will be of much value in this present experience of life. As indeed are the happenings that have taken place within your present Earth experience, for nothing is wasted. Even as a tiny child there are those happenings which can be recalled, some of great happiness, some of sadness, some of bewilderment. But nothing is wasted, and in this present experience upon the Earth plane you have had many happenings.

There have been many changes, many changes upon the Earth plane, for has not man experienced the journey to the Moon. Are there not instruments circling the Earth plane, travelling round in an orbit close to the Earth plane? And is there not an instrument that is probing forward into the Universe? It will have very far to go to even plot a minute portion of the Universe, but nevertheless these are happenings. Man is using vibrations within the ether to carry messages, to transmit pictures. You too can transmit pictures from past experiences to the present experience. Pictures which will teach you much; pictures which will tell you much; pictures which will help you to a greater understanding of those things that have happened and those things which will happen.

Meditation is a means of shutting ones self off from all that is around, then looking at pictures, and then becoming part of the picture. A part of the picture that you could never become in those that adorn your walls. They are simply to look at, to enjoy. The pictures of meditation are for you to take part of, for you to go back, or indeed to go forward, for the past and the future, and now are all one. You have one life but many experiences.

May the Love and the Light of Father God surround you at all times, and indeed it does. God bless you all.

* * * * *

Good evening. I am very happy to be with you, to join you as you sit together in harmony. I used to live in Switzerland. I used to live in Zurich. It was not as it is now, for I lived there at a time of happiness, of gaiety, of simple living. It was a place of happiness, but it was also a place of learning. I was a nurse in the hospital there and I knew Doctor Heinrick, for I worked with him before he obtained for himself his own clinic in Bekinsop.

I worked with Doctor Heinrick and saw him perform many wonderful operations on limbs that were considered beyond repair. He was one who could set bones and fractures, who repaired limbs that had become damaged. He taught me a great deal. He was of understanding and he was very strict. We learned the disciplines through him, disciplines that we never forgot, but we were also given understanding. In those days that was rare, for many a doctor put himself upon a pedestal, a pedestal where we as nurses could not touch them. But with Doctor Heinrick one could always talk to him, could ask him questions. Not to badger him of course, for he was a busy man, but he always had time and understanding to teach you those things that you needed to know.

We appreciated those teachings that he gave us and he even went so far as to hold classes to tell us about the setting of limbs and those things that could be of danger and those things to look out for. These teachings have been of great value, for they were recorded and have been passed on, but there were not many doctors at that time who did that. We noted, we learned the teachings and they helped us in our work, and we in our turn were able to help those nurses who followed on.

I worked in that hospital for many years, and I finished by being an instructor, if you like. I would teach the young nurses things I had learned in that time that I had been working in the hospital, and that is what you have to do. You are being given teachings, not within a hospital it is true, but you are being given teachings. They are not for you to keep to yourselves, they are for you to read and understand. They are for you to talk about to those who you think have understanding, on the occasions that you think are right. They are for you to use as you think best. You are teachers, you are healers, you are both things.

It is a wonderful time, this time in which you are living, although there is much darkness, but there always has been darkness. It is only because the Earth plane has shrunk in communications that the darkness has become so apparent. But you as teachers will be able to do a lot to break through that darkness in the minds of those with whom you come in contact.

Thank you for letting me be with you and God's Blessings be with you. Good-bye.

Chapter VII

HEALING
HELPING THE DISABLED

H ello. I had to have permission to come and speak to you, but I am very happy to be here. I have only just started to go round to the various groups, for it is something that we do. It is part of our progression, if you like, in the World of Spirit.

I had just started to have a knowledge of the World of Spirit when I passed, and then I got stuck somehow, for I passed quickly in an accident and somehow I didn't want to leave the Earth plane because it was still the same. And so I went on living where I was living, so to speak. And then suddenly I realised, for I saw my funeral and I knew that I was holding myself back. And when once I realised this, I went through the tunnel into the World of Spirit. This does happen, for there seems to be no difference.

There was a time whilst I had to become used to the World of Spirit, that I was sent to what was virtually a classroom, to get the balance right, and now here I am going around talking to people. When the plane crashed, everything went from fear to peace, and although things happened quickly, there was time for fear, for fear is very uppermost when in the physical body. And yet when I was around the race track, there was no fear, just the exhilaration of the race. The conscious mind was in control and it was a case of pitting skills against skills. Yet I was ever mindful that there could be a crash, that I could be disabled.

It was through that knowledge that I was led towards the disabled. It was that knowledge which made me desirous of helping those who were disabled in one way or another. I was lucky because I could walk, drive a car, swim, or do those things that I wanted to do and I realised the difference between myself and those who were disabled. Yet many of those could have had the same skills as I and the same knowledge as I, for their minds, their brains were active, intelligent, but their limbs would not permit them the freedom that I had.

And so now I go round to the various groups, but I pick particularly, for we are allowed to choose, those who have shown an interest in the disabled. You within this Group have done so, for has there not been designed a healing sanctuary into which the disabled can have easy access? And that is why I come to you, because I link in with those who have shown consideration and an understanding for the needs of those who are disabled, for your thoughts have gone towards them.

The year of the disabled upon the Earth plane has just passed. But it is only the name that has passed, for the disabled are no different today than they were yesterday, and yet it is a different year. I ask you please to go on showing your consideration for the disabled, for there will be those who will be directed to that place that has been completed with them in mind, and they will come. But things upon the Earth plane happen slowly. They start slowly and gradually gather momentum. And so it will be, for they are being guided towards that place gradually.

You will note this, but I am not talking of the immediate future. It will happen soon. So I say to you, thank you for thinking of the disabled. Thank you for listening to me, and for those who are interested, my name is Graham Hill. God bless you.

Healing

* * *

GIFTS OF HEALING

Greetings my daughter, greetings to you all, this is Thomas. There will be much enlightenment in the near future of those things that have been told you. Not all of course, for you have the understanding that some are for the future. But there will be happenings which will be an enlightenment for you, for you will realise they are as you have been told. Those words that have been spoken to you from the ones in spirit are spoken in truth, and there are two amongst you who have already received that which was advised. I will put it that way.

The time is coming when you will all have a greater understanding, when you will all realise just how much knowledge and just how great an understanding you have received of your gifts of healing. I say "gifts of healing" — for all are gifts. There are those upon the Earth plane who say that all can be healers if they so desire. That all can be clairvoyant, that all can be clairaudient. All can do this and all can do that. But it is not so. It is those who return to the Earth plane with understanding and knowledge who are the ones who go forward with these gifts, understandings if you like. For those who return to the Earth plane to learn, to correct their mistakes, so to speak, do not have the opportunity, are not given the gifts. And so you see, all do not have the gifts. All cannot be healers in this life.

If one takes many lives then that would be correct, but there are not many who will accept many lives. It is you and those like you upon the Earth plane who have returned to give teachings, to bring about and to spread the truth that life is everlasting. That those things that one does in this Earth life are reflected or are a reflection. That to progress forward one must learn lessons, for is this not true within the classroom?

If you do not learn lessons you do not progress and you never reach University. And that is so within the knowledge that is given to you upon the Earth plane. The knowledge, the awareness that you are progressing, that you have either reached the University or you are approaching the University. Think back to the time you first entered this Sanctuary to sit in this Group. It must be remembered that the knowledge and understanding then was not as now. The time is now when those things that you have learned must be spread. The time is now, when there will be directed towards you those people who will be thirsting for that knowledge, those people who will be seeking. And they will be directed towards **you**, healers and teachers in your various ways according to your own progression.

You will all hear voices in your ears, for you understand the meaning of that now. You will all receive your guidance in this way. And gradually as you become accustomed, you will virtually have a friend from the World of Spirit standing by your side conversing with you. But remember they do not tell you what to do, they merely advise, for you do those things according to your free will.

The time is indeed coming when more and more people will be directed towards you in your daily lives. Make a note of the conversations you have. Make a note of the number of people who lead into talk of World affairs and of the state of Mother Earth, and from those conversations how knowledge of the World of Spirit will come forth. It has to be thus for the teachings that you have received are not to be kept to yourselves, for now you know that always it is left to you how much you say. It is left to you to discern the capabilities and the understanding of those to whom you speak. And it is up to you to leave unsaid those things that you believe would be of a high University teaching. For those in the kindergarten would not understand the words of the University. It makes it very easy for us in the World of Spirit to be able to associate with the classroom. It is a very simple way of explanation and saves a lot of words, and thus a lot of energy.

There are teachers who are in places of great dissension. There are teachers who are in places of great problem, for they speak those words which are given to them from the World of Spirit. They stand fearlessly before a crowd, before a packed hall, before a small room, fearlessly saying the words that must be said. And in some cases in some parts of the Earth plane they say these words in great danger. But they know they must be said for seeds must be planted. Knowledge must be spread, for compassion and humility, tolerance, healing, and love must be spread upon the Earth plane.

Presently they are being pushed to one side and darkness put in their place, so now is the time for the great cleansing to begin. Now is the time for the Age of Aquarius to really show its merit and through such as you, who are the vanguard, will be sent forth the lights that will push out the darkness. It will be thus, for we choose carefully and you all know if you look deep within that you were chosen. That you accepted that which you are now endeavouring to bring about upon the Earth plane.

The Love and the Light of Father God surrounds you at all times. God Bless you all.

Healing

* * *

PHYSICAL REVITALISATION

The Blessings of My Father I bring to you. To each one of you I say, the time is coming when you will walk forth to do those things for which you are being prepared. Each one according to your own time, each one according to that which is written. I would ask you to take heed of those things that have been said to you. I would ask you not to delay that which must be, for to delay will cause regrets and it is a waste of time.

There is before each one of you work for the benefit of your brothers and sisters. Give out freely your love. Give out freely from those teachings that have been given to you. Give out freely your compassion, for there are many upon the Earth plane who are in need — in need of the understandings of others. You have the understandings for you have been given teachings, and within each one of you there is the knowledge of the need of so many. Do not expect to receive in return. But give out freely and you will find that according to the Tenfold Law of our Father, you will receive an upliftment far beyond your expectations. For to give out freely is to give out love of true value.

There are times when you yourselves will be tired and I ask you not to go beyond the limit of that tiredness. For you will achieve nothing but you will deplete your physical body. Rest when you feel tired and sit quietly. And during your quiet moments, as you have been advised, there will be given to you full revitalisation. For it will be sent to you, you who are of service.

I am not far away, for now is the time of much activity all around the Earth plane. To you all I say, be aware of the love and protection of our Father. Blessings to you all, each one.

Chapter VIII

KARMA

reetings my daughter, greetings to you all, this is Thomas. There are many changes taking place upon the Earth plane. Changes that are being recorded as 'the first time ever', or 'the first time in living memory'. There are weather conditions all across the Earth plane that should make people sit up and take notice — to record. For this is but the beginning of the changes that will take place.

It has been said that in the old days there was always severe snow in the Winter, for three or four months, and then the climatic conditions changed and the winters became mild. This of course was not recorded to any extent, but just accepted and taken for granted. Yes it is quite true, the weather does go in cycles according to the position of the planets, according to the out-flow of currents. But there are those conditions which are far more severe, whether it be intense heat or whether it be intense cold, and this is how it will be.

There is a gradual movement of the Earth, a gradual movement of conditions within planet Earth. There will of course be flooding and this is understood, for when the snows melt, the rivers are never wide enough to take away those waters. There will of course be flooding. All this is part of the plan of things. It is the stirring up and a realisation that you cannot live independently. That all are inter–dependant one upon the other in some way or another.

The thinking upon planet Earth at this time is that each one does not need anyone else. It's a case of, "I am not going to share. I have earned this and it is mine." Of course to a certain extent this is true, but if somebody had not made that which you desire to possess, you could not possess it. If you have a full larder and your next door neighbour is without, then your food should be shared. There cannot be a sharing however, where the thinking is one of distrust. And these are the barriers that must be broken through, for very often one distrusts that which one does not know.

One can easily criticise that which one does not know, and so the time is now coming when an effort should be made to know your neighbour. To understand their problems and to help if possible. I am not suggesting that you should take upon your shoulders the worries of the World, for there are those who you instinctively do not trust and this of course is really part of the karma. It is an inbred feeling. It is an inbred reaction. It is a case of putting up a barrier, for one of that type may have in the past caused you great distress, and instinctively without really knowing why, you put up a barrier. I am not going to say that you must endeavour to break that barrier down. I would say 'go round it and wait', for there will be a bringing together, and there could be understanding.

It is well known upon the Earth plane that there are those that you meet who at once you feel drawn to. There are also those who instinctively you do not like, you shy away from. This is because of experiences in past lives. And sometimes these feelings have to be overcome, and sometimes they can be put to one side. You will know within yourselves whether this is something you must overcome or whether it is something you can ignore. Each one according to their own spiritual path will be given this awareness. If you put yourselves out, so to speak, to get to know the one that you dislike or are not sure of, it could be that they will say that they felt the same about you, and this you will definitely know is a condition of past lives. Maybe at some future time you will be given the explanation, it could be during meditation. It is very interesting when this happens and it is a further step upon your spiritual path.

In the Universe at the present time there is much preparation. There are Spheres of great knowledge, of great understanding, of great advancement, and all are concentrating upon Mother Earth. There are to be great energy forces directed at Mother Earth when the time is right, but that will not be yet awhile. However there is much energy being stored, and when the time is right it will be sent as a cushion, so to speak, for Mother Earth.

There is great involvement upon the planet at this time, with electronics and all things of an electrical nature, joining together of wires and the transmitting of energies using vibrations that are around the Earth plane. Many of these vibrations are directed to what you call satellites that circle the Earth, on to which electrical energies can be focused and through which vibrations, pictures are transmitted. In a similar way there are pictures of the Earth plane transmitted to those Spheres that are concerned.

It is by vibrations, by energy forces that all things are monitored, and all things are recorded and plotted. And it is known exactly at what time there will be happenings upon the Earth plane, for energies are directed to and fro. There is much information that is stored in other Spheres within the Universe. Information which would cause the scientists upon the Earth plane great wonderment, for it is far beyond their knowledge. There will come a time when all this information is used to bring about perfect balance, not only upon the Earth plane, not only within Man, but within the whole Universe, that all **will** be harmonious. But that will not be yet awhile.

God's Blessings be yours. His love and protection is around you all. God bless you.

Chapter IX

BEACONS OF LIGHT

reetings. I bring you the wine and the bread from Tibet.
I have awakened from long sleep to come to you this
Earth evening. I wakened to find many changes have
taken place since the time that I went to sleep. There
have been many changes within Tibet, for a gentle style has
gone and the vibrations are those of aggression and domination,
and all round the Earth plane the vibrations are the same.

If you raise yourself on high as I can do, and look down
with the long eye upon the Earth plane, one can see the
greyness of the vibrations swirling around that planet. But the
grey vibrations are not complete, for pinpointed in many many
places all round the Earth plane there are small specks of light,
that lift their beams up — up into that swirling greyness. They
are the lights of the groups of people who have been drawn
together all round the Earth plane. Those who sit for prayer,
those who sit for teachings. Those who sit to attain awareness;
those who sit together in friendship and love. Those who sit
together in silence and meditate — all are lights.

When I went to sleep I knew it would be thus, for it was
written thus. And in the archives that are still safely held within
the ancient places of Tibet these things are written, and the
times that are ahead are also written. Before I went to sleep

there was much preparation, for we knew that we would sleep for a very long time, and I am not alone. There are many of my brothers who also joined me in that long sleep. There was much preparation and there are many writings of many thousands of years that are safely protected in the ancient places. They are fact, they exist, they are of material substance. But they will not be discovered until there is a true awareness, that the value can be estimated and appreciated. For upon those writings there are secrets that go back through millions of years of the life of this planet Earth.

Upon those writings there are recorded the happenings of many millions of years ago and of the civilisations that existed at those times. For in spite of those who think that they can tell all things from looking at the rocks and formations, there is much that they cannot tell. There is much that they can tell that is of truth, but many of the things are guided, that they may have knowledge and that it may be made known to those who are at present upon the Earth plane. There is much excitement when there are those who are digging discover something of ancient value. But they are but new things compared to those things which are hidden in ancient places.

There was one who built a monument in a country other than this where there were documents, various specimens and recordings made. The monument has been built on top of these, and in time those things which are hidden will be discovered, but they are of modern times. When they are discovered there will be quite a different civilisation upon the Earth plane. A civilisation of awareness, of understanding, those who can communicate by thought.

In ancient times this was also accomplished, and civilisations that **have been** and that **will be**, come and go in knowledge. But those that **will be**, will not go, for the time has come now for a speeding up of the awareness of Man. A speeding up of the development of those things that must be developed, that this Sphere may take its place with other

Spheres within the Universe. That the progression which has been made upon other Spheres can be accomplished here. That the darkness that is within Man will be lifted. It is all written in those ancient places.

There are gems there also, beyond the imagination of Man. The size and the purity is beyond the present day conception, for they were placed there in the times when all was of purity. They had been created when there was no darkness near. They are of pure light; they are of pure thought; they are of true creation. These too will be discovered.

There will be a place in the [1]Himalayas discovered during the time of an exploration. It is a place which is high up within a mountain. And within that place there will be discovered 'relics', as they are called — indications of life of great knowledge, and people will marvel. I come to tell you these things for you are a Group of learning. I come to tell you these things for it is by direction that I do so.

There are energies that are massing. There will be lightning that will strike, and through that lightning there will be an opening up of a great new knowledge. I would ask you to focus your thoughts and your prayers, as indeed you do, upon this Earth planet, that those lights that penetrate through the swirling grey mists may link up above that mist in a great beam of light. For the energies that you send forth can be utilised. They can be used tenfold according to the Tenfold Law. And you can thus see, if you visualise the planet Earth surrounded by thick and murky swirling grey mists. Then visualise pinpoints of light penetrating that mist — clear, not hazy, for they have penetrated the mist. Visualise those lights all linking up above in one great beam, and visualise also Spheres, with a great beam of light projecting down upon that which is sent up from the Earth plane.

---

[1]Himalayas — Himalaya Mountains — System of mountains North of the Indian sub-continent, containing highest summits in the world

You can then visualise that as it is returned to the planet Earth, the swirling mists will be dispersed. It is inevitable, it will be thus. It is written thus. It is recorded in our ancient places. And with the return of those energies there will be many changes in the minds of men in the physical form and in all things.

I will go. I was sent to you, I will now return. The Creator's Light is your protection. It is above you at all times. His Love surrounds you. It is thus. God be with you.

Chapter X

THOUGHTS OF LOVE
HARMONY AND DISHARMONY

Greetings my daughter, greetings to you all, this is Thomas. This is the time of the year upon your part of the Earth plane when life begins to stir within the nature kingdom. When energies are drawn from the earth to revitalise the trees and the shrubs and all the nature kingdom. The animal kingdom also receives a revitalisation, and at this time of the year upon the Earth plane there are many new creatures born. Creatures who in their turn will live upon the vegetation that is itself re–awakening to fresh life.

Upon the Earth plane those in a physical body are also receiving revitalisation. For you too draw up the energies through the soles of your feet, energies which are sent up to you from the Earth plane. There are those who would flippantly pass the comment that they wear shoes with thick soles, and how can the energies penetrate? But the energies do penetrate and this is why those who walk for their relaxation, gain fresh energy. There is nothing like walking or running or whatever it is that keeps your feet upon the actual earth, particularly when you are out in the countryside where the trees also give forth energy as they in their turn become revitalised.

The trees send forth considerable energy that is of great value to man, and it is because of the destruction of the trees that much of the aggression is taking place. For man is becoming sluggish in certain cases and therefore more likely to follow those who are of greater energy. And those who are of greater energy are very often those who are of evil intent. Thus there will be the weaker ones following one who is a leader. In many cases the leaders are of great value. There are many leaders upon the Earth plane who are of great value in their way, particularly those who help the young ones. But there are also leaders of a different kind. Leaders who are intent upon destruction, whether it be countries or whether it be of those things within their orbit.

Mother Earth is also receiving revitalisation, and there is to be a cleansing of which you have already been told. These energies as they come forth from Mother Earth, from the nature kingdom, are at this time of great value, and it should be noted that you should at this time of revitalisation, give yourself time to think. Time to stand and stare. Time to go forth into the countryside or to walk along the sea shore to get the full benefit of this revitalisation.

You will find that now there will be changes within your lives and around your lives. You will find that there will be changes because people will come to you and you will find that you will have a greater involvement in the lives of other people. Not necessarily a close involvement, but nevertheless an involvement. For people will be guided towards you, those who need the sustenance that you can give through the knowledge and the teachings that you have received, through the understandings that you have. And you will find that there are words that you will speak which will be a great comfort. Words which will be absorbed and words which will bring about a healing.

There are many upon the Earth plane who do not have a physical illness as such, but a mental illness. Illnesses which are brought about by their own thoughts, by enlarging upon instances within their lives which could be dispersed, but which have been magnified out of all proportion. For when the soul is depleted the physical body is depleted. And when the physical body is depleted then the mind is not as it should be. For those things which take part in the normal functioning of the body, in the flow of the blood, in the ebb and the flow even as the sea, are not as they should be. are not of the strength that they should be, and then within the mind there becomes a disharmony. The physical body is out of balance and therefore minor instances are enlarged to such an extent that they become as a volcano which eventually blows, even as the volcanoes upon Mother Earth.

Therefore there are being guided towards you, those people who need the words that you will speak. The words that will be given to you, or the words that you yourselves have absorbed through the teachings that you have received and the understandings that have been given to you. Thus through your words and through your guidance, those people will subside, will look upon things in a different light. Will have a greater understanding of those happenings within their lives which have magnified and magnified until they are beyond all understanding within themselves.

There is much disharmony upon the Earth plane where there should be harmony. Disharmony between man and wife. Disharmony between sister and sister, and brother and brother. All where there should be harmony. And they are all caused by disagreement — by those things which have happened in the past and which have become magnified at this time upon the Earth plane. This is a time of great cleansing and there are those who will be guided towards you who are in need of this cleansing. A cleansing which you will bring about by the words which you will speak. And you will know this because having spoken to you they will go away and say, "I feel very much better for having spoken to you. I am glad I did." That will be the proof to you, if you like, that that one has been guided to you, and these words that I am speaking are of truth. It has to be so, for there has to be cleansing in so many ways upon the Earth plane.

Those who are in positions of authority, those who are in charge of the ones upon the Earth plane who have 'gone off the rails', I believe is the expression, do not have the understanding, indeed they do not have the time to listen to the words that are spoken by those who go off the rails. But if each one were taken to one side and if each one could be allowed to speak freely and truthfully of their lives, there is always a reason for their behaviour. A lot of it goes back to childhood, to misunderstandings in childhood, because these misunderstandings fall upon one who is very sensitive. All children are sensitive, and as one grows older upon the Earth plane, so these things become magnified until they are out of proportion. And then there is a reaction, a violent reaction, for like the volcano it has to blow.

There are places where people are kept locked away for many years because it has been agreed by six or seven people, maybe more, that that person should be locked away. But in many cases there could be a great cleansing and a greater understanding if words were spoken and confidences exchanged. But of course according to the laws that have been made by man upon the Earth plane, all misdeeds must be punished according to those laws which have been made by man, and of course there then arises a distrust.

There are those who are locked away who are of great spiritual awareness, and they are very frustrated because they cannot share that awareness, for those around them would not understand. But it is those who have this awareness that prison bars cannot keep locked away, for with the awareness they have, they go forth into Astral Travel. Not all, but there are many who do, and prison bars cannot stop that, for it is something mightier than any word of man or any prison walls.

There are those who sit quietly in meditation. Very often they are called sleepy heads because the understanding is that they are asleep. But indeed they are not — they are in meditation. And through that meditation they too escape, for they go deep within and their visions are of wonderment and joy. But they are visions which cannot be shared with anyone, for if they were it would be considered that they were out of their mind. Such is the lack of understanding.

To wish to dominate is of no value. To share is of much greater value, and therefore I come back to the beginning when I say that there will be guided towards you those who are in need. Those who wish to talk, who will confide in you, those to whom you will talk and advise. And thus there will be a great sharing. And this is the beginning, for to share and to trust is also bringing about a love. A love of harmony, a harmony which will spread, providing those words that are spoken to you, the trust that is placed in you, is truly respected and is not shared by you with another. Trust and truth, sharing and love, harmony — all very much needed upon the Earth plane at this time.

God's blessings be with you. May His love and light shine down upon you. His love surrounds you at all times. God bless you. God bless you all.

Thoughts of Love

* * *

THE BROTHERHOOD OF MAN

Greetings my daughter, greetings to you all, this is Thomas. The time upon the Earth plane is advancing. There are many things that have been told you. There are many things that will take place. There are many things that have taken place in your own private lives. Your understanding now is of much greater value than it was at the beginning. You can truly say that you have had teachings of great value, teachings from those of wisdom and knowledge. Teachings from those who have come to help and to guide you in your understanding of those things that you can and should do.

There are those amongst you who know that you must be of service within [1]The Lighthouse, for that place also is a place of light. It is a place of learning and it is a place of teachings. Much has been learned, much has been taught. Much discipline has been necessary and will be necessary, for I will say once again that discipline must be learned. Desires of free will must be overcome if there is to be true oneness, a true oneness with the infinite.

There will be many changes within The Lighthouse, for there will be those of you who will make those changes,

---

[1]The Lighthouse — this was the name by which the Church was known, where most of the Group were members.

changes from routine to matters of interest, to a bringing together with laughter and happiness. Already such happenings have occurred and they have been of much value. They will expand and much light will be shed into the homes of those who need light.

Across the Earth plane at this time there is a great awakening and there is a great battle going on within the churches of all denominations. I am very happy and proud to say that the man who is now Archbishop of Canterbury is a man of far sight, a man with a mission. A man who knows that mission. A man who communes with the World of Spirit, for he is of great spiritual value. He has the understanding that there must be a bringing together of all religions upon the Earth plane, a task which he will never see completed, but a task which he is endeavouring to complete within his own sphere.

The one who is called The Pope is also of the same under-standing, he too communes with those in the World of spirit, for he is of great value also. Those of darkness do not commune with those of light. There will be much endeavour, there will be much work and much planning to bring together these men, and to bring together these religious understandings, for dogma must cease. The fear which has been handed down through the ages must be dispersed. All are children of the Universe. All are children of the Creator, a Creator who is difficult to imagine, but those of true understanding know that it is of truth.

The Master Jesus was of flesh and blood for He walked this material Earth plane. The knowledge within Him was of light. He returned to the Earth plane to bring about a dispelling of the fears, for even before He walked the Earth plane there were those who created Gods of fear. There were those who worshipped the Sun, the Moon, a certain creature upon the Earth plane. Some worshipped the water and some worshipped the hills, but all things were of the Creator, and yet many of these Gods were revered with fear. The fear of displeasing. The fear that if one displeased one was punished. There were sacrifices of those in a physical body in order to please the Gods, all brought about by fear.

Jesus returned to the Earth plane as a simple man, although a great Master. It was not the first time He had walked the Earth plane as a Master, but this time was different. This time He gave the understanding that even as a small child He knew about The Creator, my Father. He imparted much of this knowledge as a child and they gazed upon Him with wonderment and muttered and talked among themselves, but it was dismissed. He showed the meaning of compassion and love, of tolerance and healing, of service. Of true service, for He would walk many miles to tend a sick person.

He knew the meaning of loneliness. He knew what it was to be despised, hated, stoned, and in the end sacrificed. For He was sacrificed. He was sacrificed because no one would take the responsibility, no one would listen to the voice within themselves, the voice that said, "This man has been guilty of no crime. This man is Magnificent." He was sacrificed according to the methods of those days. He was sacrificed in an endeavour to bring the understanding that all men are brothers whatever colour their skin; whatever tribe or family they belong to; whatever country. All were brothers, the Brotherhood of Man, of all men. His father was the Father of them all, as His Father is the Father of all who are upon the Earth plane now. You are brothers and sisters of the Master Jesus, for you are all of the same family.

Within groups like this one the understandings are given. It is up to you to accept and follow them. For you are being told that the Brotherhood of Man must spread across the Earth plane, and therefore do not despise or turn aside from those with a different coloured skin to yourself. Do not despise or turn aside from those with a different religious understanding to yourself. Do not turn aside and despise those who do not have the same spiritual awareness that you have. For from you and the words that you speak, and your attitude towards others, can come about the vessels of love toward the Brotherhood of Man, the life giving vessels for Mother Earth. The life giving vessels for all humanity; the salvation of that which Jesus the Nazarene endeavoured to bring about. It has been said that the Nazarene will walk the Earth plane again. He has already been seen many times. **He is** upon the Earth plane, He is all around, but this time it will be beyond anyone to sacrifice Him for He is of everlasting existence. He will come to you and be seen.

The time is coming when these group meetings will cease. It is not just yet, but they will cease. It has been promised that there will be a manifestation. It was hoped that the Nazarene could have appeared before you, but it was not possible. There will be a manifestation before this Group closes, when you all have a different vision. It is very hard for me to explain, but nevertheless it will be so.

You have been given many understandings, but tonight you have been given a gift of great rarity. A gift which will be used by you. For once given it is there for all time. You have work to do, to be of service to your fellows, to the brothers and sisters who are around you. There are those who will refuse that service, there are those who will come to you seeking. All will go away with an upliftment and an understanding, and all will have the realisation of your value in varying ways.

I will go now. God bless you. The Love and the Light of Father God is with you and protects you at all times, for you are His chosen ones. God bless you all.

Thoughts of Love

* * *

OVERCOMING AGGRESSION

Greetings my daughter, greetings to you all, this is Thomas. Much is being brought about upon the Earth plane to show those of aggression that their evil ways cannot triumph. There were many prayers sent forth for those upon the Falkland Islands, for those in ships upon the seas. And the power of the prayer was very strong and those things that could have been did not happen. Those of aggression have watched other countries who are also of aggression, triumph. But the turning point is being reached and those who desire to take that which does not belong to them, who desire to expand and overcome to put in slavery those whom they have conquered, cannot be of the future for each land must put into order the harmony that must be.

There are gradually coming forward those who are of the minds of peace; those who are the minds of light; those who have the understanding of what must be. They are determined people for they have a task to complete. A task which maybe they are unaware of, but which is firmly implanted in their conscious mind. And as the spirit within rises, so the awareness of what must be done becomes of paramount importance.

There has been aggression in Israel and Lebanon, but it has not been aggression for the desire to overcome peoples. It has been aggression brought about by overcoming those who are themselves of aggression. Those thieves who steal in the night, who kill and destroy. And so there had to be aggression to overcome those of darkness, and so it was with the Falkland Islands. Those of darkness had to be overcome and removed, and so they have been.

There will be guided towards places of power, those who are with peace in their minds. Those who will seek to bring about greater harmony within their own countries. Those who do not seek to dominate but seek to work together in peace. All things will not happen at once, but gradually there will be a calming, for there have been many things of darkness within that country. Those who seek to dominate, those who rise to power with the intentions of dominating with aggression, must be removed, and so they will be. All leaders must be strong, but strong with love, strong with a desire to bring about peace and happiness within their own countries. Thus bringing about peace and happiness within man, thus overcoming the darkness that at the moment is in the minds of man.

Within your country now there is much darkness, and there is one of darkness who desires to dominate with fanatical intent. He is one who will be removed before he can put into action his evil plan. You have a leader who is very anxious to bring about peace within her country. Who is very anxious to bring sense back into the minds of men, the realisation that to think honestly and to work honestly brings prosperity. But she will not tolerate those who are cheating. For there are many who cheat, who do not do an honest days work.

Gradually there will be brought about the realisation that the party is over, that all must work together in harmony. **All** must work together in harmony whether they be in positions of power or whether they be of a lower station within life. For all are equally important in their own way, all are children of God. All have the same values in His eyes. All must be of light and love, for the darkness must be cleansed away by the light. There are many teachers upon the Earth plane now, teachers who are spreading the spiritual awareness. Teachers who do not just acclaim a God, but teachers who prove that He is there. That there is a loving God, the Creator of all things. Whose energies are pouring down upon the Earth plane to lift and to help the darkness to be dispersed. Children do not come forth from their mother's womb with evil in their minds. The evil is planted there by man. And if those around do not send love and light to that child then the evil dominates, and gradually the darkness within spreads out to those around. This must be prevented for with the spiritual awareness within the child, there will be the knowledge of what must be done. And gradually as the children grow, so will those of light guide them forward into light, bringing about a dazzling brightness which will spread across the Earth plane. In time bringing about the awareness and the oneness.

You are upon the Earth plane at this time of great turmoil, of great darkness, of despair in many places, but this is the time you chose to return for it is the time of turning point. You have already been told that you are the vanguard. You have already been told that the teachings that you have received through these group meetings must be used. They must be read in order that the words may be firmly planted in your minds, that you may recall without difficulty. For there will be occasions when you will need to quote many of the words that have been said to you, in order to teach or to guide others to go forward in a greater understanding.

Do not place your books of words away, but read them from time to time, and you will be guided to read those which will be of assistance to you. A preparedness if you like for one who will be guided towards you. You will find that time and time again you will realise that you are quoting or repeating that which has been told you in a group meeting.

And now I will go. May the Love and the Light of Father God surround you at all times, and indeed it does. God bless you, God bless you all.

Chapter XI

UNIVERSAL ILLNESSES

G reetings my daughter, greetings to you all, this is Thomas. We are now coming towards the end of these group meetings. There are several more yet to come and then, as was told in the beginning, it will close and you will go forward upon your spiritual paths, healers, teachers. Teachers because of those things that have been told to you. Teachers because of those things which are written down. Teachers because of the disciplines that you have learned. Teachers because of the understandings that you have received. The knowledge that each one of you should walk forward upon your spiritual paths, doing those things which have been advised, doing those things which are of most value. Value to yourselves, value to we in the World of Spirit and value to all those around you with whom you will come in contact.

There are many upon the Earth plane who are now seeking a greater understanding of the reasons of life, for the truths. And although there have been many complaints regarding those things which are sent forth through, as you call it, the media, nevertheless there has been an awakening of interest through those things that have been sent forth. There will come about a subtle change within those things that are presented through the media. There will come through a subtle change in those things that are seen with the eye through the pictures that are projected, through the ether. For many people are now coming forth and stating their beliefs whereas in the past it has all been kept hidden.

There is no time for secrets now, for the truth must be brought forth and people must realise that as they sow, so do they reap. It is of truth, for one cannot go forward taking all, giving nothing. One cannot go forward respecting no-one, they cannot go forward taking lives and stealing properties. Stealing lands, coveting, jealous, possessive, aggressive, all negative, for in the end they become negation.

It has been said that there are universal illnesses, and indeed there are universal illnesses — there have been through the ages. The Black Plague, fevers, consumption, cancer, and of course there are many others in varying parts of the world. But there are always universal illnesses and the next universal illness will be troubled minds, for as they sow, so will they reap. Therefore there must be a great cleansing in order that this state of mental deterioration may not prove the undoing of all.

I am not endeavouring to spread gloom and doom I am merely stating a fact, a logical fact that you can understand and see, see for yourselves. The young people of today who are aggressive, who go around destroying, who are destructive, who are negative whether they are destroying a human body, a home, a little creature, the freedom of others; unless they are cleansed they will finish in mental institutes, for that is how it must be. I am not speaking of those who are aggressive in defending something of value, such as the conservationists defending the rights of people to live freely without restriction, but according to the laws of the country.

As I have said as you sow so shall you reap, and therefore there must be a great cleansing within these young people, in order that they may realise the true values, the lessons and the understandings that they are here upon the Earth plane to learn. And then to progress along their spiritual path to learn to be of service one to the other. To learn to give out love, compassion, and many of them healing. But until they learn their lessons then there is a sad harvest ahead of them. I say sad because it will be a harvest of a wasted life, something which need not be.

There are those upon the Earth plane who suffer already from mental illnesses. In many cases they are situations that they have built up within themselves which have nothing at all to do with their surroundings or those who love them. It is a blackness within which must be cleansed out. It must be purged out, and taking drugs does not do this, for the drugs that are now manufactured do not bring about a cure, but merely seal in a box those problems that are within.

It is useless to put away priceless treasures in a locked box and never to let them see the light of day and never to let them know that they are of beauty, that they give pleasure. For mostly these things that are locked away in boxes in this way are priceless gems or treasures of gold and silver, of diamonds, of emeralds or minerals that need to feel the earth's vibrations around them in order that they may give off the energies that are of value. And so it is with those who lock away within them these problems that they themselves have created, this negation which is locked away in a box.

All should be brought forth, examined and discarded, for if examined correctly it is realised how worthless they are and how much value the things around them are. There are many such upon the Earth plane, and I am sure that you yourselves know or have heard of such people. Help them if you can when in their presence by being positive, and if they speak to you about that which is locked within, speak truthfully to them, do not hide your feelings.

It is not always a case of sending forth compassion, it is very often a case of sending forth positive thought. Positive thought which will allow the light to enter to disperse the darkness that is therein. There will come a time when you will receive a testing, a testing which will be brought about by the guidance towards you of one such person as I have been speaking. It will be from that testing that you will, or will not receive an initiation.

The time is coming when there must be a cleansing within the minds of the young people who have been led astray by those of darkness. For there are many young people who are caught up in a web within which sits a spider of great strength. They long to break free but the spider has long arms, long legs and can pull them back if they do not speak to someone who can break that web. It is that which will enable the great cleansing of young people, for it is fear that binds them. It is fear that must be dispelled and it is the fact that they must learn to be of truth to themselves and to those around them, that will enable them to be of service, to go forward in fulfilment.

You can help in many ways if a young person comes to you, for sometimes they find it easier to speak to a comparative stranger than they do to speak to those who love them, for it is because of that love that there is a reluctance. Each one of you are healers and what is that but healing. Growing up these days upon the Earth plane is very difficult, for it is indeed a testing time. A testing time for all of you when you step forward as young people, for there are always temptations placed before the young.

There is so much upon the Earth plane now that is desirous to the young and there are so many who are given everything and are not taught the values, whether it be the physical values or the spiritual values. For to respect ones self is to respect God, for is not a part of God within each one of you? It is respect that many young people do not know the meaning of. It is respect for themselves and for others that must be taught. It is a lesson they must learn, for that way their values will be justified.

May the Love and the Light of Father God surround you all at all times, and indeed it does. God bless you all.

Chapter XII

THOUGHT
POWER OF THOUGHT

Y ou who are here have been sitting before within a group, but not here in this place. You have sat before me upon the ground as I sat before you as your teacher, and once again I sit before you as your teacher. Many ages have passed upon the Earth plane since we sat together. Ages during which there have been many upheavals, calamities, successes and once again upheavals. And yet it would seem that those things which should have been learned and forgotten have not even been learned. For there are still those upon the Earth plane who seek only for their own glory, for their own power. Who seek to dominate, to cast down and destroy. Power is something that should be used to uplift all. Power is of great value in the right hands.

You have sat before me and I have told you of ancient times, of great civilisations of great knowledge. All those things that are found as miracles upon the Earth plane at this time, all of them are not new. There was the understanding long before you sat before me, of mighty travels. Not from one place to the other upon the Earth plane, but from one planet to another. There was no problem for there were teachings whereby the thought patterns 'conveyed' you, even as those within the World of Spirit can move about freely through thought patterns.

They may be great distances away from you but when you think of those who have been to this place to give you teachings, they draw comparatively close to you. They do not, as do your protectors, stand by your side for they are teachers and are not at the beck and call so to speak. But I say that in a very wide meaning. I say it to illustrate the power of thought — that movement can take place instantly. And that is how it was when I spoke to you as you sat upon the ground. We were in the hills for we were of the civilisation that was within the hills. A civilisation with great discipline, with great teachers, with great understandings of spirit communion. It was part of our lives for we were of the times before the physical body became as solidified as it is now. We were of lightness.

The time is coming when this state of lightness must be achieved as those upon the Earth plane pass along the path back to what should be; to what will be, for there is now a great escalation. We were within the hills, we were not as moles that live now upon the Earth plane, burrowing their way through with blindness. There were vast halls, there was a different type of living. There was not the need for the great quantities of food that are consumed now upon the Earth plane, for the body was of lightness. Not as the physical body is now. It was of lightness and required lightness to sustain it.

There is much that I would like to say to you, but I would say this. When in meditation I would like you to visualise the chamber of light in which the teachings that I gave you were held. I would like you to envisage that place, and if you are of stillness you will visit once again. For you will bring forth that wisdom which is within you and you will see me within that place. There will come a time when we meet again. It will not be on the Earth plane as it is now, but we will meet again.

You have had many teachings while sitting within this place. You have been very honoured for you have had those of light who have spoken to you to give you teachings of great value, to give you knowledge. Make use of these teachings.

Make use of the words that have been spoken to you. As I taught you before I say to you now, there are many wisdoms and there is much need that those wisdoms are spread. As you are, so can you teach others.

Be of purpose, determination and strength. Do not be deterred when things are not easy. You are embarking upon a path of wisdom. The wisdom and knowledge of that for which you returned to this Earth plane in this physical body, will be given to you in time. It is possible that this will be the last time that you will return to the Earth plane. It is possible that upon the completion of this task you will then pass to a different Sphere.

It is good that we are together now for this is a time of much turmoil upon the Earth plane. Turmoil of a nature that is not new. But it is as a time when there is much greed and at a time when values are sadly misplaced. It is a time of which within, you are aware that your service will take place. It is a time of much need for love to be sent forth. It is not easy to love those from whom one would turn aside, but it is necessary to lighten the vibrations around them in order that they may be uplifted into the light. To something that you may not be able to see, but it is something that does happen.

There will soon be indications in an area of disruption that the prayers that have been sent forth and are being sent forth, will be used to bring about light within an area of darkness. There will be a lifting and you will know that those things that you are told regarding the power of thought are indeed of truth. I would like you to know that I salute you in the usual way. You are of wisdom. Use it wisely. I go.

Thought

* * *

THOUGHT PATTERNS

My name is Ahmetec, I bring you greetings. There is much to be said for there is much to be done because now as then there are times of great disorders within the minds of men. The thought patterns are not as they should be.

Many Earth years ago the situation was such as it is now. A similarity, but of course with difference of the knowledge of the civilisations. The minds of men turned to desires for themselves without sending forth the love and consideration for those who were around them. The knowledge that all should work together, the knowledge that there is but one God. No, the thought patterns changed then. The evil started to take control. The desires of the lower self and the attainment of the higher self were ignored. And so it is now upon the Earth plane with many.

It is the desires of the lower self that are bowed to whilst the desires of the higher self are ignored. It is easy to seek possessions. It is easy to ignore all those things which are recognised as being part of civilisation. There must be laws to maintain order, and at the present time the laws are not being obeyed. They are being ignored and ridiculed. And those who endeavour to put right this situation are not thanked, but are criticised and ridiculed. The time is coming for a complete turn about. The time is coming when there must be a realisation that there are laws that must be obeyed, there are teachings that must be followed.

To those upon the Earth plane at the present time who wantonly kill and destroy, who wantonly cause damage, who wantonly endeavour to possess that which belongs to another claiming it as a right, claiming that possession is the law; all may seem fun to them at the moment for it would seem that everything is going their way. But no, the one thing that they cannot get away from is themselves. The realisation will gradually become dominant within them that those things that they have accomplished will reap a harvest of disease. A harvest that is inevitable, until their whole thought patterns change. And this is what will happen in the future. Thought patterns will change. The teachings that are given to the young will change. Disciplines will be learned; understandings and love sent forth.

Already there is a great awareness upon the Earth plane of the necessity for the wild life to be protected. There are many upon the Earth plane at the present time who spend their Earth lives dedicating themselves to the protection of the wild life. These people spend every hour of every day on this task, there is no time limit. And this is the beginning, the realisation that there are responsibilities for everyone upon the Earth plane towards everyone and everything around them. Whether it be in a physical body, whether it be part of the nature kingdom or part of the animal kingdom, all are necessary. All maintain the balance that must be upon the Earth plane if food is to be supplied, if there is to be happiness, if there is to be progression.

Many ages ago the thought patterns changed, but this time they changed from the higher to the lower self, and there was a [1]great destruction, for there had to be. But now upon the Earth plane there is a reversal, for gradually the understanding is a

---

[1]Great destruction — this refers to the destruction of the island of Atlantis in the ocean West of the Pillars of Hercules, which was overwhelmed by the sea because of the impiety of its inhabitants.

desire to attain oneness with the higher self, you lose the coarseness that is now within the physical body. And gradually you will find various indications appearing to you that the thinking of people is changing. There is a long way to go yet, but already there are signs. Already there are indications, already there are teachings. And you within this Group will realise through those things that you will hear and those things you will witness, that there is a change. That there is an improvement, that there is a desire to help one another. There is a long way to go, but there has to be a beginning and the beginning is now, within this New Age as you call it. It is the age of spiritual awareness. It is the age of knowledge, of teachings, of love, of compassion.

You are a group of healers. You are a group who have also become teachers, for from the teachings that you have received you in your turn can pass on the knowledge when those who are seeking come to you. You are healers, and healers are needed upon the Earth plane, for many are turning towards healers such as yourselves. All around the Earth plane there are those of special healing ability — I must clarify, they are being specially prepared — then energies of a high density can be projected through them. They are instruments of great value, and much preparation is taking place, for there must be many healings.

People must be given the realisation that within themselves lies the key to the truth, to the love that must be sent forth, to the compassion, to the understandings, to the knowledge that you just do not finish and return to dust. The knowledge and the understandings must be given that it is of truth; that life is ongoing, it is but the physical body that is left behind. That as you live this life upon the Earth plane so you reap the harvest in the next life, the life of everlasting living. It is the truth. It is not told to bring fear within the thought patterns, but to bring a realisation that everybody, everybody, is linked one with the other. That your neighbour does matter, that all should be of service and that the thought patterns should lift. That the thought patterns should be those of the higher self, the highest attainment can be achieved.

There will be changes upon the Earth plane as there were changes in Atlantis. They are inevitable, but they will be only changes, but so it will be. You will see some of those changes. You will be aware of the changing thought patterns. You will have those who will come and speak with you and ask you questions, and you will know the answers. You will bring about much comfort, much easement of distress and easement of disease, for you are all healers.

The time is coming when you will go your separate ways. But you will not remain alone for you will be drawn towards others that you may be the means of them receiving teachings. The ripples in the brook spread wider and wider. The ripples on a pond even wider, and the ripples upon the sea embrace the whole Earth plane. And so it will be. There is much ahead for you, much of value. You are of value.

There will be a time when you will feel the energies from Mother Earth flowing through your feet, your legs, you body. Flowing around your head, bringing to you the energies of the Universe, in order that you may be strengthened. In order that you may be as one with the Universe, part of and yet the Universe. I do not speak in riddles. Remember the strength of the Universe can be yours.

The Mighty One is with you. He is your protection and Divine Love.

Chapter XIII

INTERPLANETARY VISITORS
U.F.O'S

I give you greetings, I bring you love. I am intruding upon your planet Earth that I may speak with you, I have permission so to do. I am from another Sphere within the Universe, and I come to speak to you regarding that which within this planet Earth is described as 'unidentified flying objects.' I come to tell you something of the work that goes into the visits to the Earth plane. Visits which are becoming more numerous, for there are many Spheres who are sending those who orbit the Earth plane in order to bring back information.

We are not of darkness, we are of light, we are of interest. We are interested in the planet Earth for there is much that will happen and there is much that can be controlled, so to speak, through the scientific — I use that word for it is known to you upon the Earth plane — through the scientific research that is carried back to our Spheres. We are not of a physical body as you are and yet it has been reported upon your planet that our vehicles have been seen and that men in a physical body have been seen to alight; that there have been conversations; that there are those upon the Earth plane who have been removed.

My friends, we in other Spheres do not have a physical body such as you here, for we have progressed beyond the progression of the Earth plane. Much happened upon the Earth plane millenniums ago that brought about a slowing down, indeed brought about near catastrophe. Those who were on the Earth plane at that time who were of knowledge, drew together around them those who were also of knowledge, and there were those who came from other Spheres to populate the Earth plane in small groups.

From seven Spheres seven groups descended to the Earth plane, it was their chosen task. They knew what it entailed for them but they were willing, and accepted that which had to be done in order that the Earth plane would survive. Because of this, progression upon the Earth plane has been much slowed down. But everything has a purpose, and gradually there is becoming about increased awareness, and in the not too distant future the Earth plane will be lifted to a vibration of lightness. Not drastically, but nevertheless it is progression.

We return in our vehicles and as we approach the Earth plane through the outer atmospheres that surround the Earth's atmosphere which is heavy, we then adopt an armour, so to speak. An armour which protects us from the Earth plane vibrations, for they are heavy and without the armour we could not withstand. The armour we use is that of a physical body, but yet it is not a physical body. We put it around us as one would put on a suit of armour as used to be worn upon planet Earth at times of battle. But we do not come to fight, we do not come as aggressors, we come to test, we come to identify, we come to assess.

There are those upon the Earth plane who say that they have been spoken to in their own tongue by those who alight from the vehicles. But that is impossible, for we only speak through the thought pattern and the words that have been spoken have been through the thought patterns and through the thought patterns only, for one cannot make a suit of armour speak. But thought patterns are everywhere. There will be reports in your newspapers and other means of communication, that there are many vehicles visiting the Earth plane. There will be many who will say they have seen, and they will be in different countries and be seen by different people at the same time. There is a great quickening within the Universe and there are many plans that are now being put into order, for this time the planet Earth must be lifted otherwise it will be destroyed. But I say this to you my friends, it will not be destroyed, for the plans have been carefully prepared.

The task of the Spheres that are involved in this work, for it is work, it is part of the Great Plan for the Universe, is the restoration of this planet Earth. The correcting and the bringing back into line with other Spheres that have progressed to lightness. You within this room, this sanctuary, this place of light, will know when there is a quickening of these objects, of these vehicles. You will understand the reasons and it will be a proof to you and you will know. You will also know that when you are told that people have alighted from unidentified flying objects and have spoken, that it is impossible. It is impossible to speak as I do now, unless it is through a physical body of the Earth plane. I could not speak thus through the physical body which is an armour. But I could communicate quite freely through the thought patterns, for it is not difficult to identify the thought patterns of the one to whom you are speaking, they can be identified through the ether.

There are to be many visits to this country, for there is much spiritual awareness in this country, it is a centre. You realise I am sure that when you look upon the maps that you have of the planet Earth, that this country is but a dot. But it is a centre of cosmic force, and it is through the cosmic force that much can be achieved. From this country there are lines, so to speak, leading all around the planet Earth, it is the centre and therefore it is the place of much interest, of adjustment. And so there will be many sightings and much talk, and many things will be said. For many people upon the Earth plane have imaginations of great vividness and what they do not know they imagine.

Unfortunately when they speak it is as if they knew, but you have been told and you have the understanding. There are others who are also being told and there could be times when you will meet up with one or two, and when you speak together you can confirm those things that you have been told.

The vehicles that circle the planet Earth are not aggressors, they are those who are making sure that everything is as it should be. They are not interested in buildings, they are interested in lines. Lines which may lead to buildings, lines which may lead to special places. But they do not come to swoop down upon the Earth plane and carry off people. Yes there have been those who have been so-called 'removed' from the Earth plane, but they are those who were placed there, and the time had come to remove them. Those who are placed upon the Earth plane do not say so. They are specially prepared for life upon the Earth plane, a preparation which has taken a long time. But they have a task to carry out, and when that task is completed they are collected. But in order to be as one upon the Earth plane they lead a life which is called 'normal'. Thus it is that when they are collected there can be some distress. It is much regretted but it is inevitable.

There will be a time in the not too distant future upon the Earth plane when I too will be in a vehicle with a special task to complete, but I will not speak as I am speaking now, for I shall be using thought patterns. You see we do not have a voice box as within a physical body, for it is not needed, it is only needed with those who have a physical body.

It has been an experience of much interest to me to be allowed to visit you. Remember my words, your proof of what I have said will be in the print of your newspapers over the coming months on planet Earth. I go back to my sphere, I am thankful for this experiment. The Great Spirit is all loving.

Interplanetary Visitors

* * *

PLANET OF LIGHT

Greetings, I come to you from a far off land. I come to you from a place which is far removed from this planet Earth. I come to you from a planet of this galaxy. It is a place whereupon there has been much advancement. It is a place of knowledge far removed from that upon the Earth plane, and yet in some ways the links are very close.

You upon the Earth plane are beginning to have an awareness of the opportunities that are all around you in the atmosphere that surrounds planet Earth. There is much excitement because there are workshops planned where space craft may link in, where communications may be maintained, where men may live for several years — so it is planned. It is considered new, it is considered advancement, it is considered that technology is reaching a high standard. But it is not new, for all these things have been done before and all these things are already being done, but not in the clumsy way of the Earth plane.

What is the reason for workshops in the outer atmosphere of the Earth plane? What are they to achieve? What are the space ships to achieve, what are they endeavouring to do? Those things that they are seeking are already recorded in various places upon the Earth plane. Recorded by those of many many Earth years ago. These things are all recorded. Man talks about

369

many light years away, but if man had reached the understandings that should have been reached, light years away are but a twinkling, so to speak.

The Sphere, the planet I have left to visit you, to speak to you, is a place of much light. There is no darkness there are no shadows, all is light. The atmosphere is light also, for we are of light. There is no weight for it is only the physical body that has weight, the spirit when it is freed is weightless. Upon our planet all things are planned and all go about those tasks which must be accomplished. There is no question that they will be otherwise. Energies are used as once energies were used upon the planet Earth. The Universe is immense and the knowledge of the Universe upon the planet Earth covers but a small area. There will be opportunities in time for you to visit other Spheres, when you leave the Earth plane and you leave behind the body in which you are now encased to return whence it came.

Through the teachings that you have had, understandings that have been given to you, providing you go forward doing those things that will be advised, you will have earned the right to visit other Spheres. You will have earned the right for a greater understanding, an understanding which will be absorbed into your life. And at a later time when once again you return to the Earth plane, if you choose so to do, that which you have learned from other Spheres will be within your knowledge. Knowledge which you will be able to bring forth.

The Planet of Light is not the only one, for upon the Spheres there are those of light, those who have progressed, those who have reached higher understandings. But always there are teachings, always there is much to learn. The Earth plane is heavy. Those who dwell upon the Earth plane are in a physical body of heaviness. It must be so in order that they can live upon the Earth plane. It is all part of balancing, it is all part of a mighty plan. It is a chance to learn, to have understandings. It is a reason for progression. You have been advised to sit in meditation. Many people upon the Earth plane speak of meditation but there are comparatively few who really understand the real wonders that can be found during meditation.

Your lives have been varied, you have all experienced strange happenings within your lives. You have had one experience of ease and you have had many lives of hardship. Experiences of value, experiences of knowledge, experiences which have led you to the point you have now reached. The point where you have taken upon yourselves a task. a task which is **now**, for upon the Earth plane now there are to be many changes as you have already been advised. And you who have already had experiences of much value will find this particular experience upon the Earth plane of even greater value.

For spiritual awareness, is the understanding that indeed there is a great preparation for those in the physical body to walk side by side with those in spirit form. To work together in unity. To go forward at this time in many numbers. To be as is expressed upon the Earth plane, 'out in the open.' To no longer work in secret, but to let your voices be heard. To be undeterred by those who disagree, by those who seek to drag down, by those who will take hold of the Holy Book and swear that you are conjuring up the Devil. It still happens, it is those with whom you must wrestle. It is to those that you declare yourself. For it is to those that the truth may be made clear, in order that all may go forward as a vast tidal wave, to sweep across the Earth plane. To sweep away thoughts of war and aggression. To implant the knowledge which should be within every one, that you are all here for a purpose. To learn and to progress, to be of love and of service, to send out love, and to know that you will receive, according to the Tenfold Law.

When these things have been learned upon the Earth plane, then the Earth plane will no longer be required and there will be brought about in its place a Planet of Light. It will of course take time, but now is the turning point. Now is the time when there will be brought about a lightness for the planet Earth.

One day, sometime in the future I know that I will have the pleasure of welcoming you to my planet. It will be so, but not just yet. Within you is the truth, within you you know, and that will remain with you. For the knowledge is in your life and you cannot have another experience without it. And so indeed you will go forward and the lightness will be all about you. I look forward to the time when I will welcome you to my planet. Farewell.

Chapter XIV

WISDOMS FROM WITHIN
EGO

reetings my daughter, greetings to you all this is Thomas. Ego is a great stumbling block in the spiritual evolution and it has been known that there have been those who have returned to the Earth plane to complete a section within that evolution who have accomplished very little. For the ego was apparent from the time when they were small children. I ask you to remember that ego is a stumbling block whether it is within yourselves or within others. But you have the disciplines and the understandings have been given to you on several occasions, that ego is a waste of time. I ask you to look at yourselves from time to time. I ask you to check yourselves, to make sure that ego is not blocking you.

Humility and compassion, healing and love, are within you all. Let it flow from you to others, let your mere presence with those who are sick help to bring healings by listening and talking to people. Whether it be a physical sickness or disease within the physical body, whether it be a sickness within the mind. For there are many sicknesses within the mind which can bring about a great negation of physical balance through the thinking that is continually within the conscious mind.

Some people on occasion go on and on and on, and you cannot get a word in edgeways and you feel you are wasting your time with them. But no, for they will tell you they have enjoyed talking to you, they have enjoyed your company, they feel much better. And then you will know that that valuable earth time has indeed been of value and not wasted.

Check yourselves from time to time. Sit quietly and look at yourselves. Know thyself and then know man. By sitting quietly and looking at yourself you can indeed turn away that which is of no value upon your spiritual path. And through discipline you can correct that. Correct your balance and go forward to do those things that you have chosen to do. Complete those things in this Earth life, the tasks that you have set yourselves, the tasks that are within your capabilities. Go forward with a light heart and great upliftment.

Each one of you has spiritual guidance and each one of you, when the time is right, will have that awareness. The awareness of the words that are being spoken to you. Awareness of the advice that is being given to you, the guidance to lead you along your spiritual paths. Listen and you will hear when the time is right. Each one at a different time. Each one forming a long continuous service and each one remaining linked. Linked by those things that have been said to you within this sanctuary. Linked because of the love that is between you, a steady awareness, an occasional thought which is sent winging one to the other.

Communicate one with the other even when you go your own ways. Communicate occasionally to keep the link and to inform each other of those things that you are doing or those things that have happened, are happening or are going to happen in your spiritual awareness. You will be surprised at the things there will be to tell. Meet together from time to time in what is known as a reunion, for this is a special Group, a special Group that was chosen. There are many special groups who could link together in harmony and love, bringing about that great chain around the Earth plane. The life buoy, the life buoy of light, of prayer and of love. It is growing ever wider and ever stronger and is of much value in the struggle that is now reaching its peak.

It will not be those with ego, who although working in service, do so with the idea that they should be noticed, that everybody would say how good they were. It will be those who walk quietly along their spiritual path that reach the heights. It is so — it is so. The Christos walked His spiritual path knowing that the end of His physical life would be one of indignity. He was degraded, jeered at, hated, but He also received compassion, grief and love. There was no ego and He soared in exultation. He soared to the heights.

You do not have to say, "How good I am." You do not have to say, "how clever." You do not have to say, "Look what I am doing." It is all noticed, for there are those upon the Earth plane who do not miss a thing. There are those upon the Earth plane who will say those things for you and to you. But when they say them they will be sincere and that is reward enough to help you on your way. Listen to the advice that is given to you, each one in your own individual way. I cannot say, "Take it," for you have free will and your path is your path, but listen to the advice that is given to you.

May the Love and the Light of Father God be with you all at all times. God bless you all.

Wisdoms from Within

* * *

THE TREE OF LIFE

Greetings my daughter, greetings to you all, this is Thomas. The sands of the desert run dry and yet do they? As far as the eye can see there is desert, a desolate waste where nothing grows, where nothing seems to survive. But that is only on the surface for beneath that desolate scene life teems, waters flow. Beneath the desert there are cool waters. Waters which can be found, waters which can be brought to the surface with the machinery that is now available to man.

There is life beneath that desolate waste and if the waters were to be brought gushing to the surface to flow across those desert wastes, then there would indeed be a beautiful picture before your eyes. A picture of beauty, of flowers, of insects, of life. And so it is with man. That which you look upon may look barren, may look desolate, may appear to be without life. But within, the waters of life bubble and could gush to the surface if only those with the machinery of knowledge were to set out to discover those secret wells.

The wisdoms within, the treasures within, for they are one and the same, can be brought to the surface of knowledge if you so desire. For life is everlasting and although you may have had many experiences upon the Earth plane, it is the one life. And so in that everlasting life there is knowledge, wisdom, lessons that have been learned, mistakes that have been made. There have been experiences of great fulfilment, there have been experiences of darkness. All can be brought to the surface by the machinery of meditation. I wish to emphasise the importance of meditation, if you yourselves wish to bring forth those experiences which are stored within your life.

The experience of the tree of life, the knowledge of the tree of life is to give you the understanding of the progression that is made. The tree of life is comprised of many experiences, and upon the Earth plane which is the school room of life, for the short period of time that you have been upon the Earth plane, you have lived out those experiences. Those experiences have not finished yet, for the experience of this time upon the Earth plane is of great value to you, each one. It is in this experience that you gain knowledge, that you have teachings that will carry you along the next stage of your life. It is a time that you have chosen to return to the Earth plane which will decide many things.

The Earth plane will change its face. The surface of the earth will change. Climatic conditions will alter from one place to another, for in the changing of the Earth plane this is inevitable. The Sun and the Moon do not change, but the Earth plane does, and it is well within your understanding how this will cause climatic conditions to alter. The deserts will run with water and the rivers will run dry. Places will be destroyed, but fresh land will rise. And so a change will be brought about in the position of the Earth plane. A change which will lift it to a higher dimension and thus bring about a greater stability. And through these happenings there will be a great cleansing within the minds of men. All will not become of perfection, for the time is not yet, but by the lifting of the Earth plane there will be brought about a lifting in the understandings of man.

There are many upon the Earth plane who have chosen to return at this times to help to bring about that lifting through their prayers and thoughts. But there are also many upon the Earth plane who are here to undergo an experience which will be of great value to them. An experience of trauma, for fear must be wiped away from the minds of men. And with fear will go the thoughts of aggression, will go the thoughts of war. Thus, so to speak, the outer layer of the orange will be peeled away and the thinner layer of the pith will still remain.

For you all within this Group the time is coming for you to go forward. For you to read and re–read those words that are written, the words that have been spoken within this Group; the teachings that you have received. As you have already been told, each time you read these words you will be given the realisation of a different understanding. And when you see within those words things which you have not recognised before, you will know that indeed you too are lifting.

The words of peace that have been spoken within this Sanctuary are words of truth, are words of teaching. Many of them are words that have been spoken by those from higher realms. Those who are teachers with great knowledge, who have given to you some of their knowledge to help you in this experience of your life. Many words may be spoken, many understandings may be given, but if you simply chat about them at the time and then forget, they are of little value to you. It is up to you, each one of you, to take heed and to acquire a greater understanding of those things that have been said.

You have had the opportunity of asking questions and you have been given answers. You have been given the understandings to those questions, and so there must be facts within your conscious mind that will be of value to you as you progress in this experience. The time is coming when you will go forward to put to use the teachings you have received, and it is up to you to help to make the desolate wastes of the desert blossom into beauty.

May the Love and the Light of Father God surround you all at all times, and indeed it does. God Bless you all.

Wisdoms from Within

* * *

INNER KNOWLEDGE

Greetings my daughter, greetings to you all, this is Thomas. There is a path ahead for each one of you. There is a path ahead upon which you will walk if you are to be of service. Service to your fellow brothers and sisters; service to mankind; service in the name of Father God, placing your feet in the footsteps of Jesus the Nazarene. All the teachings that you have received have been guiding you along your path. We have endeavoured to encourage you, to stimulate your interest, to awaken the latent powers within you. To stir memories of different distant experiences within your life.

If you sit in meditation then you will be aware of those things that can be seen. But to go deep within there has to be regularity, for then there sets up a cycle. A cycle which brings into your lives peace and tranquillity for a few quiet moments within each day. It is the way of stimuli. It is the way of preparation. It is the way of knowledge and wisdom. It is good to go forth to seek knowledge. It is good to listen to others who themselves have spiritual guidance and it is good to listen to those who have acquired skills relating to spiritual awareness. For each one of those persons who have shown an interest in ancient methods are guided within, from knowledge that has already been acquired in a distant life. But first of all the conscious mind has to learn the skill again. For as with all things the modern thinking, the modern methods and the modern way of life do not at all resemble past experiences in your life.

Therefore you have to learn to adapt to the present day way of behaving and thinking and of life. But when once you have learned the skill which is to be of value to you, the skill which is of past experience, then the wisdoms within will come pouring forth and you will be surprised at the words that you will speak. Words that you know are not of your own conscious mind, but which come from a deeper source, a wiser source, an all knowing source. But until you place your newly acquired skill to use, until you take the first tottering footsteps, you will not be aware of how fast you can run.

Within each one of you there is knowledge of great value which can be brought forth to be used, to be spread, to be shared. You have been told those things that you should do. They are of much value if you will use them. It is of little use triumphantly climbing to the top of a mountain if that is where you stay, out of reach of all those people who are at the foot of the mountain. And so it is in ordinary life; it is not much use acquiring skills if you do not mix with the ordinary people who can benefit from your knowledge and skill.

No my children, do not set yourselves at the top of a mountain out of reach of all, but take those first tentative footsteps. Learn how to walk and then how to run, for the knowledge, the wisdoms that are your knowledge, will pour into you. It is always difficult to take the first steps; a very young child will hold on to pieces of furniture or to fingers, or to chairs that are their height that are made for them to help them to walk. Then the time comes when something interests them in the centre of the room away from all furniture, and they wish to reach it, and so the first steps taken entirely on their own are made.

Once that experience is over, the confidence is there, and so with you. Do not be afraid to go out amongst the people. Do not be afraid to let the wisdoms come forth. Do not be afraid to utilise the skills that you know are within. You will have said, "I would like to do that, I would like to help, but I do not have the time." You do have the time, you have been told this before. You will make the time for other things and you **must** make time to be of service. Otherwise all these teachings that you have received over these many weeks will be wasted, for they will be locked away and forgotten. But my children you will be the ones who will benefit the most by utilising that which you know.

May the Love and the Light of Father God surround you all at all times, and indeed it does. God bless you all.

Chapter XV

THE FINAL CHAPTER
DISCIPLINE

G reetings my daughter, greetings to you all, this is Thomas. How many times have you looked at the teachings, the words that have been written, of the words that have been said whilst this Group has sat in love and harmony? How many times have you read the words? How well do you know the teachings? How much could you pass on to others? Have you followed the disciplines, have you the understandings of those things that have been said? Have you had experiences from those teachings? Have you the disciplines? If you do not have the disciplines you have learned nothing, for we spent much time in the beginning endeavouring to guide you along that path, the path of discipline. Discipline within your daily life, discipline within your spiritual knowledge.

There are those upon the Earth plane who seem to acquire spiritual knowledge without any effort. But speak to them and those who are of value will tell you of the disciplines that they practice. The self restraint and the adjusting of their physical life to blend in with the spiritual progression that must be made if this experience upon the Earth plane is to be of true value. The happenings within this Earth experience enable you to travel forward at a greater speed than those within the World of Spirit, for this is indeed a class room, a class room from which you can go on to University. And from the University there are realms within the spirit world to which you can be taken.

There is no *time* in the World of Spirit, not time as you have here upon the Earth plane. Therefore there are those things which are not of such great urgency. But within this Earth experience there is a time limit. That is why there is time. Time in which there can be much accomplished; time in which you can cocoon yourself and stand still. Time to utilise your free will. Free will which if used as it should be, will be handed back to the Father; will be handed back to the Creator, in order that His will may be yours. And by doing so, gain your freedom.

There are many upon the Earth plane who have had spiritual experiences, happenings of wonderment. But happenings which they keep to themselves, not realising that they have been given a key. A key to unlock the door to realms far beyond their comprehension, but realms which could become home to them. There are others who have but a glimmer, so to speak, a small key which placed within their hands can open many doors. And indeed does, for they seek and they enquire and they act. They take heed of those things that they learn, and gradually the horizon expands and there is no need to carry a key any longer.

To you I say, each one of you has been given a key. It is up to each one of you to use that key, it will open many doors. As you unlock one, after you have acquired the knowledge that you need at that time, there will be another one at a later time. All things according to your needs; all things according to your understandings; all things according to your capabilities. No one accepts a task that is beyond their capabilities, but each and every one of you within this Sanctuary has accepted a task of service. You have been told that you are healers who have also become teachers through those things that have been told you within this Sanctuary, and through those things that you have learned as you have asked questions and sought knowledge.

Each one of you has much to offer, much to give in the service that is ahead of you — that should be ahead of you. It is up to you. It is indeed up to you, free will is not interfered with, for we have to stand aside and watch when that free will is used. If it is used correctly we are very joyful and draw close, but otherwise we stand to one side and wait for you to return to where we are. Do not put the teachings that have been given to you away in a dark corner. Do not *intend* to read them, but not have time. There is always time to do those things that are of the most value to this experience of your life.

May the Love and the Light of Father God surround you all at all times, and indeed it does. God Bless you all — always.

The Final Chapter

* * *

May the light of the great God [1]Ra shine down upon you. May the energies and the strength within that light, enable you each one, to go forth upon your chosen path, a path of much value, a task of much service.

Look back, look back to the first time that you sat within this Sanctuary. Has there not been a change within you? Has there not been an increase of your knowledge? Can you say now that you have no knowledge? Has not your awareness of the strength of the World of Spirit been multiplied? Have you not felt the impact of those who have spoken to you, the teachers who have come from realms of much light? Those who have come from other Spheres to bring to you knowledge of those Spheres. Those who have come to tell you of happenings that could be within this experience for you. Those who have come to renew links of ancient times. Indeed no, you cannot say in truth that you are the same as from that first time.

It is with great sorrow to know that one of your number has had an accident which has caused much pain, and which has meant that he is absent from this the last meeting of the group. The time has come for this Group to close, for you are of

---

[1]Ra — (Egyptian mythology) — Sun-god, frequently represented with head of a falcon.

knowledge. You have had teachings; you have understandings of healings that will be, if you will permit the energies to be sent through you as instruments, for you are all instruments. It is up to you whether you give permission to be used. Healing is not just a matter of thought, although I must hasten to say there is much power in thought, much strength and much glory. Each one of you within this group, as instruments are destined to have energies of great value sent through you, for which there has to be preparation. Preparation which is possible and can only be completed through discipline when you sit in meditation.

Each one of you are of great value. I speak in truth. You yourselves may be unaware at this time, but the task that you chose is a task that will show to you the truth of these words I speak. For there will be directed towards you those who will need that which you can give. The value within that healing will be proven to you by those who will seek you, and as the time proceeds so will your work increase. There has to be a time, a time that is right, and each one of you here is at a different time. One has much physical complication and all her energies are needed for the healing that she can give to her husband. My dear, I say to you there will be times of stress, there will be a time of much frustration, but it will pass, it will indeed. Endeavour to be patient, endeavour to send forth compassion and remember that a still tongue is in itself a healing on occasions.

Those of you who already attend meditation instruction, do not underestimate the value of the teachings you receive there. For the breaths that you are given are of greater value than would appear on the surface. Look deep within and know what is within. For if the breaths are correctly carried out, you will indeed feel changes within your physical body, within the Temple, the guardian of the spirit within. It was not by accident that you attend that place. It was intended in order that you could be helped and given knowledge that would be available from no other source, a source of truth, of strength and of much knowledge. It is not a waste of time by any means. You will indeed be helped along your path.

Each one of you do have the clairaudient faculty. You may say you do not think so, but I can assure you, you do. But if you are too busy to listen you will be unaware, for you have already been told that clairaudience is through the thought patterns. Yes there are those who do hear spirit voices as clearly as I am speaking to you, but it is rare. It is a faculty which has been carried through many ages within the inner mind — that which is with all life. Clairaudience is through the thought patterns and the clearness and the positiveness of your thoughts, if you send out and ask a question, enables an answer to be given. But if your thinking is muddled it is impossible to decipher the thought patterns. When you sit quietly, if you wish to ask a question, ask it clearly and positively and wait to hear the reply. It will be sent to you through thought patterns which will enter the conscious mind, to be conveyed to you.

There is much ahead for each one of you in service, one to the other, if you permit. But not unless you follow the disciplines, which is a way of giving your permission. For it is that way that you can be prepared. It all depends upon you. There are many here within this Sanctuary who have spoken to you in the past. They stand to join with you on a positive link which is possible at this time. Each and every one give to you love. Each and every one will see you when you return to the World of Spirit, if your task is completed. There will be those who you will meet in the future and it may be that you will be given further teachings through your own groups, but that is in the future. As your knowledge grows and as the clairaudience develops, so will you be advised of those things that should be.

And Now I will go. I say to each one of you, God's Blessings be with you. May you soar to the heights. The Light of Ra beams upon you. All Blessings be yours. Adieu.

The Final Chapter

* * *

CONAN DOYLE

Good evening, Doyle here. Felt I had to come and have a few words with you. Have enjoyed coming to speak to you. Understand this phase is closing, but there will be another for that is how it has to be. I will not say that as one door shuts another one opens, that is not how it is.

You will find lots of surprises ahead. Many things will happen, for the teachings that you have had here will not be wasted. You'll see to that I'm sure. I told you last time that it will not be long before I shall be speaking from platforms again, using of course an instrument. The time is coming when it will be so, I've had my time of rest. Have been around of course, been to several groups, but now I have real work to do once again.

There have to be teachings given from platforms, for many are seeking. Many young people want to know. Not content to be fobbed off with things the old fogies say. Want to know for themselves. Want to hear the words themselves, to discuss and ask questions. It's good. Many don't approve of course, would rather keep everybody shepherded into churches. Nothing wrong with churches, good institutions if the right chap's in charge.

Many of the young ones who are coming along speak words of truth from the pulpit, use their own thinking and their own guidance, even if some of them are unaware. But believe me, many of them are well aware. Many sit in meditation of the right kind. Many used to sit and doze off, but now there's a great knowledge sweeping the Earth plane. Secrets are in the open, values are changing.

Yes I know there is much destruction upon the Earth plane, but a lot of it is through ignorance. Needs strong ones to come along to give a guiding hand, to speak intelligently, to discuss whys and wherefores. People want to know and you'll find this. People will ask you questions, for the work you are to do will lead them to you. Don't be afraid to speak up to them, but always speak in truth, you can't go wrong then.

Don't make up fairy tales to tell them. Speak the truth, and if you don't know, say you don't know. Much the best way. Too many pretend a knowledge they don't have. Too many like to make themselves important. Nothing but hot air, waste of time. You'll know, I am sure that you will hear when I once again stand on platforms. Sure there'll be reports you may be sure.

Go now, make sure you go in the direction you should go. Listen to those voices you'll hear. You'll hear them all right if you listen. I say to each one of you, God Bless you all.

The Final Chapter

* * *

LAUDA

Greetings to you, this is Lauda. I have not spoken to you for a long time and I felt that on this occasion I would like so to do. I would not like you to feel that I had forgotten you. Indeed no, for at each and every meeting I have stood by the door and have listened to all that has taken place, and have been privileged to see those who have come to speak to you, and I felt part of it all.

There is much for you all still to know. You have much to learn one way and another. But then learning never ceases, for is not every Earth experience a way of learning. A way of correcting, indeed of experiencing. Each experience is of value. A span upon the Earth plane is really very short in the plan of things.

Each one of you has had many experiences and you are now reaching a point of service, for the tasks that you have chosen are of service. Realisation is part of culmination. It is really a very exciting time. This probing and enquiring, this seeking and testing, experimenting if you like. Healing for you within a physical body has to start with experimenting in order that you may gain the confidence. For after all you are within a physical body and the senses and the reactions have to be undergone in order that you may forget.

You pass through that experience, that phase if you like, to be comfortable to have knowledge, to forget yourself in the compassion that you give to others. For it is through compassion and love that healing becomes of value. You have been told that you have to be prepared, and this is so. But it does not mean that you then stand with a patient and hold out your hands and the energies flow, and all you do is stand.

You have to give, you have to give the compassion. You have to have humility, an understanding. For some patients can be very tiresome. But it is because of the disease within their bodies. But then I have not come to give you a teaching, but just once more to make the link and to say, God's Speed to each one. God Bless you.

The Final Chapter

* * *

THE CHRISTOS

I bring to you the Blessings of Our Father. I come to you with love. I stand in your midst and those with eyes to see would see me. It was promised that within this Sanctuary I would manifest. I manifest through the child through whom I speak, I am here and those with eyes to see can see me.

I send to you compassion, I send to you humility. Do not forget humility, remember all things are sent by The Father. The energies of the Universe come and go. Come and go, a continual pulsating like breathing in and breathing out. As the seas upon the shore breathe in and breathe out with each wave; as the trees rock from side to side when the mighty gales blow; as the birds that fly upon the wing, as the creatures within the seas; so the breath of the Universe is given to you to use as it must be used.

This will not be the last time that I will speak to you, for I will be with each one of you when you are completing the task that is of your choice, of your fulfilment, before you return to the World of Spirit, to that place that you have earned. You will see me upon the Earth plane, you will know that I am close, and you will see me when you return home.

Peace and Love be with you as you go forward to your destiny. The Love of Our Father and His many Blessings be yours.

The Final Chapter

* * *

THOMAS

My friends this is Thomas. I too come to bid you adieu. I also come to reassure you that you are indeed under my protection. You have the understanding of what that means. It has been my pleasure to be with you for these group meetings. Group meetings which were carefully arranged, not for amusement for that is not the way. Group meetings that were arranged in order that you may be given teachings and understandings, and so be it.

As you were told on one occasion, you will read these teachings in the future and you will read between the lines and realise the difference in your understandings. I have been very proud and happy to be allowed the opportunity of joining a group destined from their own choice to be healers. And now I will tell you, we have all been together in the World of Spirit. We have all discussed the tasks that you proposed to complete. My role has been to help you along the way to understanding when the time was right.

You were all brought together, not by accident but by careful planning. You all had free will, for you are now within a physical body. The Group became seven, at the commencement it was to have been twelve. But free will diminished, and the decision was made that the Group would be seven. It is now fact that there are many, many groups upon the Earth plane who are either of seven or of five. Those groups are carefully chosen. I speak of groups where there are teachings, I do not speak of circles where there is development. For sometimes circles are places of entertainment for some, and sometimes circles are places where some of little knowledge endeavour to teach those of no knowledge. It is a waste of time, for to develop in the correct manner there must be knowledge. The teacher of the circle, so to speak, cannot teach if they do not have training themselves. It makes sense does it not?

There are many groups upon the Earth plane as you know, and there are many prayer groups. For in ancient times those within the monasteries all sat in prayer. There are many monasteries, there are many places wherein nuns spend their whole lives, as indeed do the monks, without even venturing into the world outside the gates. But there are many, many more people upon the Earth plane than there used to be, and so now there are prayer groups. People of dedication, who sit at certain times to pray for a given purpose. And so it has to be upon the Earth plane, for Mother Earth will, and indeed must be lifted. Lightened if you like in order that man, that spirit within a physical body may also be lifted. That all may go forward in enlightenment. That the power of thought may be the means of communication and not the machinery that is now used.

Here I go giving a teaching when that was not the intention. So I will say to each one of you, it is with love that I say to each one, go your way. Remember the things that have been said. Carry within your hearts love and compassion for those you meet who are in need. God Bless you all.

Index

Index

Index

Index

Index

My Instruments

The Instruments I use, My Chosen ones,
Must ever be all pure within,
With naught to tarnish
The fair gems I send through them.
My Instruments must be all calm without,
An echo from within,
That in that calm and stillness
They may ever hear My Call
To selfless Service; and reflecting, living,
Being parts of God's own Truth
Which flows through Me to them,
And then, perchance into the outer world
Where it may anchor in the hearts
That need it most.
My Instruments I need,
With an ever increasing need,
In Service to The Brotherhood on earth.

* * *